*Making Tea, Making Japan*

# Making Tea,
# Making Japan

CULTURAL NATIONALISM IN PRACTICE

*Kristin Surak*

STANFORD UNIVERSITY PRESS

STANFORD, CALIFORNIA

Stanford University Press
Stanford, California

Printed in the United States of America

Library of Congress Cataloging-in-Publication Data

Surak, Kristin, 1976– author.
  Making tea, making Japan : cultural nationalism in practice / Kristin Surak.
     pages cm
  Includes bibliographical references and index.
  ISBN 978-0-8047-7866-4 (cloth : alk. paper) — ISBN 978-0-8047-7867-1 (pbk.          )
     1. Japanese tea ceremony.  2. Nationalism—Japan.  3. National characteristics, Japanese.
  I. Title.
  GT2910.S854 2012
  394.1'5—dc23
                                        2012021000

Typeset by Bruce Lundquist in 11/14 Adobe Garamond Pro

# Contents

# Illustrations

*Table*

# Preface

The origins of this investigation of the relationship between the tea ceremony and Japaneseness are personal as well as scholarly. In 1999, a friend, like many eager to share "Japanese culture" with foreigners, asked if I would like to visit her tea ceremony class, and I, like many foreigners eager for a taste of "Japanese culture," accepted her invitation. After watching the students make tea, I was given the opportunity to try my own hand at the intricate procedures. Though my memories of that day have worn thin, I still recall my utter confusion at how to do something as simple as pick up a tea bowl while trying to follow the teacher's directions, "Left hand, right hand. No, right hand . . ." But I went back the next week, and the week after.

More than fulfilling an exoticized image of "real" Japanese culture, the tea class offered me an entrée into wider Japanese society. At the time, I had been teaching English on a rural island for about one year, but my language skills were poor and I spent my free time with other foreigners in neighboring areas. Joining the weekly tea class allowed me to enter a local home, make local acquaintances, and, above all, learn the local language. I acquired the phrases to humbly deflect rather than complacently accept compliments, the elaborate vocabulary for marking degrees of formality and position in hierarchies, and the nuanced ways of recognizing efforts by and impositions on others. As my command of the language grew stronger, acquaintances became friends, and I felt more secure in participating in the social worlds around me.

As it has done to many other practitioners, the tea practice—the preparation procedures and modes of interaction at lessons—began to mold my foreign body into forms regarded as distinctively Japanese. Expected to be different and not to understand, newcomers to Japan are assumed to bring unfamiliar customs to local interactions that may jar locals into awareness of what is generally taken for granted. This sense of the out of place or the odd, this feeling of strangeness or discomfort, is handily encapsulated in the term *iwakan*. As my years studying tea progressed, however, I was increasingly told by people, "You don't create a feeling of iwakan. Your movements are so natural." In some cases, the compliments referred to the strict movements, determined by a kimono, used in tea practice. "You don't give off a sense of iwakan. If I look at you from the back, you look like a Japanese. The way you stand and sit is completely natural—just straight up and down." Or "You look just like a Japanese. From the back, you can't even tell you're a foreigner at all." The extended time spent interacting with practitioners and conversing at tea lessons provided opportunities to absorb the torso movements, the head nods, the two-handed gestures made with reserved expression that constitute the taken-for-granted ways the body is inhabited in Japan. Occasionally some felt so comfortable that they momentarily "forgot" I was a foreigner, complaining about the West or immigrants and then catching themselves with an embarrassed laugh, "Oh, I forgot you're American." My retooled body quietly helped to put people at ease, mediating the shock of foreignness.[1]

Yet I was not Japanese. Foreigners—particularly white Westerners—are often accorded a special status in Japan, and my research benefited from a widespread interest among the locals in sharing their culture with those from elsewhere. I received many invitations to dinner, and even to stay the night, from tea teachers eager to offer hospitality to a visitor from abroad. These opportunities to extend our encounters beyond tea spaces enabled me to better situate the role of the tea ceremony in their personal lives.[2] As a foreigner and a researcher, I was granted more mobility than most in the tea world, where a teacher's permission is often necessary to attend a tea gathering elsewhere, and where a student is expected to remain with the same instructor over the course of her or his life, unless moves or other extenuating circumstances cut short the relationship. Moreover, the people I met were often keen to introduce me to tea exhibitions at local museums, accompany me to public tea events and formal gatherings, or even invite me to often exclusive formal tea gatherings.

But over months or years, even special status fades, and at the sites where I invested the most time making tea, I was saddled with the same expectations and obligations as everyone else in the end. These are most stringent for younger women, who often lament the difficulties of negotiating the hierarchical relationships in tea classes, where "you are ordered around, you are treated as though you know nothing, and you can't talk back," as one informant described it. Eventually, however, my sympathy upon hearing such stories shifted to empathy. At one site I attended as a student I, too, began to be scolded for "mistakes" while making an honest effort. After a lesson during which we practiced the roles for a formal tea gathering, the teacher asked us what problems we noticed. I had been playing the part of the main guest—the person responsible for asking about the utensils the host making the tea had chosen for the day—and volunteered that I had forgotten to compliment the host on the silk pouch used, which had been made by a famous artisan. I had taken notice of the slip because during the preparation, the host had skipped past the opportunity to talk about the pouch in the rigid order of the discussion of utensils. But that didn't matter. As I knelt silently before her, the teacher berated me for several minutes for my rudeness and insensitivity, asking if I had learned anything at all in my years of tea training—harsh but not uncommon treatment coming from traditional teachers. Even the special pardon recognizing language difficulties was rescinded over time. When the teacher held formal gatherings, I, like every other student, was expected to read, memorize, and discuss at length the obscure names of utensils and craftsmen handwritten in ornate script on records of the gathering—and was sternly scolded if I failed. Sometimes, to my regret, I was treated like everyone else.

The Japanese are well known for hyperbolic compliments: an obvious foreigner who utters a simple *arigatō gozaimasu* as "thank you" may be applauded for speaking perfectly fluent Japanese. Certainly I have received my fair share of this sincerely offered flattery not to be taken literally. But experience also cultivates the sensitivity for knowing when their phrasing reflects the platitudes of social graces and when it expresses a more genuine surprise or deeper impression. Sometimes the practitioners I talked to would never get past offering pat explanations of the tea ceremony crafted for foreign ears, but with experience these are easy to spot and, reflexively analyzed, offer useful clues to wider social processes. Occasionally, with time, such formalities would segue into more sincere discussions. In such cases, I was treated as a fellow tea practitioner, who understood the gritty reality that lay under the sheen of spiritual ideals, recognized in the aside, "You know how it is."

Not only was I a foreigner, I was also a tea practitioner, and the balance and overall relevance of these two ways of identifying me shifted both between and within interactions. As a foreigner, my tea network was more diverse than that of most, with even recent acquaintances eager to take on the mantle of cultural ambassadorship by sharing their interest in the practice. Because I was almost always asked about what I was doing in Japan, sometimes a conversation with a stranger on a bus could lead to an invitation to a tea gathering. The uncle of an acquaintance might have attended high school with the head (an *iemoto*) of a particular school or style of tea preparation. The friend of a friend might take me along to a local tea festival. As I got to know people involved in a number of tea organizations, I asked them to introduce me to other practitioners—both typical and notable—in order to explore the tea world's variety. The personal introductions were essential for chipping away at the barrier often erected between "Japanese" and "foreigners," with its idealized explanations, and making possible more matter-of-fact conversations.

The accumulation of time and information led to a change, as I was treated less as only a foreigner and more as a foreign researcher, a foreign tea practitioner, or even simply a researcher or a tea practitioner. My own tea training—ten years of lessons leading to a teaching certification—also aided this process. When visiting a class, I would often help out with preparations behind the scenes, where the formality of the tea room (and the formality of a visit by a foreign researcher) is broken and everyday conversations and complaints are heard. Washing tea bowls was often as informative as watching the tea being made. Extra hands are appreciated at larger tea gatherings, and I volunteered to help at as many as I could. When longer conversations emerged during slower moments, I told people I was conducting research on the tea ceremony and asked about their experience. In such cases, I was treated as a (foreign) tea practitioner, who could be relied upon for competent help in the back or front room.

A decade of tea training also helped me understand the often specialized talk that occurs in tea settings as practitioners converse about utensils, artists, and tea masters. But, more importantly, it enabled me to see how people act within, or manipulate, the strictures and structures of the tea world. The years spent kneeling in front of the boiling kettle were essential for differentiating between a genuine compliment and a back-handed compliment, or recognizing when a mistake has been made but purposefully ignored. The time also cultivated a deep awareness of the embodied practice of making tea, on which I draw heavily in this book.

But no matter how "natural" my bodily comportment became, and no matter how much tea expertise I accrued, I was still a foreigner in Japan carrying out fieldwork. To the extent that I have examined how these identifications affect the data produced and collected, they have been not hindrances but resources. Because my very presence primed the relevance of Japaneseness in interactions, I draw heavily on occasions when my involvement was peripheral or nonexistent: tea demonstrations by Japanese for Japanese, tea books written in Japanese for Japanese, tea television programs produced in Japanese for Japanese. Explicit references to Japaneseness are common in all of these sites, providing rich material for studying the relationship between this practice and national identity.

## Data Collection

The book that has resulted draws on several years of historical and ethnographic research in Japan, subsequent to my initiation into the tea ceremony. The bulk of the fieldwork was carried out between August 2006 and February 2008, supplemented by evidence gathered on earlier and shorter trips during the summers of 2002, 2003, and 2005. To ensure some exposure to regional differences, I chose three locations for the ethnographic and interview research: Tokyo, Kyoto, and Awaji Island, representing the country's metropolitan center, traditional capital, and rural hinterlands. I also carried out brief fieldwork trips to Niigata on the western coast and Aomori in the north.

The ethnographic work set out to map the tea world from multiple points. Four classes, which I attended for one year or more, became bases for my exploration, and these were supplemented by an additional four sites, where I visited lessons less regularly but multiple times. In some cases I recorded informal group discussions with the participants, and at two places I videotaped classes. One-shot visits were carried out at an additional ten sites, including community centers, hotels, private homes, and the headquarters of several tea schools, and I observed several high school and college tea ceremony club meetings, as well as junior high school tea performances. Public tea demonstrations were another focus of ethnographic inquiry, and I attended a number as a visitor or a participant, including community tea performances sponsored by municipal governments for local residents, tourist tea performances at hotels and temples for Japanese and foreign travelers, and ritual tea services at temples held in celebration or remembrance. Becoming a member of one tea school's national association, I took part in official meetings and training sessions, and got to know the organizations that structure the tea world from the inside. I also attended or assisted at numerous small formal gatherings (*chaji*) and large-scale gatherings (*chakai*) that dot the calendar of most tea aficionados. While many of my observations were with people affiliated with the Urasenke school of tea, which accounts for a majority of practitioners, I spent extensive time at lessons, gatherings, and in conversations with tea participants of other schools, including the Omotesenke, Mushanokōjisenke, Edosenke, Dainihon Sadō Gakkai, and Sekishū schools.[3]

In addition to this ethnographic work, I conducted semi-structured interviews with over one hundred tea practitioners, including housewives, students, policemen, school teachers, office workers, real estate agents, monks, geisha, and the simply rich and leisured, in addition to the iemoto heads of tea schools and others formally employed in the tea ceremony industry and related sectors, including tea producers, sweet makers, and museum curators. The participants ranged in age from their late teens to their early nineties, and included over three dozen men. I also informally interviewed fifty people from similarly diverse backgrounds involved with tea. Finally, to develop a picture of the relationship of nonpractitioners to the tea ceremony, I took field notes after several dozen informal conversations with those not directly involved in the tea world, including bartenders, hair cutters, taxi drivers, and regulars at the local pub.

The historical investigation was carried out in Kyoto at the Chado Research Center, where I collected information from tea ceremony periodicals, and in Tokyo at the National Diet Library, where I examined tea ceremony depictions in etiquette books. The Textbook Library in Tokyo and the Tokyo Women's Christian University Library provided additional sources, including school textbooks and women's magazines from across the twentieth century.

*Acknowledgments*

In the process, I accrued many debts to the scholars and friends who aided me along the way. Rogers Brubaker has provided indispensable guidance since the project's inception, and his penetrating insights and criticisms improved the work beyond what I initially thought possible. Combining acumen and affability, Andreas Wimmer offered invaluable suggestions, while Morgan Pitelka cheered me on as he read several in-progress drafts. Christine Guth and Joshua Mostow took the time to give detailed feedback on the entire manuscript. Other scholars in the United States and United Kingdom provided intellectual and moral support, especially Adrian Favell,

David Fitzgerald, Nazgol Ghandnoosh, Wesley Hiers, Angela Jamison, Rob Jansen, Jack Katz, Jaeeun Kim, Justin Lee, Herman Ooms, Iddo Tavory, the participants in the Comparative Social Analysis Seminar at UCLA, and the members of the Japan Research Centre at SOAS. While carrying out the fieldwork, I benefited from the academic assistance of several scholars in Japan, including Kobayashi Yoshiho, Satō Kenji, Satō Shigeki, Tanaka Hidetaka, Tanimura Reiko, Ueno Chizuko, and Yoshino Kosaku.

Friends in Japan made me look forward to every opportunity to return to the field, and I am particularly grateful to Aragaki Kaeko and family, Kunita Akiko, Maejima Akiyo, the Nishioka family, Takashi Aiko and the Kida family, Toyoda Maho, Uchida Keisuke, and the bunch at Petticoat Lane. Others outside Japan were consistently encouraging, especially Giulia Andrighetto, Kheya Bag, Jodi Blumstein, Sung Choi, Theo Christov, Nick Elliot, David Koussens, Alex Malthias, Irene Padavic, Raj Pandey, Federico Rossano, Barbara Schmenk, Yasemin Soysal, Sarah Teasley, and Michelle Tierney. For their support over the years, I am thankful to my family: John, Judy, and Sarah.

My research benefited from generous grants or fellowships from the Fulbright-Hays Program, Japan Foundation, Terasaki Center for Japanese Studies, Sasakawa Foundation, and UCLA Graduate Division. The book was written in London and Florence while I was a Robert and Lisa Sainsbury Fellow at the Sainsbury Institute for the Study of Japanese Arts and Cultures, and a Max Weber Fellow at the European University Institute.

This project could never have been undertaken without the generosity of the numerous tea practitioners, teachers, and friends who opened their doors to me, took the time to talk with me, and shared a part of their lives with me. I am grateful for their kindness. *Okagesamade.*

# A Note on Transliteration

I follow the standard English-language academic conventions for transliterating Japanese. Names are written in the Japanese order of the family name before the given, and words common in English, such as Tokyo, are written without macrons. Unless otherwise noted, all translations are my own.

*Making Tea, Making Japan*

# Introduction

## *Nation-Work*

Few practices are simultaneously as exotic and representative, esoteric and quotidian, instrumental and sensual, political and cultural as the Japanese tea ceremony.[1] While most Japanese have never participated in a formal tea gathering, and to many its arcane procedures remain alien, the tea ceremony is all but universally recognized as a defining constituent of Japanese culture, integrating arts, manners, and sensibilities deemed peculiarly characteristic of the nation into a single, striking form. The paradoxes of the tea ceremony offer an unusually rich ground for considering some of the still unresolved questions of nationality today.

### *Nationalism and Nationness*

Broadly speaking, two kinds of literature have dominated thinking on this topic. On the one hand, and starting much earlier—at least four decades ago—scholars have examined the rise and spread of nationalism as a political mobilizing ideology and movement, aiming to create or expand a nation-state. Opinions have divided over the origins of nationalism—whether it is a purely modern phenomenon, going back no further than the era of the American and French Revolutions, or whether it has much older and more primordial roots. But common to this body of writing, whose landmarks include Hugh Seton-Watson's *Nations and States*, John Breuilly's *Nationalism and the State*, Benedict Anderson's *Imagined Communities*, Ernest Gellner's *Nations and Nationalism*, Anthony Smith's *The Ethnic Origins of Nations*, and Eric Hobsbawm's *Nations and Nationalism since 1788*, is a macro-historical focus on processes of nation-building or destroying and the agents that have driven them. Such studies have shown how myths, symbols, customs, memories, and beliefs that more or less loosely bind members of an ethnic community together have provided raw material for nationalists to work into representative cultures, which then have been used to establish the identity and uniqueness of the nation as the legitimate grounds of its political sovereignty. Traditions were invented, holidays consecrated, and representative dances, landscapes, foods, or sports designated emblems of the country as the state sought to secure the loyalty of its citizens, and as supporting institutions—museums, exhibitions, pageants, statuary, and the like—reinforced the supposed natural congruence of its cultural and political borders. During the originating phase of nation formation, modern school systems—along with military conscription—played a central role in patching together an overarching community effacing regional, class, religious, and other differences, and forging a collective identity so potent that those who came to share it would willingly give their lives for it in battle.

On the other hand, over the past two decades, there has developed a growing body of work, spanning sociology, critical theory, and media studies, that has begun to look in meso- or micro-analytical focus at productions and expressions of nationhood, or "nationness," in everyday situations, where no overt ideological mobilization or political pedagogy is at stake. Directing attention away from the elite projects that galvanize nationalist will or passion for the ends of state, it has investigated the forms in which the nation is experienced or enacted in the commonplace routines of ordinary lives. In works like Michael Billig's *Banal Nationalism*, Tim Edensor's *National Identity, Popular Culture and Everyday Life*, Robert Foster's *Materializing the Nation*, and Richard Jenkins's *Being Danish*, studies of seemingly inconsequential facets of day-to-day existence have explored the internally shared, nationally bounded ways of seeing, thinking, and acting that can form an unconscious doxa of the community.[2] This is an optical shift that has also increased sensitivity to the ways in which what may appear relatively solid, smooth, and coherent when viewed at a distance appears much more variable, textured, and differentiated when inspected close up.[3] Turning a critical eye toward the quotidian, this strain of research has raised awareness of the often unnoticed yet pervasive "forgotten reminders"—the faded flags at the post office or the symbols on money—that embed the nation in everyday life. It has explored how the proliferation of first-person plurals in the press can point through a "national deixis" back to the homeland, which not only serves as their referent but is reproduced and reinvigorated by them. Like other identities, national belonging too has also become commodified, the consumption of food, music, media, and other products defining and affirming unspoken national sensibilities.[4]

Though they should in principle be complementary, these two strands of research have, on the whole, evolved independently of each other, studies of nationalism training their eye on major historical developments, and studies of nationness on contemporary practices.[5] To date, little work has attempted to bridge these literatures, with a notable exception in Rogers Brubaker and colleagues' *Nationalist Politics and Everyday Ethnicity in a Transylvanian Town*, which moves between the two perspectives. The lacuna is due in part to differences in the temporality and the phenomenal expression of their objects of investigation. While studies of nationalism usually adopt historical methods to inquire into the emergence or resurgence of nations over long swathes of time, research on nationhood has typically turned to ethnographic evidence to explore how nations are instantiated in routine practices and the moment-to-moment unfolding of social interactions. Only occasionally have the tensions between these differing approaches surfaced in open debate.[6] And even then, the most sophisticated attempts to bridge the two mainly present evidence of a disjuncture, without moving toward integration.[7] Yet both arenas concern the subjective practices and agencies that give objective reality to the nation.[8] This social labor of objectifying the nation—that is, of making this abstract concept identifiable and tangible—may be termed *nation-work*.[9]

### Bridging the Divide

Nation-work is a material condition both of nationalism, as a movement or ideology, and of nationness, as a form of collective existence.[10] Analytically, it allows the two fields to be unified in a single framework, but as a concept it must be first fleshed out itself. Politically, the legitimacy of the nation-state is typically based on claims to the ethno-cultural uniqueness of a territorially delimited group of people. A range of practices, objects, events, or figures will conventionally be identified as markers of the asserted culture.[11] Characteristically, the underlying relationship between such cultural markers and the nation is synecdochal, the part standing for the whole. Scholars have long noted that the elements in question may be arbitrarily chosen, but they have less often looked at the different ways selected cultural features may relate to the totality. If we consider these, nation-work can be subdivided into at least two general types: *definition/explanation* and *embodiment/cultivation*. The distinction between the two is heuristic: definition and explanation spotlight the linguistic acts of designating the identifying characteristics of a nation, and embodiment and cultivation its physical enactment.[12] Since language is an embodied capacity and what is corporeal relies on linguistic interpretation to move beyond tacit understanding, the difference between them is not hard and fast. But it is useful in distinguishing between principally expository and principally performative ways of concretizing nations. While the former can be precisely enunciated and qualified, the latter are less open to questioning or challenge, as they operate through the body and are therefore less clearly articulated.[13]

Definition designates characteristics that identify the nation. These may be highly elaborated, or abbreviated and elliptical, but they are always selective, highlighting some features while ignoring others. Though they rely on explicit or implicit comparison with external others, the definitions do not necessarily stand in a neutral relationship to members of the nation: they may contribute to the production of what they seem to designate. To describe can be to prescribe. Authorized definitions create standards to which the world is expected to conform, obliging the beholden to comply.[14] Debates and disagreement may result, but these often enliven national imaginings even as they are contested.[15] The importance early studies of nationalism placed on the intelligentsia recognized the potency of these articulations, but once they are taken for granted, even small talk can perpetuate national understandings.[16] Though some definitions are all-encompassing, others select particular—often classed or gendered—cultural elements as typecasts of the whole, intertwining national assertions with nonnational categories.

Nation-work is particularly potent in pedagogical situations, where definition appears as explanation. In this case, the contours of the nation are not so much clarified as motivated, in the form of new information for the edification of those instructed. This will vary not only according to the level of knowledge assumed among its recipients, but also their responsibility for the new information, which is conditioned by their imputed relationship to the nation. Not simply Americans but men in particular may be expected to know more about baseball than French counterparts. A primary locus of pedagogical nation-work is schools, where the state crafts the young into good members of the community.[17] Nonetheless, definition and its variations operate across a range of sites that includes advertisements, magazine articles, political debates, pamphlets at tourist sites, and even everyday conversation. Differences, commonalities, and disagreements in characterizations of the nation can by tracked by examining what the definitions select and how this material is organized, presented, and debated across time and space. Attention to the various clusters of categorical distinctions and differentiations can reveal how descriptions are used to establish who "we" are versus who "they" are, how these definitions are inflected by class or gender, or how they are generated through comparison with inadequate or exemplary members.

While the work of defining a nation is expository, that of embodiment is performative and sensual, acting on and through the corpus. Its modes encompass the perception of recognizably national sensory experiences and the enactment of recognizably national movements, postures, and modes of interaction. As a performative representation, it is distinct from what some might consider the unconscious dispositions of a "national habitus"— a modal way of doing things.[18] Though such enactments may occur alongside definitions of the nation, they are, in the first instance, dependent on them to set out the national significances. Embodiment, as an objectification of nationness, requires a measure of distance from the consummately mundane to identify the relevant enactments or sensations as physical encapsulations of what is deemed exemplary of the nation.[19] Yet it is a somatic sensibility or performative capacity, and thus its acquisition may involve an investment of time and effort. Because this type of nation-work operates in and through the body, intersections are common with other social categories, such as gender and class, that are sustained in part through physical enactment.

Embodiment's pedagogical formulation—cultivation—works to transform people into better or idealized members of the nation, generally by mimicking a practice or sensibility previously defined as national. As an uneven process of skill attainment, cultivation highlights differentiations within membership.[20] Indeed, it is precisely because all members of the community do not equally perform the characteristics or qualities indicative of national culture that refinement of these becomes necessary, transforming—for example—some Japanese into "real Japanese" or "better Japanese." Embodiment and cultivation can be examined at a range of public sites and cultural performances, as well as in subtle expressions in everyday life. Once the crucible of schools is left behind, these bodily practices in which nationhood is in-corporated and enacted become one the most powerful forms of nation-work.

## Nation and Categorization

The nation-work approach builds on the recent cognitive shift in studies of nation, race, and ethnicity, conceptualizing these phenomena as matters of categorization and classification rather than as substances or traits.[21] Early studies of ethnicity often took for granted a view of the world in which identity, culture, and community were neatly coterminous: ethnic culture was coherent, ethnic communities were bounded, and ethnic groups could be clearly identified by the unique culture they bore. While such Herderian assumptions still inform many common understandings of not only ethnic groups but also nations, analysts over the past forty years have embraced constructivist views of ethnicity as a fundamentally relational process of boundary negotiation.[22] Fredrik Barth's 1969 introduction to *Ethnic Groups and Boundaries* contributed the most substantial push dislodging static notions of ethnicity, replacing them with the interactional, processual, situational, and relational formulations.[23] Proposing that ethnicity emerges as groups are constituted through negotiating boundaries between them, Barth argued that ethnicity should be understood as fundamentally transactional and rooted in the ways such self- and other-ascription canalizes social life.

Since Barth, it has become a truism that ethnicity springs from we–they distinctions drawn in contrast between a collective self and a dominant other or multiple others to create a social distance between "us" and "them." But a danger lies in too keen a focus on the action at the boundaries, which can lead to a neglect of the variegations that they enclose and their impact on ethnicity formation. The underlying assumption a simplistic boundary-approach courts is that all members within a division are functionally interchangeable: they can be transposed with each other without altering the ethnicity construction under investigation. Certainly other differences may be apparent, but these are treated as irrelevant to the boundary relationships of immediate analytical interest. The we–they division is, to put it in strong terms, totalizing for the task at hand. But the image of homogeneity that ethnicity projects is often constituted in part through internal heterogeneity, as illustrated in Yen Le Espiritu's evocative study of a Filipino community in the United States, in which she shows how the moral distinctiveness of the group is claimed vis-à-vis Americans through branding promiscuous Filipina teenagers as "more Americanized" or "more Westernized" than others. Labeling these "bad girls" helps constitute an image of internal homogeneity that defines the ethnic community.[24]

This is to suggest that not only differences across ethnic boundaries but differentiations within them are critical to group formation. Membership in a group may be a matter of degree or qualified in particular ways, as theorists stretching as far back as Max Weber have noted.[25] Yet analytic engagement is brief, and the implications of this promising line of inquiry remain underdeveloped. This may be due in part to the paucity of words in English that can be honed into analytic tools for examining degrees of ethnic—and a fortiori, for our purposes, national—membership.[26] While intensities of religious faith are captured by the term *religiosity* and qualifications of gender attributes may be expressed by *femininity* or *masculinity*, there are no equivalent English terms such as *ethninity* or *nationalosity* to convey relative degrees of membership in ethnic or national categories. Although observable, these differentiations have received little sustained study.

Consideration of nation-work, however, suggests that these may be captured by noting three possible operations it can involve. The first is simply *distinction*—that is, the identification of traits that distinguish the nation from other nations, as in the classic we–they contrasts studied by Barth. The second is *specification*. Membership in a given social category is not always direct, but may be mediated by other categories, as a substantial literature on the way intersecting axes of social categorization, such as gender, race/ethnicity, and class can construct one another, has shown.[27] Historically, as is well known, nation formation conditioned the relationship between the individual and the state by gender: men could serve the state as soldiers, and therewith in many cases enjoyed the right to vote, from which women, who could serve the state as mothers, were excluded.[28] What is national may also be specified through class categories. Invented national traditions were, as Eric Hobsbawm has shown, often originally practices of the upper classes that filtered downward.[29] The middle classes could also supply nation-defining characteristics, as with German *Bildung* and *Kultur*.[30] In other cases, practices originating among the lower classes could become national symbols, like the Cuban rumba, though these—the Argentinean tango would be another example—might need their origins to be obscured to acquire this status.[31]

Nation-work, however, may also involve a third kind of categorization—*differentiation*. Who "we" are may be established not only vis-à-vis "them," but also other members of "us."[32] A person may be a particularly good or bad member, a typical or strange member, an exemplary or phony member, of the national community. Here the contrast is with neither an external other nor even an internal other. Indeed, there is no "other" in such cases—the comparison is with fellows precisely as fellows, for it is shared membership that enables the differentiation.[33] Often such evaluations are crafted against a standard ideal—patriotism measured by the gauge of a war hero who has risked or sacrificed his life for the country, a *real* American showing up those who are, in a pointed adjective, *un*-American.[34] But if in some cases what makes a good compatriot is clear enough, conflict over judgments of this kind may also occur.[35]

Distinction, specification, and differentiation are not simply alternative modalities of ethnonational categorization, but constitutive of the broader category itself. An individual may be Scottish by being decisively not English; a woman may be a good citizen through procreation; a Canadian may prove her colors by striving to be a good Canadian. Capture of we–they distinctions made across national boundaries, nonnational categories mediating national identities, and differentiations internal to a national community can sharpen analysis of just how nations are evoked and enacted. Nation-work, operating as it does by definition and explanation, embodiment and cultivation, typically involves these further gradations.

## The Tea Ceremony

These considerations may serve to bring the peculiarity of the tea ceremony in Japan into sharper comparative focus. To a rare degree, as an object of investigation it stands at a juncture between the two levels at which nation-work has normally operated: nationalism and nationness. The tea ceremony, as we shall see, played an integral role in the construction of an ideology of Japan as a nation-state, reaching a pitch of political intensity as the country plunged into overseas expansion. But if it rose to this position in an epoch of "primary nationalism," when the nation-state was still being erected, it has survived into the period of what the sociologist Kosaku Yoshino terms "secondary nationalism," that is, "the type that preserves and enhances national identity in an already long-established nation-state."[36] There it retains an exceptional position among the range of emblematic practices, places, and objects that in Japan, as elsewhere, define cultural nationhood: the characteristic venues, food and drink, clothes and interiors, sports and spectacles, traditional customs, not to speak of the arts or language itself, that distill the distinctive life of the nation. That tea has been able to bridge successive epochs and forms of nation-work with such éclat has in part been due to the remarkable metamorphoses in its primary social carriers—moving from an aesthetic pastime of aristocrats, to a political tool of warriors, to a salon for business elites, to become, in the twentieth century, largely a hobby of middle-class housewives. Unlike most other practices that came to occupy comparable positions in the symbolism of emergent nation-building, the tea ceremony was not, and is not, a recently "invented tradition." But its longevity is not its least astonishing feature, for it offers a case of extraordinary stability in the face of change—the actual *doing* of the tea ceremony has altered remarkably little over the past four hundred years.[37]

Tea thus offers a striking site for observing how people may do different things by doing the same thing. Originally an accoutrement of power politics in a premodern society, *chanoyu* as it was known, was recast as a symbol of Japan as a modern state and employed to unify a national community. Transformed into a hobby, it retains enough of this past to project Japaneseness in ostensibly banal conditions, continuing to condense and give form to a pregnant vision of the essence of the nation. As a practice of nation-work, at a nexus between high-flying nationalist discourses and mundane expressions of nationness in everyday life, it is unlike many others. Today, it is a leisure activity like sports, but has no spectators. It is a hobby, but encased in a rigid hierarchical organization. It is a ritual, but also a business. It is an art, but also a routine. It exists in a deliberate, negotiated apartness from everyday life, yet lays claim to a synthesis of everything that is Japanese. It is practiced now mainly by homemakers, among the least prestigious groups in society, yet reaches upward to the political stratosphere of prime ministers and state visits.

The country where tea holds such sway appears—on the surface—to be an unusual example of a strongly bounded monoethnic community.[38] Japan is conventionally listed as one of the only two large societies in the world—the other is Korea—where ethnic minorities make up less than three percent of the population.[39] Because the ideological habits and beliefs that reproduce national understandings are embedded in the everyday routines of this relatively stable society, it might be thought that nationality need not be constantly indicated or explicitly reinforced. Yet in a surprising number of instances when the national could be taken for granted or merely implied, it is not, and uncovering the uses of such explicit markings can tell us something about the procedures of nation-work at large. Although contrasts with other nations always contribute to the construction of nationality— whether multiethnic or otherwise—a largely monoethnic case draws out the ways intra-national differentiations may also underwrite its production and reproduction. Thus in Japan what is at stake is less *whether* someone is Japanese, a question that nearly always allows for a clear and automatic yes-or-no answer, but *what kind of* Japanese that person is.

The tea ceremony, as a complex practice involving a combination of traditional arts and exercised within a highly developed organizational structure, offers material of unusual fascination for examining nation-work. Although in principle, symbolically laden objects, events, figures, and practices all enter the repertoire of such work, practices and events—the tea ceremony includes both—offer particularly strategic sites for exploring its operations. Objects can only in a limited sense become a part of the body, supplying at best indirect supports for physical in-corporation of the nation. The same applies to public figures. Practices, such as dance and sports, and events, such as holidays and parades, however, provide abundant material for the study not only of national representations, but also of how national meanings are experienced through and potentially transform the body. The boundaries between the various sites of nation-work are amorphous—practices can be performed at or as events, events often incorporate particular practices, and both frequently include nationally representative objects or public figures. The tea ceremony, as a skill that is formally taught and learned, favors pedagogical formulations and expressions of nationhood, where explanation of what otherwise might be taken for granted is at a premium. But these by no means exhaust it as a medium for nation-work. Chanoyu is richly multifaceted—it physically transforms the participants, requires a large number of material components, and rests on an elaborate written philosophy. Because it is so widely understood as archetypically Japanese, it provides an exceptional variety of angles for exploring how and with what effects Japaneseness is produced.

It would be surprising if a phenomenon as striking as the tea ceremony had not attracted a substantial literature. Academic treatment of it, however, is relatively recent.[40] In Japan, Tsutsui Hiroichi's *Chasho no Keifu* opened the field in 1978 for the pioneering work of Kumakura Isao, *Kindai Chadōshi no Kenkyū* (Research on the Modern History of the Tea Ceremony)—covering its development from the late Tokugawa to early Showa periods—which first appeared in 1980, followed by a series of monographs by the same author over the next two decades. Following Kumakura, other Japanese historians producing important contributions to the field include Tanihata Akio, whose *Kinsei Chadōshi* starts with the Muromachi era, and whose *Kuge Chadō no Kenkyū* explores the tea practice of aristocrats since the Middle Ages; Tani Akira, who provides a close analysis of tea records in his *Chakaiki no Kenkyū*; and Tanimura Reiko, author of a penetrating study of the tea involvement of Ii Naosuke, the last statesman of the shogunate.[41] The mingling of tea practice and power politics, and the evolution of collecting and taste, have provided the impetus for much of this scholarship.[42] Foreign historians have for the most part worked in a similar vein, yielding two distinguished collections, the first edited by Paul Varley and Kumakura Isao, *Tea in Japan: Essays on the History of Chanoyu*, and the second by Morgan Pitelka, *Japanese Tea Culture: Art, History, and Practice*, which brings together some of the best recent research in the field. Outstanding studies of particular forms or figures in the history of tea include Christine Guth's *Art, Tea and Industry: Masuda Takashi and the Mitsui Circle*, Patricia Graham's *Tea of the Sage: The Art of Sencha*, and Pitelka's *Handmade Culture: Raku Potters, Patrons, and Tea Practitioners in Japan*. To date, the historiography of the practice has provided the major contributions to our knowledge of it.

Anthropological approaches, the other leading branch of literature on tea, have been more sporadic. Produced principally by foreigners, they extend from Dorinne Kondo's structuralist analysis of the ceremony, through Herbert Plutschow's geomantic reading, to Rupert Cox's investigation of Zen elements in the practice, and—at greatest length—Jennifer Anderson's *Introduction to Japanese Tea Ritual*, which treats it as essentially a cult, whose functions are closest to those of a religion.[43] Sociological studies of the contemporary tea world are still less developed, though here two scholars have broken fresh ground; Barbara Mori argues that the practice offers women an affirmation, however ambiguous, of their role in society,[44] while Etsuko Kato's compelling *The Tea Ceremony and Women's Empowerment in Modern Japan* claims, more emphatically, that it has become a means for improving women's social status.

A feature common to much of the literature, historical or anthropological, on the tea ceremony has been its close intellectual relationship with, and at times material dependence on, the most powerful institution of the postwar tea world, the Urasenke Foundation. This is a connection that has affected, and constrained, research in the field. The foundation is an arm of the iemoto system that essentially controls the practice of tea in Japan, as will be discussed in Chapter 3. In the aftermath of the Second World War, this system was frequently criticized as a vestige of feudalism. But voices objecting to it were fading by the late fifties, when the first serious study of the iemoto as a traditional pattern of organization in the arts appeared: Nishiyama Matsunosuke's 1959 *Iemoto no Kenkyū*, which remains the standard treatment to this day.[45] In English, Francis Hsu's *Iemoto: The Heart of Japan* followed in 1975, projecting the iemoto as the core of Japanese social life. Neither work specifically addressed the business interests undergirding the iemoto in the tea world, and there can be little doubt that the lack of a more critical distance from these grand authorities has inhibited research on the tea ceremony.[46] A notable exception, Robert Kramer's trenchant dissertation, "The Tea Cult in History," never saw publication.

Recently, this situation has begun to change. Morgan Pitelka's treatment of the legends surrounding Raku pottery in his *Handmade Culture* is a sterling example. *The Ideologies of Japanese Tea* by Tim Cross, focusing on the role of tea in nationalist mobilization before and during the Pacific War, and its cinematic representations since, follows in Pitelka's path. This is a work that owes much, in turn, to Tanaka Hidetaka's collection of essays, *Kindai Chadō no Rekishi-Shakaigaku*, which examines the way intellectuals— among them the author's ancestor, founder of the first explicitly nationalist tea association in Meiji times—retooled the tea ceremony as a distinctively Japanese tradition in the early twentieth century. Yet the historical coverage remains partial in most of these studies, and neither the historians nor the ethnographers offer a sustained analysis of the relationship between the national meanings of the tea ceremony and actual tea practice.

## Looking Ahead

Profiting from the work across disciplines that has appeared since the eighties, this book tries to remedy some of the lacunae in the literature by at once offering a more rounded account of chanoyu and analyzing it as a signal example of nation-work. The two aims are not identical, but neither can be approached without the other. In his famous essay on the gift, Marcel Mauss argued that it had to be treated as a total social phenomenon, though the actual expression was the more Durkheimian *fait social total*. His examples were the potlatch and the kula ring, in what he called "archaic" societies, before the advent of a state, let alone a nation. It is therefore not surprising that in Mauss's enumeration of the various institutions he had in mind—including the legal, the economic, the religious, the aesthetic—he did not at first include the political.[47] Today, in a case like the tea ceremony, that would be harder to do. For much the same reasons, Mauss's agenda also omitted an historical examination. That too would scarcely be feasible in the case of tea. This work will attend to these dimensions. That it is unlikely to satisfy Mauss's full program goes without saying. What it will attempt is to combine a number of angles of vision that have not hitherto been brought together in the same way.

As Max Weber observed nearly a century ago, the concept of "nation" incorporates an almost analytically crippling range of social phenomena, from the multiple definitions and determinations of the collective belonging it denotes, to the great variability in the strength of the emotional attachment of membership, across both time and segments of a population.[48] Only a many-stranded methodological approach can begin to do justice to this diversity.[49] Each chapter of this book therefore applies a different interpretive lens—phenomenological, historical, institutional, and ethnographic—to capture the ways Japaneseness crystallizes in the tea ceremony. Here historical reconstruction will seek to establish the events and actors enabling that crystallization in the first place. Institutional analysis will turn from originating to sustaining conditions, to show how national meanings can become invested in organizational structures that facilitate their perpetuation. Phenomenological description will explore the ways that such meanings, in the case of the tea ceremony, are encoded in spatial structures, material objects, and corporeal forms that urge—even mold the body into—a sentient experience of Japaneseness. Ethnographic inquiry will ask how those concerned invoke or enact these national valences in everyday life. Yet whether across long stretches of historical time and wide expanses of collective identity, or more fleeting rhythms of individual experience and interpersonal interaction, a similar repertoire of action can be observed. Nation-work is the cord pulling together these varied dimensions into an overall pattern in what follows.

To bring home at the outset the sheer intensity of the tea ceremony as an instance of nation-work, Chapter 1 offers a phenomenology of it as a performance, treated as a flow of spaces, objects, and movements. Descriptions of tea rooms and the actions within them are readily found in the tea literature, but these typically remain schematic summaries of a complex experience that requires more meticulous subjective reconstruction if its sense and effects are to be analytically understood. Contrasts with everyday life evoke distinctively national resonances, creating a Japanese space within Japan, sustained by connections to other practices marked as Japanese.

Changing register, Chapter 2 looks at the history of the tea ceremony in Japan from premodern to present times, without which its contemporary phenomenology is incomprehensible. As noted above, this history is the dimension of the practice most thoroughly researched, both within and beyond Japan. But it has rarely, if at all, been recounted as a full narrative. The reasons for this, though no doubt in part due to gaps in the record, have more fundamentally reflected the role of the practice in the modern trajectory of the country. While its evolution from the Muromachi to Meiji eras—the fifteenth to early twentieth centuries—has been documented as one of the splendors of a now uncontentious past, its transformation into a national symbol in the inter-war and postwar periods of the last century pose more controversial questions, which tea scholarship has often preferred to avoid. Without pretending to any comprehensive coverage, this chapter tells a more continuous political story than has hitherto been recounted.

One of the impediments to such continuity has been the power of the iemoto system in postwar Japan. No study of the tea ceremony can ignore this formidable reality, which dominates the tea field today to a far greater extent than ever before. Yet the contemporary iemoto, who patronize much writing about tea, do not welcome investigation of their own operations, which remain a closed book in most of the literature. Chapter 3 attempts to remedy this lacuna with an institutional analysis of the structure and activities of the iemoto. Here sociological emphasis falls not only on the ideological and social, but also on the economic operations of the iemoto system, now in effect a set of modern business corporations invested in the Japaneseness of the practice they sell.

Chapter 4 shifts register again, moving from institutional to ethnographic terrain, to look at the ordinary practitioners of the tea ceremony: who they are, how they learn the ceremony, and how they invoke Japaneseness not only as they validate the authority of the iemoto, but also in their routines in the tea room. Even securely within a well-established nation, tea aficionados nonetheless occasion and employ the national inflections of the practice in their endeavors, and this chapter examines how.

Chapter 5 concludes the book by turning to the salience of the ceremony in the surrounding society at large as it is projected in the various systems of a media-saturated society. It ends by offering some comparative reflections on chanoyu, drawing on other classic venues of nation-work—gymnastics and music—in Europe and Asia, and returning the different dimensions of the tea ceremony to the overall framework under which they are viewed: as an exceptionally vivid and concentrated illustration of one of the fundamental processes of modernity, the work of making nations.

CHAPTER I

# Preparing Tea
## Spaces, Objects, Performances

To the foreign eye, the tea ceremony may seem unavoidably Japanese: a kimono-clad woman kneeling on tatami mats, gracefully preparing the beverage by means of a dense array of arcane procedures. But to outsiders, much in Japan is read as an expression of a foreign culture, from the politely crowded subways, to the exquisite yet simple aesthetics of prepared food, consumed with the eye before the mouth. For Japanese, most of these experiences are taken for granted as simply how things are done—people are more concerned with getting on the subway and getting fed than reading a cultural specificity into their activities. Yet even to many, accustomed to the quick preparation of simple green tea, consumed on tables and chairs while sporting Western clothes, the tea ceremony often connotes the traditional and evokes images of a fading cultural heritage. How is it that for the Japanese in Japan, where Japaneseness can be taken for granted, such an experience can be maintained?

## Japaneseness within Japan

Delaying for a moment the question of origins—where these national inflections came from—which will be addressed in the next chapter, let us consider the positioning of the practice. The tea ceremony does not serve the work of signifying Japaneseness alone, but is situated within an assemblage of other practices and objects that also represent this diffuse concept—a cultural matrix, as Tim Edensor terms it, that "provides innumerable points of connection, nodal points where authorities try to fix meaning, and constellations around which cultural elements cohere."[1] The complexity and reciprocity of these associations give rise to the "nebulous condensation," to use the words of Roland Barthes, that is Japaneseness.[2] Some items of the matrix display qualities akin to those of chanoyu—such as the delight in asymmetry found in flower arrangement—while others offer contrasts, as in the military self-sacrifice of Nitobe's *bushidō*. In this interconnected field, the tea ceremony occupies a privileged position, for it alone combines so many different practices and objects of the assemblage—clothing, cuisine, craft—into what its theorists describe as a "cultural synthesis."

A second axis of connection and contrast weds national meanings to the doing of tea. For the ceremony is at once an expression of the rhythms and aesthetics of ordinary existence, and detached from such unreflective lifeways as a consciously focused objectification of what is traditionally Japanese. It is through the alternation of parallels with and contrasts to common features of everyday life in Japan that tea condenses the nation. Barthes described a similar process when he remarked of houses in the Basque region of France that they do not strike the eye as particularly Basque in their local setting. But transposed to Paris, in a simplified, clarified form omitting many of the practical details (the barns, the external stairs) that made them functional dwellings in their homelands—such houses impose their Basqueness on the viewer.[3] In modern urban Japan, women in kimonos kneeling on tatami-mat floors invite a similar gaze. The Japaneseness encoded in tea places, captured in tea objects, and patterned into tea movements can be interpreted and experienced as quintessentially Japanese by the Japanese themselves because it is different—but not completely removed—from mundane aspects of life unmarked with national significations.[4] As we shall see, the apartness and deliberateness of the tea room and the objects and actions within it concentrate and purify aspects of the community diffusely lived elsewhere, but bent through the prism of tea. In Barthes's telling terms, the Japaneseness of chanoyu is "neither a lie nor a confession: it is an inflection."[5]

How tea "just *is* Japanese" can be conveyed by taking a tour of an actual tea room. We will begin by examining how its architecture molds the body into recognizably Japanese forms and corresponding sensory experiences, and go on to look at the objects used in tea practice and their cultural significations. Finally, we will greet the practitioners in a chanoyu performance.

## Tea Spaces

The tour begins at the tea complex Mushin'an,[6] designed by a successful architect in the early 1990s for his daughter, a tea aficionado, who was delighted when her father converted her apartment into a compact but versatile tea complex as a marriage gift. Adhering to the numerous detailed standards of tea architecture, Mushin'an has not only appeared in magazines, but is also rented by high-ranking teachers for their classes. Many lessons do not take place in such authentic spaces—what practitioners emphatically label *real* tea rooms—and teachers hold classes in their homes or public tea rooms at community centers or schools. When "making do" in these cases, adjustments are often accompanied by apologies, measured against standards represented by places like Mushin'an. Thus even if not a typical example, this tea complex is a good example, for its seriousness—as well as that of the lessons that take place inside it—renders in sharper detail the ideal to which tea practice is held.

Mushin'an is tucked away in Roppongi, one of Tokyo's many hubs, known as a center for consulates and foreign businesses and as a popular nightlife district. Emerging from the subway, one is beset by ten-story highrises lining the street and an elevated highway blocking the sun. The megalithic Mori Building—symbol of the decadent Tokyo architecture planned during the economic bubble of the 1980s that combines shopping, working, and entertainment—beckons in one direction, and Tokyo Tower, a red steel TV transmission station inspired by Eiffel's Parisian creation that serves as an architectural symbol of the city itself, guides the way to the tea room. Visiting a lesson on a Saturday morning may require dodging a few still-drunk revelers emerging from one of the numerous nightclubs and bars that dot the district. During the week, however, one is more likely to weave through the packs of shoppers and workers overfilling the sidewalks while trying to avoid volunteers requesting charity donations stationed at the subway entrance. A short distance down the street, the tea room is tucked away in an unremarkable multistory building, a few signs advertising the businesses inside speckling its narrow front, just like most edifices in the neighborhood. It is hard to imagine from street level that a tea room complex would occupy a significant part of the top floor in a building shared with a restaurant, an architectural firm, and a dance school. The owner of the complex even commented once on the strange juxtaposition as we walked to the subway station. "I sometimes wonder what is normal and what is not normal when I'm going between the tea room and here. Is this really everyday life? Sometimes the tea room seems so much more normal."[7]

The urban infrastructure of Roppongi, Tokyo

Entering the building, the ground floor with its narrow hall, linoleum tiling, row of mailboxes, and potted plant looks like any other small, multi-purpose office building. Up the elevator to the eighth floor and a short trip down the hall, the standard gray outward-swinging metal doors give way to a wooden lattice portal that slides to the side with the *garagaragara* sound often mimicked in traditional *rakugo* comedy sketches.[8] Visitors are greeted by the name of the tea complex, engraved in flowing calligraphy written horizontally in the traditional style of right to left on the wooden name plate that hangs on the wall opposite the entrance.[9] The three characters of Mu-shin-an, or *Hut of the Empty Spirit*,[10] are followed by the signature of the Urasenke iemoto, who christened the complex with this Zen-infused name. Only tea rooms meeting standards of excellence are granted an appellation by the iemoto, an honor applied for, and subsequently compensated for, with thousands of dollars in financial contributions.

In the small entrance space, guests leave their shoes on the slate flooring before rising up on a single wooden step and then onto the tatami mats that cover the floor of much of the complex. While most modern shops and businesses have done away with formal entranceways, a change in elevation between the threshold where shoes are removed and the interior proper is still common in many houses, restaurants, and schools, though the difference is typically a mere five inches or so. However, like many older or traditional buildings where the change is much greater, Mushin'an includes a long wooden step to bridge the almost 1.5-foot gap between the levels, and on which shoes may be set for guests about to depart. Because the distance is so large, brief greetings that do not require the visitor to enter the complex are met by the person on the interior kneeling rather than standing. When tea sweets are delivered, for instance, the difference in height beckons the person collecting the parcel to move to the floor or else tower awkwardly over the deliverer. Kneeling at the entrance—a scene invoking hospitality sometimes featured in tourist brochures at traditional inns[11]—is not only considered the most polite way to greet people at the door, it is almost required by the feeling of space. And once on the ground, a formal bow, rather than a polite head-nod, flows easily from the body as the hands slide from the lap to the floor.

The complex itself is constructed in an interlocking layout, with every room connected to others by at least two doors—an openness that facilitates the adaptation of the space for multiple purposes. Proceeding through the entrance, one comes to a narrow room with shelves for storing coats and bags, and a hook on the wall where a scroll might be hung if it is transformed into a waiting area during a formal tea gathering. The space—like most tea spaces—remains empty unless in use, but the absence of objects draws attention to how it is enclosed. The walls are made of high-quality *kabe*, a mixture of clay and sand that was a staple in building construction before plaster—easier to install and less prone to cracking—came to cover most walls after the Second World War. Along one side, the textured, earthen comfort is disrupted by a set of sliding doors connecting the space to a small tea room. The off-white papered portal is dotted by elegant pearl-colored prints of a chrysanthemum and paulownia pattern—a traditional combination that the knowledgeable will identify as popularized by the sixteenth-century warlord Toyotomi Hideyoshi.

A second sliding door—this one of translucent rice paper stretched across a wooden lattice that stages a play of shadows when the sun is shining—leads out to a small garden.[12] Here a flood of light greets visitors through a floor-to-ceiling wall of glass defining outdoor and indoor sections. Bearing little resemblance to the typical rooftop or yard packed with flowers and carefully

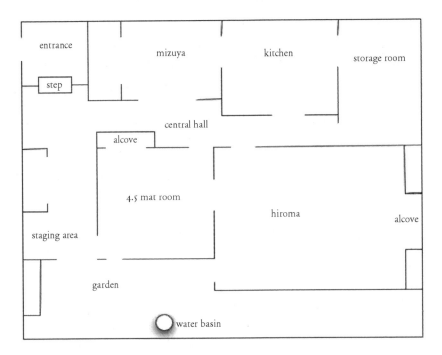

Floor plan of Mushin'an

A guest at a tea gathering entering the garden

sculpted trees, the tea garden is laid out on a bed of round pebbles strewn with irregularly shaped stepping stones that are interspersed with islands of small plants and moss. At the visual center stands a large stone basin, about two feet tall, and kept constantly full by the slow drip of water from a bamboo fountain. To the side sits a simple wooden bench where guests attending a formal tea gathering wait until invited to enter the main tea room.[13]

When the garden is in use, an earthy scent creeps into one's awareness from the slowly evaporating water sprinkled judiciously across the stones and path—a symbol of welcome still performed outside some storefronts and restaurants, particularly in Kyoto. Because the guests have left their shoes at the main entrance, sandals of woven straw are provided for traversing the uneven stepping stones. These are slipped on and worn with relative ease by those in a kimono, their split-toed socks fitting snugly into the thong-style slippers, though guests in Western clothes wearing socks usually have a more difficult time both putting on—and keeping on—the slippery straw sandals. Still, they manage to walk to the stone basin, where they purify their hands before entering the tea room. Here they encounter a bamboo scoop placed diagonally, the cup resting on its side, across the basin for their use. Almost all Japanese will have some familiarity with ladling water to purify the hands and mouth, a symbolic activity carried out whenever visiting a shrine. But at these sites less attention is paid to the fine details of movement than is demanded in the tea ceremony, where novices are instructed in how to hold the ladle to pour water over their left hand, their right hand, and then into a cupped left hand to use in rinsing the mouth. Afterward they may be gently reminded to return the scoop as they found it, on its side.

Two tea rooms stand at the core of the complex, a 4.5-mat room—the nine feet by nine feet classic size of a tea space—and a larger 8-mat room, or *hiroma*.[14] A sense of confinement in the smaller chamber is moderated by the numerous doors leading into it: two sets of sliding panels connect it to the waiting hall and to the larger tea room, a diminutive white papered door used by the host leads to the preparation areas, and an opening so narrow that one must crawl through it—a classic symbol of a tea room—leads to the garden. Explanations at temples and in history books, as well as by tea practitioners themselves, often point out that the crawl-through entrance was initially designed so small (approximately 28 by 28 inches) that samurai were forced to remove their swords before entering the tea room, symbolizing the equality of all in the space. More immediately consequential than its historical associations, the crawl-through door compresses the body such that, when entering, one is automatically positioned to kneel on the floor, the space spreading ahead with a deceptive impression of capaciousness. The transition between the inside and outside, created by the momentary tunnel, thus provides a smooth segue into the sensory and behavioral orientations of the tea world.

Defining the room is an alcove built into a wall and used for display—typically an arrangement of flowers resting on the slightly raised floor under a scroll inked with the bold characters of a terse Zen phrase. Once considered such a central part of interior architecture that debates raged on whether these recesses—superfluous from a utilitarian point of view—should be included in the public housing hastily erected on the rubble of

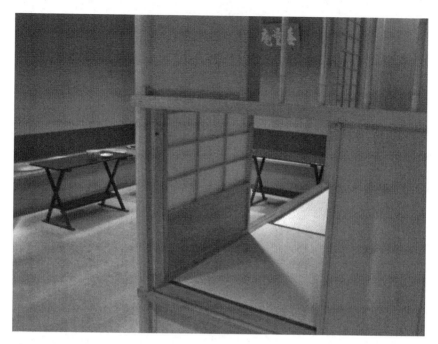

The crawl-through entrance of a tea room built within a room at a hotel

World War II, alcoves have become less common in recent years.[15] Along with sliding doors, tatami mats, and clay walls, alcoves are a definitive element of *washitsu*, literally "Japanese rooms," found in homes, restaurants, and hotels.[16]

The alcove marks the upper end of a nonlinear hierarchy of positions that locates all guests on a scale of importance, anchored at the other end by the host's door. Such negotiated orders of interior space may be disregarded in more mundane aspects of daily life, but still appear in both business and formal etiquette.[17] Trainees at large companies will learn the "high" and "low" positions in a waiting room or car, and are expected to develop a subtle skill for sliding toward the control panel marking the most honored place within an elevator to hold the "open" button for a social superior. Tea gatherings, however, stand out for the degree of deference displayed. Guests do not simply assume a seat, but position themselves in this unequal space through active, energetic (and even tiresome) negotiations. Experienced practitioners are remarkably adept at displaying the much-lauded value of modesty by situating themselves on the lower rungs of the spatial hierarchy—an inversion that even newcomers know not to tolerate. At larger gatherings these "no, after you" refusals can continue for so long that the host may step out and appoint a guest to the place of honor.

If one is standing, it is not hard to notice the wooden ceiling, which looms lower than in the rest of the complex. Over the guests' area rest patterned slats of wood, their upward slant contributing a sense of spaciousness while maintaining intimacy. A second section made of unfinished branches hangs flat above the place where the host sits. Hovering close to anyone standing up in the space, the low-lying ceiling prescribes a seated position as the most comfortable. Indeed, anyone approaching six feet tall must bend the head slightly when walking upright through the doors. The host's portal is cut even lower, around five feet high. Demanding the entrant bow the head when passing through, it configures the body into a position of humility upon entering the tea space, calling for an awareness of this action and attitude. Teachers may do so as well, but more explicitly. When students unused to low lintels perform tea in such spaces for the first time, they often pass through with a slight bend at the knees that keeps the torso upright—a posture typically corrected with the instruction to think humbly and bow at the waist.

The room is arranged for appreciation from the floor. When hanging the scroll, the host sits back on her heels while adjusting it so that the writing is best viewed from below. This orientation also drops the line of sight, increasing the feeling of spaciousness. The guests' eyes fall naturally on the hands and movements of the host preparing tea on the floor, which opens up as a working surface shared by everyone. Novices who spend most of their days in rooms with tables and chairs may be told that "tatami are not just the floor, they are like a tabletop on which you place the things you use, like a tea scoop. The perception of them is different from that of a floor. That is the sensation of a *Japanese* Japanese room."[18]

Within a tea room, people generally do not simply sit on the floor—they kneel. This way of installing oneself, called *seiza*, literally "correct sitting" in Japanese, is widely considered the most formal seated posture, and though Japanese may be accustomed to settling on the ground, most kneel only on particular occasions. Annual work-place parties, which often take place without chairs in the large tatami-floored rooms of restaurants, provide such opportunities. Here many of the participants may sit on their knees during the solemn opening speech and toast, relax into a cross-legged position for the heady revelry, and then return to kneeling for the closing speech. Children, when reprimanded, may be commanded to listen and apologize from a kneeling position, and formal requests, like a daughter's hand in marriage, may be offered from seiza. Yet kneeling is considered not only a *formal* way of sitting, but also a *Japanese* way of sitting. Books on the Japanese body frequently contain sections describing how it is perfectly made for kneeling, how seiza has affected Japanese culture, and so forth.[19] Indeed, such contortions are purported to foster the pigeon-toed style of

A tea practitioner kneeling to view a scroll at a tea gathering

walking regarded as the most elegant way for women in kimonos to move, and many attribute the country's prowess at international judo tournaments to the robust knees that result from seiza.[20] Of course, kneeling for an extended period—or even at all—is uncomfortable for anyone unused to the extra pressure on the legs, and even if most Japanese are accustomed to sitting on the floor on some occasions, many—perhaps most—nowadays find seiza painful.[21] The putative decline in the national ability to kneel is often bemoaned by purists, lamenting that "young people today can't even sit seiza," or that "since a Western lifestyle of tables and chairs has taken over, no one can kneel properly any longer."[22] Tea practitioners, with time, increase their endurance, cultivating the ability to sit in both a formal and a Japanese manner.

Kneeling serves functional purposes in small tea rooms as well. While one could sit cross-legged or with the legs to the side of the body, seiza facilitates movement by scooting. Placing the hands in front of the body and bringing the lower part into alignment with the upper half offers a means for getting around the room without standing up. Folded legs also enable as many as five people to occupy the narrow space. During tea preparation, the guests sit lined along the walls and, although only six inches or so may separate one from another, this close proximity is not experienced as particularly invasive, for with the body anchored at the bottom, the freest movement occurs along a front-back axis. Planted in such a position, guests face each other, at best, only at an angle by turning at the neck or waist. The arms, of course, may extend outwards, but their range of movement is restricted to a frontal arc, occupied largely by one's own lap. Although most novices will attempt to kneel at least initially, those unused to the posture often hastily shift to sitting either cross-legged or with their feet extended to the side—positions that take more space and lead to apologies acknowledging their impropriety.

The larger eight-mat room looks deceptively like a standard *washitsu*. As mentioned above, it is not unusual for houses, schools, community centers, and even businesses to possess at least one, with its hallmark tatami-covered floors, sliding doors, and alcove. But these "Japanese" rooms are hardly the unmarked standard in Japan, and even in buildings with a washitsu, most of everyday life occurs outside them—in homes they typically serve as storage spaces, spare rooms, or places for receiving guests.[23] Because of the particular demands of tea preparation, the hiroma differs slightly from garden-variety Japanese rooms: the floor is cut for a sunken hearth that can be opened in winter, the ceiling houses a hook for hanging a tea kettle at certain times of the year, one wall hosts a gong for use at formal tea gatherings. Yet even without such accoutrements, most washitsu can easily substitute if a purpose-built tea room is not available. With a ceiling of standard height, the hiroma feels more capacious than its intimate neighbor, and although the 4.5-mat room is considered the classic size for the tea ceremony, most lessons take place in the more spacious arena, preserving the smaller chamber as a region apart.

Although the hiroma does not boast a crawl-through doorway, tea practitioners nonetheless do not approach it unceremoniously. Most beginners learn early on to always enter a tea room by first sitting and then sliding across the threshold on the knees, before standing again. This traditionally "proper" way to enter a washitsu is rarely applied in other contexts and is easily forgotten even by experienced students, who may be reprimanded when they nonchalantly stride into the space. But while uncommon, this glissading entrance is not unknown. Kimono-clad employees at Japanese-style inns and restaurants,[24] where sliding doors separate the spaces, may set

A hiroma-style tea room with a sunken hearth and water container on display, in addition to a scroll, flower arrangement, and incense container in the alcove

down their tray as they sit on the floor to open the door and edge in and out
of the washitsu. But this formality is rarely observed by customers, even in
the most traditional inns, who simply open doors while standing and stride
directly through.

Tatami mats define not only the shape and size of tea rooms, but also how
to cross the space within them. While the details of walking vary from tea
school to tea school, all strictly proscribe treading on the silk borders of the
tatami mats—an injunction intended to preserve the appearance of the cloth
and, though rarely exercised in contemporary life, traditionally taught as a
part of good manners. Until patterned into the body and carried out mind-
lessly, steps must be carefully measured so that students do not make unusually long strides or short shuffles to avoid the borders. Furthermore, the
feet are not lifted and planted, but rather slid in small steps across the mats,
conforming to the demands a kimono makes on one to prevent its front flap
of cloth from opening indiscreetly. The resulting *zaaza* is an onomatopoetic
standard that refers to the sound of feet shuffling under the traditional garb.
Historical dramas, such as the popular television series on sixteenth-century
concubines, *Ōoku*, may project a thundering *zaaza* and a close-up of glissading split-toed socks when showing the women of the inner chambers on
the move. No less attention is given to turns, which too are carried out with
the same expectations of the "proper" way of walking in a kimono. To avoid
indecorously spreading the legs, left pivots, for example, are begun not with
the left foot, but with the right crossing in front. Cultural purists—and the
industry of schools teaching customers how to dress in a kimono—often
observe that as "Western" clothes, and the relatively free movement they
allow, have prevailed, many people no longer wear kimonos with comfortable conformity to the dictates of the wrap. Relearning how to walk in the
tea ceremony prepares the body to inhabit the antiquated garb with seemingly natural ease.

Behind the two tea rooms lies a *mizuya*, or preparation room, a space
unique to tea quarters. Lining one wall are cedar shelves on which white
cotton towels are stretched and the utensils meticulously arrayed. These are
pulled from a small closet set into one of the walls, where the implements
are stored. In preparation for a tea service, tea bowls rest equally spaced and
diagonally ordered in an economic arrangement that ensures they do not
chip each other. Tea scoops are grouped together on the shelf above, lined
up vertically beside the bamboo tubes that encase them when not in use,
and next to an array of lacquered tea caddies and ceramic tea containers.

Larger and less delicate objects—the feathers, baskets, and metal chopsticks used to prepare the charcoal fire—can be found on the upper shelf, and below this array is a copper faucet set into the wall, accompanied by a large, almost two-foot-tall clay basin holding water for immediate use. Ladles, brushes, tea whisks, and towels hang from knobs set into the wall around this sink area. A bamboo grate covers part of the floor and serves simultaneously as a countertop and drain into which waste water may be emptied. In the mizuya, again kneeling is necessary, as the water is easily accessible only from the ground—the only preparation space available.

Those accustomed to the back rooms of tea spaces will find no surprises here. Down to the copper faucet, nothing is specific to the mizuya in Mushin'an just described, patterned, like most in the Urasenke tradition, on the one found at the school's headquarters. Numerous pictures of this archetypical mizuya and textbooks on how to arrange and carry out preparations within it provide models for practitioners to follow at home. The meticulous standardization facilitates interchangeability: those trained in one place can enter a new tea compound and immediately know the location of utensils and necessary preparation tools—knowledge useful when hands are short. Because the space is small, motions must be coordinated for the smooth organization of the backstage preparations supporting a tea lesson or gathering. The standardized order of procedures expedites work as experienced practitioners, glancing around, can anticipate what a person will need next: if someone reaches for an empty tea container, a colleague may quickly hand him the powdered tea to place in it. Efficiency is not the only outcome of this anticipation, which also indicates an ability to read the needs of others—a skill cultivated and put into practice in the main tea room and esteemed in Japan more widely as proper adult behavior.

The preparation space links to a kitchen—a marker of the formality of the tea complex no less important than the mizuya to its side. Though many tea rooms do not offer immediate access to a place for food preparation, proximity is a boon because formal tea gatherings include a multi-course *kaiseki* meal, whose enjoyment hinges on strict timing. With its vinyl wood flooring, plaster walls, white ceiling, even a small table with chairs, the kitchen resembles many found in Japanese households. But precisely this mundaneness distinguishes it from the other rooms in the complex. A sink set into a waist-high counter ensures that standing (rather than kneeling, as in the mizuya) is the only possible way to prepare items, and the doors of the cupboards even open outwards rather than slide sideways. As such, the room calls for a different physical comportment than in other areas of the complex. It is a place where practitioners stand or sit on chairs, rather than kneel, and chat and laugh, rather than talk in low voices.[25] Grubby preparations—sifting the tea powder that can leave a green film on surfaces, washing the black dust from sticks of charcoal—are often undertaken here, preserving the cleanliness and symbolic purity of the mizuya. A convenient compromise, the kitchen incorporates the expediency, efficiency, and comfort afforded by modern designs within the larger, more traditional, complex.

Next to the kitchen, at the far end of the tea house, lies a storage room. Like those of its modern neighbor, the walls and ceiling are of white plaster, the floor is of laminated wood, and the door connecting the two spaces swings outward rather than sliding sideways. Here, larger utensils—wooden stands for preparing tea, cushions for the floor, flower vases, scrolls—are kept in closets and cupboards, but the space also serves as a changing room and storage area for personal items belonging to students and teachers. A bench along one wall offers respite to practitioners longing to sit rather than kneel during time-out moments. Like the kitchen, the storage room is a pragmatic concession that facilitates mundane tasks, such as answering phone calls, and preserves the more traditional tea spaces solely for their dedicated purpose.

Connecting the storage room to the rest of the compound is a narrow passageway running through the center of the complex. Less a room than a collection of doors, the hall is indispensable: without it, the tea spaces would open immediately to the mizuya and kitchen, offering a view of the preparations in progress each time the host enters. While any restaurant owner knows that masking the back room is essential to high-quality entertainment, this staging area is, critically, floored with tatami mats, which enable the person preparing tea to slide in and out of the room on the knees and to set the tea utensils on the ground without suggesting contamination.

With these eight chambers, Mushin'an offers, in Gaston Bachelard's terms, a "particular case of the possible"—and a particularly good one in the eyes of tea connoisseurs, as its appearance in magazines confirms. Not all places are as well appointed, and more often than not, practitioners must make do with what they have. Tea rooms in homes are usually installed by converting an eight-mat washitsu, but they often lack full mizuya, and those in schools rarely include access to a garden where the hands are ritually purified. At community centers, tea classes may even be held simply on a few tatami mats spread on the floor. Many modern buildings do not have sufficient ventilation for burning sticks of charcoal, leaving practitioners to make do with electrically heated kettles, though many are thankful for their low cost and easy maintenance. When a sunken hearth is unavailable, a portable version of the same shape may be placed on top of the tatami— a compromise that enables students to learn the positioning of the body and arrangement of utensils for tea during the "winter" half of the year, but one that leaves them to scoop and pour hot water at an awkwardly high angle. If a 4.5-mat room, required for the most esoteric forms of tea preparation, is not to be had, students are told to pretend that a larger room is of smaller measure, and to mime opening a door positioned much closer to the sunken hearth. All of these adjustments are made as compromises looking toward and simultaneously establishing tea rooms like Mushin'an as "more authentic" standards. Adhering to the numerous expectations that make for a good tea room, places like Mushin'an are often present in other situations when inadequacies are assessed against benchmarks exemplified by their architecture.

Tea spaces have long been saluted as representative of a distinctively Japanese architecture—indeed Takeda Goichi, a leader in the formation of a national building style, in an 1898 treatise lauded tea rooms as its epitome.[26] They continued to provide inspiration as the "modern Japanese style" of construction crystallized in the 1920s, and still today serve as a touchstone.[27] Yet the depth of this association goes beyond symbolic claims. The tatami mat floors, the earthen walls, the sliding paper doors stand out against the mundane modern architecture of everyday experience, yet they share commonalities with other locales seen as storehouses of tradition—such as temples or *ryokan* inns—that reinforce their Japaneseness. The exceptional materials, relative emptiness, and infrequent use of tea rooms define them as a space apart, where details and discrepancies catch the eye and afford a legibly Japanese experience to tea participants drawing on connections and contrasts beyond their immediate environment. Their architectural features craft the body into emblematically Japanese positions, from kneeling to obtain a proper view of the objects in the alcove, to sliding on the knees as a means to get around a small space without the disruption of standing. Otherwise rarely assumed postures incite awareness (if only the pain of kneeling), naturalized through the physical environment, while the structure encourages smooth segues into the habitation of the space. The low door shepherds entrants onto the floor, where their seated position limits movements that might disturb others and their eyes fall naturally on the low space of tea preparation. Quietly, the architecture channels a flow of movements that obscures the complex triumph of transforming the body and perceptions to create a physical experience of Japaneseness.

## Tea Objects

During tea preparation, the rooms are enlivened by an eye-catching array of utensils. Bowls, caddies, whisks, scoops, feathers, baskets, vases, incense containers, trays, picks, cloths, pouches, kettles, ladles, cushions, pipes, and jars are some that are easier to translate, but such a list omits an enormous number of specialized implements necessary for the back-room preparations during a tea gathering. The most crucial implements, of course, are the visible components in the tea preparation proper. To introduce these, we will follow a group of five tea practitioners through their rounds as they prepare for a lesson at Mushin'an.[28]

The first hour of class is dedicated to the cooperative transformation of the empty space into an active tea arena. Upon changing her shoes for white socks at the entrance and shedding her bag in the storage room, the first to arrive heads for the kitchen to place a large pot of water to boil on the stove. When steam issues forth, she removes a hefty cast-iron kettle—about a foot in diameter—from the tea room, and placing it on the bamboo grate on the floor of the mizuya, she carefully ladles the boiling water into it. With the kettle absent from the hearth, another student prepares a bed of ash—a three-dimensional landscape waiting to receive the warm body of the cauldron—lining its bottom. She heats a few precisely measured charcoal sticks, still retaining the shape and texture of the tree branches from which they were hewn, to a red glow over the kitchen stove, and then places them carefully in the ash according to a standard pattern, and accompanied by a sliver of incense.

Meanwhile, another student, kneeling on the floor of the mizuya, takes a small wooden spatula and metal sieve to sift the *matcha* tea, eliminating any lumps from the fine, green powder. Made from finely pulverized leaves, the dark green tea becomes an opaque suspension rather than a translucent infusion, and bears few similarities to its common counterpart that accompanies most meals in Japan. Whipped, not steeped, the matcha is mixed with a small whisk of around one hundred tines cut from a single piece of bamboo. The tea powder itself is high quality, torn from only the sweet tip of the tea leaf, and sold in a variety of blends that are targeted for two types of tea. The "thin" variant is rapidly whisked until a sheen of froth appears on its top, whereas thick tea, with its much greater powder-to-water ratio, is slowly mixed to yield a viscous blend approaching the consistency of yogurt. Both drinks, though known, are a rarity in Japan, and indeed the opportunity for a sip may serve as a selling point at tourist sites in traditional centers. In recent years, the beverage's exotic taste has fueled a boom in matcha-flavored products—ice cream, coffee drinks, cakes, crackers, and the like—often marketed with distinctively Japanese inflections, with women in kimonos proffering the drink alongside labels declaiming "taste the tradition." Yet though matcha-flavored products are increasingly common, bowls of actual matcha tea are not, and when they appear in the tea room, as elsewhere, they are accompanied by a few handmade sweets delicately shaped to invoke a theme or a season.[29]

Once the tea is sifted, a student, usually of more advanced rank, transfers the verdant powder into a tea container. The approximately three-inch-high caddies for thin tea are typically crafted from wood lacquered with designs in gold leaf that shimmer against a somber black background. Making regular appearances on these receptacles are traditional motifs, including figures found frequently in older art, such as irises and rafts; meaningful clusters like the pine, bamboo, and plum blossoms, which represent freshness and the ever-lasting; and vintage patterns such as the stylized arrow feathers that were once a popular choice for kimono cloth. The wide mouths of the caddies leave the tea powder on display for guests, and therefore care is taken when filling them. Slowly turning the container, the student gently deposits scoop after scoop of powder to create a perfectly smooth hillock—a landscape marred by no stray flecks, which would be immediately wiped from the sides of the receptacle.

Thick tea powder is stored in small ceramic containers shaped like the Chinese medicine bottles that were employed for the same task several centuries ago. Their fine glazes and ivory stoppers suggest the antique, and their narrow necks render unnecessary the attention to form applied when filling thin tea caddies. When displayed, these canisters are sheathed in pouches of thick silk brocade woven with ornate designs that likewise derive from traditional patterns.[30] The dual packaging and delicate manipulation of the vessel and pouch supply an additional layer of inaccessibility and rarefication to the powdered thick tea. Once the container is filled, a student transfers it to the tea room for exhibition on a small wooden stand waiting in the preparation space. Here it is complemented by a large ceramic water jar, typically around nine inches tall. The colorful designs brushed on the por-

celain, or the more subdued patterns emerging from the natural glazes, provide a background and balance to the tea performance that occurs before it.

As the preparation area assumes a working form, one student selects a
few tea bowls from the storage closet, sifting around for four or five with designs or colors appropriate to the season. About five inches in diameter and
three inches high, the vessels bear a closer resemblance to rice bowls than
the smaller cups that are the staple for steeped tea, and novices are often
hesitant when confronted for the first time with drinking from such a large
object. Though they come in a variety of shapes and pottery styles, from
finely painted porcelain to the unfinished asymmetry of Bizen ware, bowls
made in the rough, thick style of black Raku pottery are emblematic of the
tea ceremony.[31] While everyday teacups may be quite costly if old, crafted by
a well-known artisan, or fired in a famous kiln, the value of tea bowls derives
from additional sources. The pedigree of prior ownership, authentications by
respected authorities, and even an evocative name bestowed on the piece add
symbolic significances that contribute to the conversation at tea gatherings,
though at a cost: a high-quality vessel used at a formal gathering will carry
a price tag of a few thousand dollars. With more prestige value in the hierarchy of pottery than their quotidian counterparts, tea bowls—though used
only rarely—are as likely as teacups to be displayed at ceramic exhibitions,
a marker of the potter's prowess. Indeed, the status of these pots is so great
that particularly prized specimens have been designated national treasures.

Though often-used tea bowls wait uncovered in the storage closet, prized
ones are housed in boxes—finely crafted cedar cases, tied with a thickly
woven ribbon, that may even be stored in a yet larger box.[32] Yet not the container itself but the lid is the most valuable element, as this carries the name
and origin of the utensil in vertical brushwork, which bestows a pedigree

Tea bowls displayed alongside a tea scoop and tea container

and identity on it. For this reason, box covers are displayed at tea gatherings as a matter of course, sometimes with a person stationed by them, not only to explain the meanings encoded in the flowing brushstrokes, but also to ensure that the lids do not end up in a guest's kimono sleeve. With all of the information about the object's symbolic value, the container may be worth more than the item it holds, which would be rendered anonymous if separate from its case. Indeed, boxes are so central to the identity of an item as a tea utensil that when a found object is employed—a nineteenth-century British silver tray used to serve sweets, for example—a cedar house will be made for it.[33]

Once the bowls are arrayed on the mizuya shelf, a student will complement them with one or two bamboo scoops, lined upright, that are used to precisely measure the tea powder without disturbing the carefully crafted mound. To the uninitiated, the scoops appear more or less alike and seem hardly worth what may be a several-hundred- to several-thousand-dollar price tag for a light piece of curved bamboo. Aficionados, however, are largely concerned with their symbolic value. Those whittled by famous monks and tea masters are standard fare at formal gatherings, and invoke the presence of such spiritual figures in the tea room. Carvers also bestow monikers on the tea scoops, carried in black ink on their cylindrical bamboo cases. These "poetic names" (gomei), often borrowed from classical poetry or ancient texts, convey oblique references to the seasons or to spiritual concepts, imbuing these physically anonymous objects with an evocative personality.

With the kettle, tea caddy, and water container now in the room, an empty alcove looks amiss. Not simply in tea spaces, but in most washitsu, flowers and prized objects are exhibited in these niches, and a scroll hung on their back panel.[34] In traditional flower arrangement (ikebana) the blossoms are angled according to strict rules passed down within an iemoto-headed school, but only a handful of explicit dictates guide the placement of flowers in the tea ceremony (chabana). Practitioners, for the most part, do not attend separate classes to learn the skill, but simply pick up a feel for "good sense" through the accumulated experience of viewing such displays over time. Often it is the teacher who positions the flowers—sometimes a single bud in the colder months or a larger bouquet in the warmer ones—to ensure that the subtle arrangement is expertly accomplished. But this comes after a student, usually of senior rank, has suspended a scroll, unrolling the easily sullied composition of silk and paper with care. While hangings with Chinese-style landscapes or longer pieces of poetry may be found in alcoves more generally, the scrolls displayed in a tea room are limited in kind. Most common are ones bearing a Zen phrase of five characters or so, inked in a single column. Rich in potential meanings and difficult both to read and unravel without experience, the phrase sets the theme of a tea session. Experience and study aid in interpreting the expression, and its ambiguity allows a host to use the same scroll on multiple occasions for evoking different atmospheres. At lessons, the laconism offers teachers the opportunity for short lectures on the philosophical and spiritual orientations appropriate to tea.

As this suggests, much of any utensil's value resides in its symbolic significance, and a seasoned practitioner will be fluent not only in its handling, but also its origin and import. Copies of famous utensils, a staple at lessons, encourage a historical bias to this cultural knowledge. When a thin-tea container, striped with bands of red, yellow, and black, makes an appearance, a teacher will typically clarify that the design recalls a spinning top, which was favored by the warlord Toyotomi Hideyoshi, who employed this emblem on one of his family crests. A student who selects a tea bowl with a long base and a small hole at the bottom will be told the "horse riding" vessel was modeled on one used by samurai, who would sling a string through them and drink with one hand while astride their steeds. A copy of the ceramic tea caddy "Spindle Tree" will lead to the explanation that its name comes from a verse in the *Kokinshū* collection of poetry, a Japanese classic, that concerns the yellowing of the spindle tree's vines, as suggested by the amber color of its glaze. The teacher may add that the Hosokawa family, one of the most powerful daimyo houses during the Tokugawa period, possessed the original, which can now be viewed in the Nezu Museum.[35] Such glosses are not left to chance: scripted into the formal tea-making procedure is a segment for discussing the utensils, as we will see in the next section.[36] Whether political, social, or cultural, the information conveyed is often of a distinctively Japanese history, though not always an accurate one, refracted through chanoyu. As students learn to handle utensils, they acquire a detailed knowledge of cultural practices, aesthetic awareness, and historical events and figures— high cultural expertise—that enables their deployment and decoding, skills essential for appreciating the utensil selection at a gathering.[37]

To this is added a refined comprehension of seasonality, necessary for the appreciation and appropriation of utensils. Though seasonal change marks the cultural life of many parts of the world, it has been embraced in Japan as a national hallmark, and inculcation begins early. One textbook produced by the Ministry of Education informs junior high school students in a section on patriotism that "nature in our country has the distinct seasons of spring, summer, autumn, and winter, and a beautiful climate. Each season has sights, sounds, colors, and winds that reverberate in our hearts."[38] Such lessons are carried over to English classes, where textbooks routinely contain sections on seasonality as something Japanese must be prepared to explain to foreigners during moments of intercultural exchange. Adults can continue learning through the vast number of specialized books and magazines detailing the symbolic references to, pointedly, "Japan's seasons." Indeed, so fundamental is it that even manners manuals commonly feature a segment on seasonality. One of the most popular, produced by the Ogasawara family, etiquette advisor to the political elite for over seven centuries, begins a section on "seasonal awareness" with the assertion, "There are few countries that have such clear changes between the four seasons as Japan. Japanese culture is distinctive in that it does not oppose nature, but adeptly brings in and co-exists with nature in everyday life."[39] Unsurprisingly, traditionalists lament that the shift to urban lifestyles and the Westernization of living spaces has dulled such sensitivity.[40]

Because tea rooms lie empty when not in use, the scrolls, flowers, and dishes are selected specifically for the occasion, and a preference for objects evoking the time of year encodes seasonality into the array. A tea scoop evocatively named "spring fog"—a poetic reference—may be used in April when cherry trees are in bloom; a tea caddy lacquered with a flowing stream may be employed during the hot summer months to suggest coolness; a rusted yet repaired kettle may appear in October, as the leaves begin to wither and fall. The freshness of the ever-shifting décor makes the choices topical, creating opportunities for conversation or instruction concerning the seasonal significance of the particular objects employed that day. Yet the selections are not made with complete liberty, as codification has firmly fixed these seasonal associations to the calendar—even if they are late on the trees, plum blossoms appear in the tea room in February. Similarly, May is the month for irises, June for hydrangeas, and August for cicadas. Kyoto, as the capital of culture, is treated as the dominant referent for seasonal changes not simply within the tea world, but in Japanese society more broadly, trumping the dictum that tea should be made in harmony with the surrounding environment.[41] When little is to be found in their own gardens, practitioners in the snowy north may frequent flower shops to purchase buds in accordance with Kyoto's seasons. Although the famous irises at the Meiji Shrine in Tokyo bloom around the middle to end of June, tea enthusiasts in the capital avoid references to the flower at that time because of its association with May, the month it typically appears in Kyoto.

An additional axis constrains choice. Utensils are selected with an eye toward both their individual properties and the way they work together—meaningfully and aesthetically—in combination with other utensils, known as *toriawase*. At gatherings, this serves as the host's primary means for creative expression, and as the central draw for experienced practitioners who have seen the standardized tea preparations hundreds of times.[42] Pairing a bowl bearing a likeness of the goddess Benten with an incense container in the shape of a lute, her attribute, might draw a knowing nod, particularly if the Benten festival is approaching, but the precise nuances of more obscure combinations may require explanation.[43] Repetition is avoided (chrysanthemums on the tea caddy, kettle, and sweets would be boring) and asymmetry embraced—a dark wooden stand steadied by a bright water container—in this aesthetic sensibility acquired through observation and injunction.[44] Teachers may warn a student preparing for a lesson, "That bowl won't work with that tea container. You should choose something more vertical to balance out the container's squatness." Or, looking over the shoulder of a novice arranging the morsels that accompany the tea, a teacher may caution, "The

Visitors at a large tea gathering examine and discuss the utensils selected for the occasion

sweets are pretty on their own, but don't look good in that dish. You have to take that into account as well." The sense for asymmetrical harmony that is valued in everyday life—the variegated display of food in bento lunchboxes for example—is heightened in tea practice, evident when teachers instruct students to arrange the two varieties of sweets offered on a tray into contrasting piles of different numbers, or to arrange the flowers in an enchantingly angular array. Yet within these agreeable irregularities, the levels of formality are rarely crossed: modern glass bowls would appear out of place if combined with ancient Chinese ceramics or ivory tea scoops, for example. Though a site of creative expression, the toriawase must nonetheless fit within the normative guidelines of "good taste" within the tea ceremony.[45]

## Tea Performances

Though the utensils are meant to impress, the most visually striking aspect of the ceremony is the controlled gestures of tea preparation—*temae*—which are divided into hundreds of styles that vary with the utensils, tea room, and time of year. The simplest of these requires a minimum of implements and about twenty minutes from start to finish, while more elaborate variations can stretch over an hour, with two types of thick tea mixed using a host of objects, esoterically handled and purified. Yet whether intricate or unadorned, all procedures follow the pattern of set-up, utensil purification, tea preparation, and clean-up, and similarities among them render interference from kindred temae a lingering threat to smooth maneuvers. A tea scoop that is usually wiped only twice during the cleanup may on occasion be swabbed three—sometimes four—times. A bowl that is typically set out with the right hand will be placed with the left in some tea rooms. If particular value is attributed to the vessel, two hands may be necessary, but only until the tea is served, after which the one-handed standard again applies—though sometimes not, if the bowl is of Chinese origin. In the flow of preparing tea, students face the challenge not of remembering "in this case, the water scoop is set down with the thumb on top, and the fingers are not raised," but of unthinkingly allowing the motion to flow from the body. Without the hesitation of decision-making, the self is transformed into a lived expression of the practice.

Because tea preparation is so punctiliously regulated, a detailed description of an idealized temae can illustrate the forms of bodily discipline, corporeal communication, and sensory attention that constitute expert tea performances, regardless of the particularities of the space and utensils.[46] Although now representative of the ceremony, a single temae is only one element of a formal tea gathering (*chaji*). These four-hour-long affairs are planned weeks in advance and include a multi-course kaiseki meal, rests in the garden, two formal charcoal preparations, and services of thick and thin tea. Needless to say, because of the time, effort, and cost involved, formal tea gatherings are relatively rare, and the lessons that are the focal point of tea practice concentrate on temae.

The most basic preparation, *hirademae*, begins with a controlled arrangement of the space. As a wooden stand for displaying utensils is not used, only the guests, a tea kettle, and a tray of small sweets wait in the room for the host, who slides open the door, bows, and enters with a water container. Walking and turning with measured steps, she kneels to place the jar beside the kettle, her back straight while she sits and stands, with an even distance maintained between the carried object and her body. She exits and returns twice more, retrieving and positioning a tea container and bowl, and finally a container for waste water and a ladle. The utensils are set down directly, without further adjustment, in a balanced arrangement on the empty space of the tatami, whose lines of woven rush serve as aids in obtaining the precisely regulated spatial balance: five lines should separate the portable brazier from the wall, and fifteen lines distance it from the

A practitioner prepares tea at a formal gathering

A practitioner prepares tea using a portable brazier in an arrangement commonly employed in October. Also visible are a tea container, bowls, scoop, whisk, and cold-water container.

knees. The gap between the tea bowl and tea container should be the size of the caddy's lid, and the scoop resting on the tea vessel should not protrude beyond the curve of the water jar to maintain a sense of balance from the main guests' point of view.

When the utensils are arranged, the host pauses, exhales, and then commences an extended purification of the items. She moves the bowl closer to her knees in three steps, guided by an imaginary clock-face. Careful not to disturb the tea caddy beside it, she lifts the vessel with her right hand at four o'clock—thumb on top absolutely straight, hand curved around the side, fingertips aligned at an angle—and holding it over her lap, she adjusts her grip, left hand at nine o'clock, and sets it down with the right at three o'clock. To move the tea caddy closer, she grasps it from the top, shrouding only half the lid with her hand as she transfers it in a smooth arc to the front of her lap. Removing a twelve-inch silk cloth from her kimono belt, she folds the heavy fabric and wipes the lid of the tea caddy with a few stately strokes. Though the movements are distinct, they flow in rhythm from one to another. As the right hand grasping the folded cloth comes to repose on the lap, the left extends to replace the tea caddy, torso tilting in pursuit to restrain an awkward stretch, and then moves directly from the relinquished container to the tea scoop. Lifting the light object as if it were heavy conveys gravitas, and the slight spoon is hefted by raising first the handle and then the curved cup. Returned to the front of the body with the scoop in delicately curved fingers, the left hand remains motionless while the right, cradling the silk cloth, sweeps the body of the bamboo stick three times to purify it, slowing toward the end and hesitating briefly in the final moment to convey a sense of closure. As the right hand comes to a rest on the lap, the left sets the scoop on the tea container lid; the host exhales as first the cup, then the handle, meet the lacquered top, and inhaling, withdraws the hand. With the same precision, the host examines the tines on the tea whisk, opens the lid of the kettle, and warms the bowl, as the rhythmical flow and economy of movement convey relaxation.[47]

At last the scoop is hoisted to make the tea. Touching her fingers to the tatami mats with a slight bow, the host invites the first guest to sample one of the sweets presented before the procedure began. She reaches for the tea caddy, and in bringing it to the tea bowl, she traces an arc to prevent a kimono sleeve—real or imaginary—from dipping inside. Clutching the scoop with the final fingers of the right hand, the same hand removes the tea container's lid—straight up, no wrist turning—and circles the bowl to deposit it before her right knee. She re-grips the tea scoop to measure two heaped mounds of the matcha into the bowl. Preserving the delicate hill of tea, she draws out a portion of powder from the side, her breath measuring a solemn cadence: exhaling as the scoop is sunk into the mound, and inhaling as it is withdrawn. The spoon tips the powder into the bottom of the bowl, with a movement originating from a rounded arm—not a twisting wrist—that departs from the body at the shoulder. Finally, a gentle tap on the side of the vessel dislodges any remaining clumps of tea. Caution, however, is foremost, for too firm a strike may provoke a hairline crack. Thus, to forestall concern among knowledgeable guests, the host produces no sound when the bamboo meets the bowl.

Next, the host adds water from the steaming kettle to the powder, while ensuring that the ladle's cup remains suspended in the same mid-air position—slightly above the bowl—to avoid a sense of contamination. After returning

A practitioner prepares tea using a kettle placed in a sunken hearth

the residual hot water to the kettle and replacing the ladle with aplomb, the host grasps the bamboo tea whisk, and securing the bowl with the left hand, she whips the tea into a frothy suspension with rapid flicks of the wrist on the end of a steady arm. The beating slows, and she removes the whisk with a circular motion to sculpt a faint mound of foam on the surface of the drink. With the bowl on her left palm, she turns it twice so that its front faces the guest, and places it out for consumption.

The moment her hand departs from the object, her eyes turn briefly toward the main guest—the first in the line of three—who, still kneeling, scoots up to retrieve the tea. Upon returning to his seat, he offers a series of acknowledgments before imbibing the beverage. Placing the bowl between himself and the next guest, he apologizes for drinking first: head tipped in a semi-formal bow, his fingertips resting only partially on the floor. He then moves the bowl before his knees, and with a formal bow—hands fully on the floor and the torso dipping deeper—thanks the host for preparing the tea. Finally he lifts the vessel onto his left palm, and stabilizing it with his right, faintly raises it as he bows his head in a final show of gratitude. Turning the bowl twice, he drinks from its back as an indication of humility, but for the moment he takes only one sip, as the host will inquire about the taste, which he will invariably certify is delicious. These memorized greetings, like many in the ceremony, employ elevated, if archaic, terminology that is comprehensible but rarely used in everyday life. Without setting down the bowl, the guest will finish the remaining two ounces of tea with a few more sips—heedful of the time, as the other guests are waiting. But the carefully selected vessel must also be admired, so he wipes the lip of the bowl clean with a pinch of the fingers, and places it on the floor for viewing. With both hands on the ground, he first absorbs the overall appearance. Leaning forward, he then takes the bowl in both hands, the elbows resting in his lap to stabilize the inclined position, to examine it more closely. Turning the container to the side reveals the stamp of the artist who made it, though the guest does so cautiously, careful of stray drips. The bowl remains close to the ground throughout, for flipping around the fine ceramic piece from a greater height might transmit a ripple of anxiety across the room. Finally he returns the vessel to the floor to again admire its shape and glaze before sliding on his knees to return it to the host.

Waiting until the first guest returns to his seat—he shouldn't feel rushed—the host moves the bowl to her knees, ladles some cold water, and begins to clean it. Either further servings will be made for the remaining attendees or, at the request of the first guest, she will begin the closing sequence. For this, a slightly quicker tempo applies, and the implements are wiped and replaced in an abridged variation of the purification procedures. Once the initial order is restored, the first guest will typically ask to more closely examine the tea scoop and container—these having been carefully selected by the host, but seen until now only at a distance. The host symbolically purifies the pair once more and lays them out for the guests before removing the other utensils from the room one by one. The moment she departs from the tatami mat where the preparation has taken place, the first guest slides to retrieve the implements, but waits to view them until after the host has withdrawn the other objects—grasping, standing, returning, sitting—and closed the door behind her. The examination proceeds much as it did earlier with the bowl, though now the first guest passes the treasures on for the others to see. When the final attendee has finished, placing the scoop aside, the first guest—alert to this cue—looks over, and with an exchange of glances and bows, the two slide to the center of the room for a hand-off that permits the main guest to return the implements to the host. She has been sitting outside the closed portal, listening intently for the sliding (or monitoring the timing through a crack), and opens the door the moment the guests have returned to their seats. She installs herself before the utensils to answer a series of questions posed by the first guest—again in formal phrasing—about their origin and name. A bow of gratitude thanks her for her trouble, and as she removes the remaining implements, the host turns and kneels on the floor for a final, measured bow that lingers slightly longer than the others, before she slides the door closed with a concluding rap.

Following such a meticulous script, the tea ceremony is not to be confused with a casual call at a neighbor's house for a cup of brew, though here, too, ritual elements are evident: visits occur in select spaces, tidied or hastily made so; greetings bookend the conversation, which touches on delimited topics; a small snack can be expected to accompany a drink, along with the offer of a second serving—even if social graces anticipate refusal. In the tea ceremony, such mundane routines take heightened form in submission to its strict sequence, precise placements, and controlled motions. Formalism is the result, but one softened by the stylistics of action, marked by a restrained grace in movement, attention to rhythmic intervals, and vigilant consideration of others, discussed below.[48] Marked as national qualities both within and outside tea settings, these mundane actions are refined through tea practice—training that transforms disciples into consummate examples of Japanese comportment.

The tea ceremony reconfigures the most elementary activities—standing, walking, drinking—into an elegant expression that tames any extraneous motion. Congruent with the movements and manners dictated in etiquette textbooks, the re-incorporated dispositions are widely recognized as the "proper" ways of behaving. At a formal tea gathering, a pedagogy of culinary behavior teaches learners that their casual chopstick handling will not do: they must *correctly* heft them from the top with the index finger and thumb of the right hand, then grasp them with the left, while deftly sliding the right around the side to re-grip them from below. The procedure replays the lessons taught in the "Japanese dining" sections of manners manuals, with morsels of rice grasped by kimono-clad models, that are distinct from the "Western dining" segments where cutlery usage is addressed by figures in blouses and jackets, eating soup with spoons and sampling wine.[49] One book in this genre, while noting that Japan is not alone, still ascribes a national uniqueness to its cutlery: "Asian countries such as China, Korea, Thailand, and Indonesia also have a custom of using chopsticks, as do the Japanese, but they also use spoons" and thus "the

Japanese are unique in the world for eating only with chopsticks."[50] Still, many have become negligent, according to the manual, which prescribes as the antidote the same procedures as followed in the tea ceremony.

Bowing offers another iconic example. Meeting in the streets, adult friends typically exchange slight bows—these, of course, are much deeper when greeting a superior—and a quick nod of the head often accompanies the "yes, yes, I understand" replied to instructions. So pervasive, yet unnoticed, even bowing by people talking on the phone turns no heads. Little wonder that many textbooks for English classes, a required subject in school, contain images of bowing Japanese and handshaking Westerners. But being able to bow routinely and unthinkingly, does not mean that one knows how to do so correctly or formally. Indeed, it is one of the first things taught to beginners at tea lessons. When bowing from a kneeling position, novices often curve their backs, bend their necks, and bring their faces nearly to the floor in a fledgling attempt at formality. Typically a teacher must walk them through the proper variant: maintain a straight torso, bend only at the waist, move just far enough to allow the hands to transfer smoothly from the lap to the floor, where the fingertips form a small triangle, toward which the face is aimed but doesn't touch. Following the same strict procedures in etiquette books, initiates also learn a troika of formality, each grade distinguished by depth, as well as the degree of contact between the fingers and the floor. Employed during the greetings that commence and conclude lessons, as well as throughout the tea preparation proper, these bows, over time, become second nature to participants. But unlike greetings in everyday life, those in the tea room must be explicitly taught even to adults, who commonly make mistakes along the way. New students, and even some experienced ones, may forget how deeply to dip on a given occasion, and consistent precision can take several months to master—curved backs are an easy lapse. Though the variants of bowing and chopstick-holding incorporated in tea practice are recognizable as the proper versions of distinctively Japanese behaviors—as manners manuals and English textbooks remind— they nonetheless must be cultivated, as inclusion in etiquette books in the first place suggests. Carrying this pedagogy into practice, tea lessons become a venue for producing a properly Japanese figure.

A distinctive re-patterning is also visible in the ways that the kimono structures the movements of temae. Although a kimono is typically worn only on formal occasions, the basic motions of grasping, placing, sitting, and standing are channeled by the dictates of the long sleeves, open flaps, and tube-like bottom of the garment.[51] Teachers alert students to these exigencies, for most will have worn this increasingly archaic garb only a handful of times—college graduations and weddings offer opportunities. They project the garment onto the learner's body, cautioning students in casual skirts and blouses, for example, "When you turn, don't bounce up and down. That just looks careless. Move smoothly, so you don't disturb the air around you, and keep your right hand at your left knee so that the front flap of your kimono doesn't fold open." And they may warn learners in short-sleeved shirts, "When you put the tea caddy down, you need to move it around, not over, the bowl or else your sleeve may dip inside." Learning tea prepares students for natural movement in a kimono, as learning how to move in a kimono does so for tea—two symbols of the nation enlivened through a homology of gracefully retooled comportment.

This flow of movement is propelled by a rhythm structured by *ma*, meaning interval, gap, or the space between two things. Closely linked to the traditional arts, the term's aesthetic importance appears in the third definition offered by the *Daijirin* dictionary: "the temporal interval between beat and beat (or movement and movement) in Japanese traditional arts (music, dance, theater, etc.)."[52] As the description suggests, national associations for this interstitial suspension are strong. Indeed, the country's leading etiquette expert has declared that it "represents the tempo of life that constitutes the Japanese."[53] The concept even found expression in the first major Japanese architectural exhibition in the West: a self-declared exploration of "Japan-ness," innovatively interpreted by Isozaki Arata in New York in 1976.[54] Tea training instills a deep sensitivity to these structuring absences, as the movements flow with a distinct rhythm.[55] The water poured into the tea kettle at the end of the tea preparation slows to a deliberate trickle of a single drip, drip . . . drip. When the tea scoop is wiped three times from the base to the tip, the hand slows toward the end of the first run. The gesture proceeds more smoothly and swiftly the second time, and on the third round, the hand again slows. A momentary hesitation at the tip finalizes the purification, as the folded silk cloth departs from the scoop. Measured timing when handling utensils projects onto them an aura of importance, encouraged by teachers who tell students to remove their hand from an implement "as if leaving a cherished friend."[56] They may caution a student withdrawing a tea whisk too quickly from an inexpensive bowl, "You have a very valuable and famous bowl there, and you don't want to hit it. You need to take your hand away slowly. The movement *after* setting down a utensil is extremely important. That's what experienced practitioners notice most." Or they may warn, "If you don't have a good rhythm, then the guests won't be relaxed. You need to place that rhythm into your body."[57] With a consummate sensitivity to timing, experienced instructors can even correct actions they do not see. A slight difference in speed can be enough to indicate whether a student who exited a room turned to the right or the left before sitting, and the pupil may be surprised to find herself corrected even on such "blind" occasions. But more than a pedagogical aid, a refined sense of rhythm is crucial to maintaining the flow of coordinated action. The tempo catches the participants in its stream, sweeping them from one point and depositing them at another, smoothing the experience of this unnatural ritual. Attention to *ma*—and rhythm more generally—contributes not to making good tea, but to a good experience for the guests through a delicate sensitivity to nonverbal communication.

And this, too, carries national inflections. Although the ability to read between the lines is an essential skill for adults anywhere, indirect communication is frequently claimed in Japan as a particularly national characteristic, and the *Nihonjinron* books celebrating the country's uniqueness trumpet this quality.[58] The top-selling book of 2006, *The Style of the Nation*, even began its list of uniquely Japanese qualities with "unspoken understanding, intuitively knowing what others are thinking, non-verbal communication, respect for one's elders, duty, and mutual obligation."[59] Cross-cultural business manuals for Japanese working with foreign clients are rich with such examples as well, and titles such as *Japan's Power of Ambiguity* (*Nihon no Aimaichikara*) sell copies based on the self-congratulatory fascination with implicit communication.[60]

Although indirectness may be regarded as a distinctively Japanese trait, internal regional differences are recognized, with the traditional capital Kyoto representing the extreme in empathetic communication. A common joke about a non-Kyoto-ite's visit to a traditional house in the old capital captures the danger of miscommunication presented by these tacit transferals of intention. As the visit grows long, the host offers the guest a small snack, which the guest, wishing to leave but also wanting to be polite, accepts. This draws a frustrated sigh from the local, for in Kyoto a small snack is offered in hope that the guest will not want to burden the host yet further with preparing food and will take the hint that the exit door is open. What would elsewhere be a difficult-to-refuse invitation to prolong a visit becomes a polite way of showing someone to the door with the additional layer of nonverbal consideration.

It is not uncommon for practitioners to describe the communication in a tea room as retaining a strong flavor of such intuitive understanding, even if it is not evenly distributed across the nation. At a class introducing chanoyu at a culture center in the contemporary capital, a kimono-clad teacher explained to the group, "We in Tokyo are quite abrupt. We say things clearly and directly. But that's not the case in Kyoto. If I were to take a tray for sweets like this one [a low-quality platter] to the iemoto and ask for his signature of endorsement, he would say something like, 'Aaah, yes, maybe that can be used.' But in reality it would mean 'No, that's not good enough.' In Tokyo when people say, 'I'll think about it,' they really mean it. But in Kyoto, it means, 'No way.' The tea world is the same—it's like the way people in Kyoto speak."[61] Though the indirectness and allusiveness frequently lauded as Japanese traits are not evenly distributed, tea is proffered as a means of cultivating this sensitive mode of behavior.

Consideration is achieved through putting oneself in the position of others to anticipate their desires. A touchstone of the Nihonjinron literature, Doi Takeo's *Amae no Kōzō*, translated into English as *Anatomy of Dependence*, invigorates the national associations of this attitude on its opening pages. The author relates his disappointment upon arriving in the United States, where his host asked him if he was hungry, rather than foreseeing his stomach's needs. Books on top-quality service explain that rather than offering an array of options, servers ought to anticipate a customer's desires and pre-select what she is likely to prefer.[62] Drawn in opposition to Western-style customer-oriented service (*saabisu*) in which the demands are depicted as largely one-way, this genre portrays a Japanese-style hospitality (*omotenashi*) that relies on the cooperation of both the customer and server to produce a harmonious alignment though nonverbal empathetic understanding. Not surprisingly, the indirect empathy of omotenashi is generally marked (and marketed) as a distinctive form of Japanese hospitality, still found in traditional inns (*ryokan*) and restaurants (*ryōtei*), unlike their mundane counterparts, *hoteru* and *resutoran*.

Similar demands inform what is lauded as "good tea," in which actions are managed with an eye to the effect communicated. Not to appear greedy when the drink is set out, the guest waits until the moment the host removes her hand from the tea bowl—but not so long as to appear inattentive—before moving to retrieve the tea. And when the bowl is returned, the host, careful not to convey a sense of rushing things, waits until the guest is again seated before she collects the bowl. The same sensitivity is expressed when she takes care not to jar the observers by tapping the tea scoop too sharply on the bowl's rim.[63] As one practitioner explained, "Learning tea, you learn how to think about others. It's not just about making tea and putting it out, but making tea in a way that will make the other people feel relaxed. If your movements are too abrupt, they'll notice and not feel at ease."[64]

Failure leads to correction, and teachers remind remiss students to take those around them into account. Sprinkling too much water in the garden, for example, may evoke the reprimand, "You must think about the kimonos the guests will be wearing." Some lament that nonverbal consideration of others has attenuated with younger generations. As one tea-practicing monk bemoaned: "Too many people now say things directly." But, he continued, the tea ceremony stands as a bastion against this trend and offers a remedy, for "the tea world is not about saying things with words, but creating a harmonious group." This association, widely shared, lies behind the claim of a popular design magazine that the tea ceremony is a place where "the host and guest become of one body," which is "the ultimate in Japanese hospitality."[65]

During tea lessons, however, such references may be implicit. At a class in Tokyo, the rhythmical flow of the temae came to a halt when the last guest finished her tea and set down the bowl. Pausing, she quietly waited for the first guest to ask to examine the pottery more closely. Noticing the disruption, the teacher sharply reminded her classmate, "You need to ask to see the bowl." The target of her reprimand, a middle-aged woman, known more for her kindness than discipline, responded with surprise and then a chuckle, "Oh! Wow, well this is really a busy job!" The older, silver-haired student beside her commiserated, "Yes, so many things to do." The teacher explained, "But you have to be able to sense what is going on with all the guests. You have to be aware of everyone around you." The first guest chuckled again, saying, "I guess you can't be K.Y. if you do tea," which sent a ripple of laughter through the other students. The teacher queried, "K.Y.?" The youngest member of the class replied, "Oh, you haven't heard of it yet? It means you can't read the situation (*kūki ga yomenai*). I think some TV star made it up. It's a sort of sickness that people who are just too dense to get what is going on have." The teacher checked her understanding: "K.Y.? Yes, well, you really can't do tea if you are K.Y. You have to be very aware of what is going on around, being able to read others. That's one of the things you can learn through doing tea." The lesson was followed by dinner, during which I asked the teacher, who had lived for several years in the United

States, what she had found difficult in her time abroad. "Well," she replied, "there everyone is—what was it?—K.Y. You don't have to really worry about what others are thinking. You just act based on what you want to do, but it works because everyone is like that. Japanese people who live there a long time become like that as well. I think that's why I ended up making a lot of Japanese friends who do tea, because they're different. That's really one of the most important things in tea—finding friends to do it together with, who really understand what is going on."[66]

To make "good tea," the participants must transform the ceremony's unnatural ritualized procedures into an unaffected social stream, achieved by engaging aesthetic sensitivities and social awareness charged with national resonances—the restrained grace of comportment, the temporal articulations of *ma*, and a subtle consideration of others. These distill qualities from everyday existence into a refined variant and transplant them into new surroundings, enabling juxtapositions with the everyday to spotlight their clarified Japanese significations. The demands of the space and the constitutive elements of the practice conspire to dilute individuality and reconfigure the bodies of participants into distinctively Japanese postures and perceptions. Yet none of this can be taken for granted. Acquiring and enacting refined forms of Japaneseness—bodily gestures, social orientations, cultural knowledge—does not come easily, but requires cultivation.

## Conclusion

A delicate interplay of distinction, differentiation, and specification watermarks the constitutive elements of tea—its spaces, objects, and performances—as Japanese. From the moment of entry into the tea room, its natural materials and architectural features stand out in contrast with the mass-produced components and modern layouts of most of the spaces of daily life, while the ritual forms demand refined versions of mundane behavior—properly held chopsticks and executed bows—that may be labeled symbols of the nation but are often not experienced as such in everyday life. Behind this quiet Japaneseness commonly stand "Western" variants that serve as a foil for defining national qualities, conveyed by Nihonjinron texts and the popular media.[67] But once these distinctions can be taken for granted, internal differentiations with quotidian counterparts can elicit national resonances. Not only are distinction and differentiation at play, but specification as well. The refined aesthetic sensibilities, the carefully controlled comportment, the exquisite material components of the tea ceremony instantiate an upper-class version of traditional Japan. Like many high cultural forms, the tea rooms and utensils are delicate, difficult to maintain, and come at a steep price. Yet even if practitioners do not possess costly implements of their own, they acquire the cultural know-how to appreciate and appropriate, as well as maneuver with and within, these lavish objects and spaces. Enacting the ritual with aplomb requires practitioners to transform themselves into a lived expression of cultural sophistication, tinted in national hues.

Sustaining the Japanese tinges are homologies with other items carrying similar valences. The water sprinkled on the stones in the garden as a sign of welcome recalls analogous practices at traditional stores and temples. The alcove and tatami mats of the tea room suggest the washitsu in homes and hotels. Adding to their resilience, the forms may reinforce one another: it is easiest to slide into the archaic straw sandals in the garden when wearing the split-toed socks accompanying a kimono, and scrolls rather than framed pictures decorate the alcove. These elements offer an experience beyond themselves—one of Japaneseness—sustained by a matrix of items and practices whose analogous characteristics, defined as Japanese often through the same media at work in the tea ceremony, reinforce these significations through mutual reference.

Such affiliations inhere not in the objects themselves, but emerged through the historical elaboration of indicia of the nation. Here the degree of consensus of what belongs is striking, underwritten not only by the thriving Nihonjinron industry that profits from the proliferation of such associations, but also other institutions—movies, popular literature, magazines, textbooks—that offer succinct articulations of what this national essence entails. For while life in Japan is heterogeneous, as are possible definitions of what is Japanese, only certain variants of architecture, objects, and manners have been stamped with national colors. What gets selected through the lens of the tea ceremony is a Japaneseness of a particular sort: not that of anime, manga, cosplay, and otaku youth culture, nor of the overtime-working, dark-suited salarymen, but a markedly traditional formulation of the national essence. Drawing on long connections with a consecrated past, this version has greater impact and wider import than variants from contemporary culture. Not only members of a subgroup, but *all* members of the nation—the incumbents of national history—are projected as accountable for at least a basic knowledge of, if not actual competence in, the practice. Asked by a foreigner about manga or anime, a Japanese uninterested in the genres will simply apologize, but if the question concerns the tea ceremony, the same person is far more likely to express embarrassment for her lack of expertise.[68] The historical grounding of tea as a pediment of Japanese culture, a rope tying the present to the past, secures its position as a part of a national identity. Why these connotations are so strong can only be understood by unearthing the historical association of the tea ceremony with the apex of political power, to which we now turn.

## CHAPTER 2

# Creating Tea

*The National Transformation of a Cultural Practice*

If the tea ceremony today furnishes a potent emblem of the nation, it is because it can draw on a long and hallowed past in premodern Japan. Yet for all its prestige in historical times, it would be a mistake to think that it was identified as essentially Japanese before the coming of modernity, since the category of the nation as an inclusive community was still absent. The practice of tea may be preeminently nation-work now, but the nation itself had to be created and tea made national before it could help make the nation. That in turn could only happen because of its often dramatic earlier history, which lent itself especially well to symbolic appropriation in the modern period. The transformations of chanoyu that eventually brought it to this position stretch back over half a millennium, and no understanding of its present role is possible without some reconstruction of them.

## Origins

Like that of writing, law, and Buddhism, the story of formal tea drinking on the Japanese archipelago begins in China. During the Tang period (618–907), a solid cake tea, roasted and then pulverized, was added to boiling water—sometimes accompanied by sweet onions, ginger, jujube fruit, orange peels, dogwood berries, cloves, peppermint, or salt—a process requiring around two dozen implements. The popularity of the beverage spawned a vogue for tea parties, where guests were expected to conform to a strict etiquette, and lack of knowledge of decorum brought dishonor. Heightened concern with proper tea preparation gave rise in turn to a class of professional tea masters. Employed by the emperor, powerful mandarins, and single-family households, these men procured the finest leaf, experimented with the best modes of preparation, and ensured that utensils were of the highest grade. But the focus was on the quality of the tea. While compliments went to the host, the tea master often received a tip from the guests upon leaving.

Song period (960–1279) tea masters pushed the form forward with the development of powdered tea, a substance costlier and more difficult to produce, which—free of spices—was combined with boiling water and whisked to a frothy foam. This suspension flourished among Zen monks too, who sometimes became itinerant tea masters, hired by merchants who could not afford a full-time specialist. As a bridge between people, tea was celebrated for the leisure, friendship, and sociability it engendered. The upper classes found delightful diversion with tea contests, in which participants guessed the geographic origins of different teas as they vied for expensive prizes. Public tea houses proliferated alongside, rivaling taverns as business and social centers where deals could be cut, marriages sealed, and competitors for games of dice or mahjong found under the din of actors staging plays and storytellers recounting tales.[1]

It was during this time that tea was introduced to the Japanese archipelago by monks who had studied in China, though these monastic channels failed to carry the Chinese culture of conviviality around tea consumption. Initially the beverage remained largely confined to temples, where its high caffeine charge was used as a stimulant by votaries consigned to long hours of meditation, who incorporated a formal preparation and consumption of the beverage into their Buddhist rituals. With the spread of *shingi*, or regulations structuring the daily routines of monks in the mid-fourteenth century, so too came rules governing their comportment when drinking tea. By the fifteenth century, enjoyment of tea radiated out from the temples, as elites began hosting elaborate gatherings around the beverage. In lands where lords were captivated by the accomplishments of Chinese civilization, these sumptuous occasions offered an occasion for the display of prized Chinese wares—scrolls, vases, and bowls—that represented the ultimate in taste. Sometimes raucous affairs that could last through the night, they included among pleasurable diversions, such as poetry writing and incense appreciation (*kōdō*), both tea drinking and tea contests in which the participants attempted to identify the origins of blindly introduced tea. But unlike their Chinese counterparts, in such Japanese gatherings it was the objects, rather than the tea, that held the limelight.[2] Artistic specialists served both as advisors in the display and employment of utensils, and as instructors in proper drinking procedures. Warrior leaders frequently hosted such affairs, with the Ashikaga shogunate setting a standard with monthly gatherings.[3]

During the early sixteenth century, Buddhist channels diffused tea drinking beyond the military elite, and by mid-century successful merchants, particularly in the urban areas of Sakai, Nara, and Kyoto, were hosting tea gatherings at which they expanded the repertoire of utensils, aesthetic standards, and preparation procedures.[4] In smaller spaces, the merchants made tea for three or four invitees in a setting of carefully constructed intimacy and conviviality. While aristocratic tea gatherings revolved around the appreciation of rare Chinese objects, with the tea prepared in a back room by attendants, wealthy commoners incorporated more accessible local items in creative juxtaposition with valuable treasures, and themselves prepared the tea before the guests. With the host also on display, the tea ceremony shifted from an event to a practice, carrying the stamp of the person responsible for inventing a singular experience permeated by his individual taste, personal style, and attention to social graces. The guests were an active audience, creating a site not simply for networking but also for fraternity and community. In this development, the objects in the tea room began to take on meaning beyond their economic value, expressing a sense of artistic choice, as extravagant Chinese *karamono* artifacts were combined with plainer and more somber Japanese *wamono* implements. So pivotal were the selections of utensils that they dominated the tea diaries kept by the merchants, who carefully recorded these—in addition to the names of the guests—with only occasional mention, if at all, of the etiquette, conversation, or food.[5] The inclusion of intriguingly asymmetrical, rough or imperfect wamono pieces shifted the aesthetic taste of the period toward the values of the "cold and withered" to be found in the flourishing worlds of *waka* and *renga* poetry, yielding what was known as *wabi* tea, practiced in a quasi-rustic setting— though at no small cost to its carriers, who spurred a vibrant international and domestic market for these misshapen wares.[6]

A portrait of these gatherings was left by João Rodrigues, a Portuguese who arrived in Japan as a boy in 1577 and remained for thirty-three years, serving the Jesuits as an interpreter. In a compendium on the local culture he devoted four chapters to the tea ceremony, which he described as follows:

> The chief and most esteemed social custom among the Japanese is meeting to drink *cha* [tea], and so they spare no pains in constructing a special building for this purpose. Emphasis is laid on a frugal and apparently natural setting; nothing fashionable or elegant is used, but only utensils in keeping with a hermit's retreat. Social distinctions are not observed in this wholesome pastime, and a lower-ranking person may invite a lord or a noble, who on such occasions will behave as an equal.

In a later chapter on the "General Way in Which the Japanese Entertain with Tea," he observed:

> This manner of entertainment differs greatly from ordinary social dealings, for much modesty, tranquility, and quietness are observed. . . . They do not make use of spacious rooms or rich apartments for the occasion, nor do they use costly China dishes; there is no artistry or elegance, but only natural neglect and old age. . . . But although the small house and its utensils may appear rough, people spend large sums of money on them. Some earthenware utensils may be worth twenty thousand crowns—something which will appear as madness to other nations. In keeping with their melancholy disposition and with the purpose for which they collect such things, the Japanese find such mystery in these *cha* [tea] utensils that they attribute to them the value and esteem that other people place in precious stones and gems. This pastime was much influenced by the shogun Ashikaga Yoshimasa, who on his retirement from office withdrew to a quiet life in Higashiyama in the eastern part of Kyoto. He built there a small house which was used exclusively for gatherings to drink tea. . . . The purpose of *cha* is courtesy, breeding, moderation, peace of body and soul, humility, without pomp or splendor. *Suki*, the new way of performing *chanoyu*, originated in Sakai, and the wealthy merchants there acquired many rich utensils. . . . They consider *suki* as a wealthy poverty and an impoverished wealth, because the things used therein are poor in appearance but rich in price. They see to it that such objects are more valuable than they look and do not possess any glitter, luster, or contrivance. . . . Thus this poverty is in reality rich and wealthy, so much so that even the wealthy can maintain it only with difficulty.[7]

Tea gatherings of this kind became arenas where prosperous men from a range of backgrounds could mix relatively freely, display refined tastes, and diversify their social networks, in a liminal space—one of *mu'en*, or "no relation"—providing momentary respite from the commitments of a highly structured society.[8] Thus the tea ceremony of the late sixteenth and early seventeenth centuries was a central venue for the production and reproduction of social and cultural capacities that could be parlayed into political influence or economic capital. But though tea contexts allowed status divisions to be suspended, they reinforced class distinctions, as it was largely the well-connected and financially successful who had access to such gatherings.[9]

## Power Politics

In these conditions, decisive for the future of chanoyu was its annexation by the two most powerful figures in the land, the military hegemon Oda Nobunaga (1534–1582) and his vassal successor Toyotomi Hideyoshi (1536–1598). Like other ruthless warriors of the period, neither possessed the accoutrements of the court or the aristocracy—Hideyoshi, indeed, coming from origins so obscure they remain uncertain to this day. But as de facto supreme rulers, both sought consecration as men of culture. Poetry, the highest of the arts, required more literary training than either could hope to acquire, though Hideyoshi tried his hand at it, as at Noh drama. Tea, by contrast, required less painfully assembled knowledge, and offered social opportunities in two directions—emulation of older aristocratic forms of display, and appropriation of the more recent and restrained aesthetic of commoners. Of these, the second was the more important. Socializing with merchant tea experts offered a means to win the favor of urban commercial establishments, particularly those trading in military supplies, staples, and metals—essential during this battle-riven time of territorial consolidation.

Nobunaga's interest in tea seems to have crystallized when bringing the important merchant city of Sakai under his sway, which he accomplished through negotiations with the prominent tea master Imai Sōkyū, who was not only an influential member of the city's governing body, but also the owner of ammunition factories.[10] Nobunaga knew that legitimacy as a political ruler depended in part on fluency in aesthetic practice. Adopting chanoyu not only lent him the requisite veneer of cultivation, but linked him to the pleasures of the Ashikaga shoguns, while at the same time placing him within a web of powerful traders who could aid his expanding military ventures. As such, the tea ceremony became an indispensable political tool during the Momoyama era (1573–1615): utensils served as war prizes, small gatherings functioned as networking opportunities, and large celebrations marked military victories. Amid the chaos and violence of the period, the tea room remained an oasis of order, between whose four walls no assassinations—abundant outside them—were ever recorded. By the time Oda Nobunaga occupied Kyoto in 1568, chanoyu had become such an axis of power politics that the defeated party presented him with a tea container reputed to have belonged to Ashikaga Yoshimitsu (1358–1408). This diminutive ceramic became one of the greatest trophies in his fluid collection. Recognizing the symbolic potency of utensils with famous pedigrees, Nobunaga attempted to control their circulation completely, demanding the surrender of prized items after military victories and distributing them among his favored generals.[11] In Hideyoshi's words, "The tea ceremony was the lord's [Nobunaga's] way of doing politics."[12] During his time, the practice became a medium for negotiating rivalries, a tool for demonstrating wealth and power, and a space for forging important cross-class contacts, with merchants-cum–tea masters such as Sōkyū or another such figure, Sen Rikyū, serving as his intermediaries off the battlefield.

In 1582, Nobunaga died under attack from a rival warlord, just after a chanoyu gathering with a group of court aristocrats, and his most capable general, Toyotomi Hideyoshi, gained control over both his territories and his utensils. Soon after his ascent, the new hegemon cemented his legitimacy with several prominent tea demonstrations and utensil exhibitions in key sites of power—Osaka Castle, Daitokuji Temple, and the Imperial Palace in Kyoto. For the emperor, Hideyoshi constructed an entirely gilt tea room in which he personally prepared tea with prized utensils from his collection, using the ceremony to enact a union of the chrysanthemum of the court and the paulownia of his own house. On a more monumental scale was the Grand Kitano Tea Gathering of 1587, held at a shrine on the outskirts of Kyoto in celebration of recent military successes in the southern island of Kyushu. In contrast to Nobunaga, who granted permission to participate in tea only to his most trusted vassals, Hideyoshi invited all aficionados, publicly advertising the event on major thoroughfares. Over a thousand visitors gathered for the occasion (those who did not attend were threatened with a ban from all future participation in tea), which was held in as many as 1,500 tea huts assembled on the shrine grounds. Hideyoshi and his attendants served over eight hundred bowls of tea during the first morning to guests chosen by lottery, with others viewing the full array of Hideyoshi's utensil collection. The many fine pieces amassed from the holdings of the earlier Ashikaga shogunate offered a visual link between the new power holder and his predecessors, legitimating his supremacy by historical association.[13]

At Hideyoshi's side during this spectacular event, as well as at other key tea gatherings, was Sen Rikyū, his appointed tea master, who for a time was so powerful that it was reported that "no one can say a word to him [Hideyoshi] without first going through Rikyū."[14] With Hideyoshi's brother Hidenaga officially responsible for external affairs and military operations, Rikyū took charge of subtler transactions, using the tea room as a space to negotiate confidential matters for the hegemon, out of sight of interested others, without compromising him. While taking wabi tea to new levels of refinement, Rikyū had simultaneously to minister to Hideyoshi's displays of ostentation, helping him construct a portable gold-plated tea room—the flamboyant antithesis of wabi restraint—in which the regent (tairō) received emissaries from China and prepared tea for the emperor. Ultimately condemned to commit suicide,[15] Rikyū was succeeded as tea master to Hideyoshi by the warrior Furuta Oribe (1543–1615), who promoted a glitzier aesthetic, known as *karasuki*, that employed many ornate utensils of Chinese origin, more in keeping with the grandeur of the daimyo lords.

After Hideyoshi's death, the division between daimyo- and merchant-style tea practice became entrenched under the early Tokugawa shoguns, who appointed as their most trusted tea master the daimyo Kobori Enshū (1579–1647), followed by the daimyo Katagiri Sekishū (1605–1673). These two domainal lords-cum–tea masters set out to reform chanoyu in a manner more suited for warriors. Under their influence, the tea room became a site for reaffirming divisions between ruler and ruled, adopting the classical aesthetics of court culture, and developing rules of comportment that enforced social rank. The *sankin kotai* system, which required daimyo to divide their time between Edo (Tokyo) and their domains, ensured the transfer of the practice as a key form of sociability from the entourage of the shogun to lesser lords. Thus even shoguns who had no particular affection for tea, such as Tokugawa Ieyasu (1534–1616), still used tea masters as intermediaries in negotiations with daimyo. By the end of the seventeenth century, proficiency in chanoyu was expected of any elite warrior, and most turned to daimyo-style tea, rebuilding the hierarchical lines of authority within the tea room that had been suspended in the Momoyama period.[16]

Still, merchant-style tea persisted. With the stigma of ritual suicide quickly fading, Rikyū's grandson Sen Sōtan (1578–1658) continued and expanded tea practice as a family business. A social climber who used Rikyū's name to construct a sprawling network of tea associates and disciples, Sōtan employed his elite connections to garner appointments for three of his sons as tea masters to major domainal lords. These patrons solidified the reputation and wealth of the ensuing trio of Sen family branches: Omotesenke, Mushanokōjisenke, and Urasenke.[17] Though they were commoners serving in prominent warrior houses, the Sen families enjoyed a special status, including permission to retain residences in Kyoto and supplement their income by instructing well-off commoner clients in tea practice. Yet while their influence grew as the seventeenth century wore on, they were not the most important tea leaders, for the more prestigious forms remained the warrior-style ceremonies patronized by Hideyoshi in his last years.

The founding association of the tea ceremony with the pinnacle of political power in Japan, on the eve of the country's unification under the Tokugawa, would be critical for its subsequent history. A sense of Japanese identity, as distinct from Chinese, was found among the elites. Hideyoshi had even claimed that the purpose of his projected conquest of China, for which his invasion of Korea was intended to clear the way, was to bring Japanese culture to the (less enlightened) Middle Kingdom. Forms of tea preparation as well were generally distinguished based on the Chinese or Japanese style of the utensils employed. But it would be anachronistic to suppose that in the Japan of the time the tea ceremony had come to possess any "national" connotation, since there was no nation in the modern sense of an inclusive community of inhabitants sharing a national identity.[18] What it did acquire—and what inflected it decisively thereafter—was a symbolic association with the *state* in its emergent neo-feudal form, as a concentrate of legitimate political authority.

By the mid-seventeenth century Tokugawa rule had become a stable political order and in the extended peace that followed, most warriors no longer practiced their military calling, becoming in effect gentlemen bureaucrats, trained not only in swordsmanship, archery, and riding, but also in calligraphy, Confucian philosophy, poetry composition, and flower arrangement. Within this matrix of polite practices, the tea ceremony continued as a venue for political networking and gathering of confidential information on other domainal lords. For the daimyo themselves, good governance took on the idealized figure of the "model ruler" (*meikun*), who encouraged frugality, promoted scholarship, and patronized the arts—duties and obligations couched in moralistic terms.[19] Three prominent such rulers of the later

Tokugawa period, all of whom wrote treatises on the tea ceremony, singled it out as a crucial means of acquiring the qualities of good political leadership, instilling respect for the social order, and upholding the legitimacy of the state. Matsudaira Fumai (1751–1818), the daimyo of the Matsue domain, lauded for his economic reforms and enormous utensil collection, compared the role of tea in Japan to that of rituals and music in pre-Qing China, as a means to maintain proper status hierarchies and bring harmony to society. Critical of what he saw as the corruption of the ceremony by wealthy commoners, he compiled a catalogue ranking famous tea utensils held by past rulers, standardizing their value and re-inscribing their historical importance through the pedigree of their owners—a task he carried out in the name of the country.[20]

The masterful Matsudaira Sadanobu (1759–1829), the Tokugawa chief minister of state, instituted with the Kansei Reforms (1787–1793) a campaign to reinvigorate the shogunate. An administrative and economic disciplinarian, Sadanobu was also an aesthete and tea connoisseur, as well as a driving force behind the construction of a self-conscious "Japanese culture," albeit one with limited penetration to the lower classes. Critical of the profligacy of tea cognoscenti who squandered their fortunes on famous utensils, he produced four tracts expounding the virtues of the tea ceremony, interpreted in a Confucian rather than Zen register, as a means to solidify social position and secure the stability of the state.[21]

Six decades later, Ii Naosuke (1815–1860) became the last statesman of the shogunate, whose dramatic two years in power (1858–1860) saw the Harris Treaty opening ports to the United States, the management of a succession crisis in the Tokugawa family, and a great purge of disloyal government officials, before he was assassinated. An unexpected heir to the Hikone domain (he was the fourteenth son), Naosuke penned five treatises on tea before assuming the helm of state and three as governor of the country. In these, he promoted chanoyu as a means for improving society and reviving the warrior spirit, which, as the referent of "samurai" shifted, was now understood not as a component of a military status passed down within a house, but as a more narrow ruling class of elite politicians and bureaucrats. Naosuke conceived the tea gathering as a cure for the worst social ills—a microcosm of the ideal state in which all fulfilled their proper roles for the benefit of society—and a way to cultivate both the self and the principles of good governance. Where Sadanobu called for openness and freedom in how tea was actually prepared, Naosuke insisted upon a rigid formula—bodily movements generally taken for granted, such as opening doors or bending forward, were elaborately detailed in his texts, inscribing micro-class boundaries into elite male comportment.[22]

## Under the Tokugawa

The use of tea to package political ideals for members of the warrior class makes clear how widespread knowledge of the practice was within it. Tea training, for these men, cultivated the knowledge necessary to serve in one's "proper place" within the social hierarchy, as the relatively free mixing at merchants' gatherings of the Momoyama age, in which status frequently did not determine the most honored guest, was eclipsed by the elaboration of rules and procedures for exceptional treatment of high-ranking nobles and aristocrats in the tea room. Not only was the warrior stratum expected to master tea as part of the repertoire of sophisticated manners that structured interaction, but such cultivation was held to refine character and instill self-discipline. The elevation and preservation of daimyo tea required that it be distanced not only from excessive focus on the objects of the tea room, but also from either mimicry or degradation of it by prosperous commoners. For urban merchants continued to enjoy tea practice, amid the economic growth and improved transport and communication systems of the first half of the Tokugawa era,[23] and wabi styles of tea came under scornful attack from some spirited samurai, mocking its valorization of broken tea vessels, the baseness of crawling into the tea room like a dog on its belly, and the unhygienic drinking from the same bowl as others.[24]

In the same period, moreover, a rival to matcha-based chanoyu emerged in *sencha*, a form of tea preparation in a Chinese mode that used steeped leaves and was associated with Confucian scholars and literati in bohemian settings.[25] Pitting sencha against the rigidities and corruptions of chanoyu, its champions promoted it as a freer and more relaxed form of sociability, with the prestige of the Chinese example behind it—powdered tea having been completely replaced by steeped tea after the Song. While connections to China were drawn through Zen Buddhism in matcha tea consumption, Confucian learning served as the linkage in sencha. Though at first an iconoclastic practice, by the mid-nineteenth century steeped tea advocates had diffused sencha among a wider swathe of the population by borrowing characteristics from chanoyu itself—rigid etiquette, standardized preparation procedures, instructional texts, fetishized objects—even if its tenets remained rooted in Sinophilia.[26] But steeped tea—consumed, of course, in less refined versions as a normal beverage throughout the country—was never a match for powdered tea at the highest levels of power, where chanoyu remained entrenched.[27]

At full stretch, the matcha tea ceremony was an almost exclusively male affair. But from at least the mid-eighteenth century, both elite and wealthy commoner women could learn its rudiments, etiquette manuals encouraging them to gain a thin knowledge of some of its procedures.[28] The widely read late-seventeenth-century pair of lifestyle books for women and men, *Onna Chōhōki* (1692) and *Nan Chōhōki* (1693), which contained sections on the ceremony, illustrate the contrast. In these, men received much more detailed instruction in a practice presented—complete with illustrations—as a form of training necessary for properly cultivated adults, while for women tea was simply listed as an appropriate hobby or pastime.[29] The guidebook granted them social approval for enjoying tea, but did not foster an understanding of the ceremony's essence, and only sketchily outlined a full tea gathering.[30] Ladies-in-waiting in daimyo families were often of urban merchant origin, sent by their parents at great expense for basic training in the arts to refine them for such service. For them, "learning tea was a way of learning to be graceful."[31] As for Momoyama men, tea for Tokugawa women was a vehicle for improving social status while reinforcing class barriers. But in their case, it was an introduction to comportment rather than a practice of the ceremony itself that was learned.[32]

Thus by the nineteenth century, tea was promoted among elite men as a way to cultivate the disciplined body and mind of a good leader, and among elite or upwardly mobile women as a means to develop social graces, refined comportment, and genteel femininity. But while tea could make good ruling men and good society women, it could not yet make good *Japanese* men and women. Yet in two critical ways the premodern history of the practice predisposed it to become such an evocative symbol of Japan during its transformation into a nation-state. The first was its aesthetic elaboration in a society that in all strata placed a premium on beauty. Under the Tokugawa, horizontal networks connecting people across the social spectrum in group activities such as poetry, flower arrangement, incense appreciation, and the tea ceremony flourished as a type of substitute—tolerated by the state—for a public sphere of the political kind in Europe. In this place of an order apart, where status divisions were momentarily suspended, merchants, monks, warriors, and even villagers could gather together in collective pur-

suit of aesthetic pleasures. The effect of this was not only to make a sense
of beauty an instinctive value among broad layers of the population, but
to smooth interactions between people in less committed social contexts,
creating a distinctive "civility without civil society."[33] By the late seventeenth
and early eighteenth centuries, a status system was firmly in place that incorporated a general image of the appropriate comportment and standards
of good behavior—from language, to movements, to dress. The sensitization
to aesthetic values it inculcated could later be reworked into an ideology of
national identity for internal and external consumption in the Meiji construction of a purported natural *Gemeinschaft* defined by aesthetic awareness, encompassing the archipelago and stretching back for centuries.[34] In
this edifice, the tea ceremony would come to hold pride of place.

But if tea could eventually occupy this position, it was because of its intimate associations not just with beauty, but with power. By the end of the
Tokugawa period, no other communal art stood as a competitive rival. Tea
alone had accumulated such a noble past as the cultural accoutrement of
the central figures of a glorious national history, once the innovative styles
of successful Momoyama merchants were co-opted and recast by the military leaders and model rulers of the age—producing bountiful material for
constructing a lineage of the practice intertwined with the political history
of the archipelago. The prestige of the ceremony was underwritten by the
devoted practice of it, across three hundred years, of the outstanding states-
men at the apex of power: Nobunaga, the hammer of sectarian divisions;
Hideyoshi, the founder of a pacified Japan; Sadanobu, the great reformer
of the shogunate; Naosuke, its final heroic defender. Nor did this grand
genealogy stop even there. Amid the turmoil of 1868, as the Meiji Restoration was taking form, Kido Takayoshi (1833–1877)—one of its principal
leaders—was noting in his diary the tea gatherings he continued to attend.[35]
The connection between power politics and tea practice held up to the
threshold of modernity.

## Modern Japan I: Connoisseurs

By the early nineteenth century, the Tokugawa shogunate was succumbing
to a fiscal crisis, and its outmoded military apparatus was no match for Matthew Perry's gunpowder superiority when his ships entered Yokohama Bay
in 1853.[36] Naosuke's reforming purges were not enough to keep rebellious
daimyo and samurai like Kido in check, and by 1868 the shogunate was

overthrown and the emperor "returned" to rule. The political, economic, and cultural upheavals wrought by the Meiji Restoration devastated the economic underpinnings of the tea ceremony world. In 1871 the abolition of the feudal status system dismantled the domains whose daimyo had been patrons of the ceremony, and not a few of the politicians and bureaucrats of the new era came from lower-level samurai families, less versed in the practice. Traditional aesthetic pastimes of every kind were threatened by an out-with-the-old, in-with-the-new fervor attacking what were seen as vestiges of a conservative ancien régime, and an attempt was made to reclassify tea masters, along with geisha, as mere "entertainers," to be taxed accordingly.

But by the 1880s a reaction had set in, and once-decried practices were reevaluated in a positive light, often with the help of Western enthusiasts reframing traditional aesthetic activities as native arts. In this climate, from the mid-Meiji period and with growing enthusiasm from the turn of the century, tea found new practitioners among the emerging business elite—the captains of industry whose rise was one of the commanding features of the time. These came to include such prominent figures as Mitsui director Masuda Takashi, shipbuilding magnate Kawasaki Shōzō, Tobu railroad founder Nezu Kaichirō, silk baron Hara Tomitarō, and Mitsukoshi department store director Takahashi Yoshio. In the Tokugawa era, merchants had never enjoyed a high social standing, and these men were determined to establish a superior position, in keeping with their importance to state and society as modern industrialists rather than mere traders. To enhance their social prestige, they followed the model of the cultivated elites of Tokugawa and pre-Tokugawa times, and took up chanoyu, emulating aristocratic rather than commoner forms of the practice. Daimyo tea thus returned to the upper altitudes of society as these millionaire *sukisha*— "tea connoisseurs"—developed latter-day versions of its style. By adopting the cultural practices of prior rulers, the new businessmen aesthetes could hope to temper their image as ravenous economic animals, and appropriate legitimizing links to past elites. As Masuda put it, "Tea is one of the leisure arts I enjoy. . . . Nobunaga, Hideyoshi, and other heroes were impressed with this art and came to find it deeply rewarding. Since the Genki and Tenshō eras [1570–1575], all great men have had a taste for tea."[37]

Reminiscent of feudal lords who mixed business and pleasure in their tea rooms, the sukisha used tea to further their corporate networks. From small clubs of bankers, bureaucrats, art dealers, and physicians sharing an aesthetic interest in the practice, grew large-scale gatherings that dotted the social calendar. The most spectacular, the Daishikai, was a major tea event that from the turn of the twentieth century brought together dozens and later hundreds of prominent members of different elites in a melding of the tea ceremony and high society. Such gala tea gatherings—at once grand and intimate, attended by the powers-that-be and lavishly covered in the press—where captains of industry knelt on the floor and prepared tea before their guests, also provided opportunities to advance business networks, negotiate deals, or secure marriage alliances. At the Mitsui conglomerate, whose operations in banking, trade, mining, cotton, paper, electricity, and armaments handled over a third of Japan's international trade by 1914, one contemporary observed that "no aspiring company executive could afford to be ignorant of *chanoyu*."[38]

Begun in 1896, the year after Japan's victory in the Sino-Japanese War, the Daishikai gatherings were staged in a period of burgeoning national pride. Whereas individualistic collecting and ostentatious display of utensils were frowned on in the early and mid-Meiji period, by the turn of the century the sukisha began to host spectacular public displays. Throughout, tea utensils seen as works of art were the focal point of their activities. Competing for prized items, these men supported a flourishing and volatile market in which circulated not only famous teaware, but also antiques, relics, and other objects all fetching exorbitant prices. At a time when the Western category of "art" had just arrived and the native formulation, "Japanese art," was still finding its feet, these collectors invested heavily not only in the financial but also the cultural worth of their acquisitions.[39] Moving though the tea room, Buddhist relics—only a short while before regarded solely as sacred icons—obtained a new sheen as objects of art linked to a long and distinctively Japanese history of elite tea practice.[40] Collecting, displaying, and employing utensils that had belonged to great figures in what was now a national history—Ashikaga Yoshimitsu, Oda Nobunaga, and Toyotomi Hideyoshi—these magnates inserted themselves into an archetypically Japanese historical narrative through association with this noble past.[41] For many collectors, such as Masuda, this stockpiling and display was a "patriotic duty," preventing the country's aesthetic treasures from falling into the hands of avaricious foreign buyers. Before the advent of museums, their formal tea gatherings served as salons where prominent businessmen, art dealers, and others could handle fine works newly defined as art—indeed, participation became the sine qua non of membership in Japan's business elite.[42] Inscribing their interest into the landscape, the sukisha even built chains of tea huts on their private estates: Masuda's contained thirteen tea buildings, and the gardens of Hara's seventeen-hectare estate were laid around numerous tea rooms.

Engaging in debates on chanoyu in wider intellectual circles and publishing books on tea utensils, philosophy, and aesthetics, the sukisha generally stressed that the tea ceremony was essentially a demonstration of taste and an aesthetic pursuit improving oneself and fostering exchanges with friends.[43] Assertions otherwise could be vociferously rejected. When tea dilettante in the Ministry of Justice Takaya Tsunetarō asserted that the ceremony was "the ruling policy of the country" (kokka keirin, shortened to the neologism chadō keikoku), offering a way to develop "our spirit and the national intellect," and occupying "the most prominent position with national morals,"[44] he was ridiculed by Takahashi Yoshio, director of the Mitsui Bank, who retorted, "Recently people have been saying idiotic things about tea, connecting it to the training of morality and cultivation of patriotism, and spreading the exaggerated claim that it is 'the ruling policy of the country.' That is not what the tea ceremony is. Tea is essentially connoisseurship. Enjoying tea as a connoisseur is enough. . . . I, as a true Japanese gentleman (shinshi), follow my heart and enjoy tea as a matter of taste."[45] Tanaka Senshō, head of the Dainihon Sadō Gakkai (Great Japanese Society for the Way of Tea), responded that Takahashi's typical sukisha position resembled that of elite tea practitioners of the past, but had no connection with the general population, for whom tea was a means for cultivating manners, as well as body and soul. For, as he would repeat throughout his career, "the tea ceremony is the basis of national morals and national manners."[46]

Striking in this exchange is that while the idea that the tea ceremony served the Japanese state or nation could be contested, that it was fundamentally Japanese was not. Takaya expressed what was by then a common nationalizing image of tea in etiquette textbooks, and Tanaka maintained his long-held view that tea was a means to craft good national subjects. Takahashi, on the other hand, dismissed usages of tea for anything—including nationalist endeavors—beyond enjoyment of the practice itself. But in bolstering his argument with the avowal "I, as a true Japanese gentleman, follow my heart and enjoy tea as a matter of taste," he clothed the aesthetic claim in national form. It was the properly *Japanese* man who, almost instinctively, enjoyed tea as part of civilized life, and it was a properly Japanese *gentleman* who practiced tea as a connoisseur. The choice of the term "gentleman" signaled the distinctively male associations of a nonchalant connoisseurship—by contrast with the stiff training involved in women's tea practice—and the implicit limitation of this particular form of masculine Japaneseness to the upper classes.

Comparable overtones are audible in other sukisha writings. In 1936 Masuda Takashi, who stood at the center of the business world of tea, wrote on a fold-out page in the introductory volume to the first encyclopedic work on the tea ceremony, *Chadō Zenshū*, that "the essence of the tea ceremony is enriching the heart, warming exchanges with friends, and promoting harmony in the world. . . . It is essentially a form of pleasure."[47] Noteworthy in this formulation is the innovative way Masuda writes "tea ceremony," normally referred to as chanoyu (茶の湯), preceded sometimes in written documents with the honorific *o* (お), yielding お茶の湯. Masuda, however, chose to write *ochanoyu* as 夫茶の湯, combining a character pronounced as *o*, but meaning "male," with the word for the tea ceremony. The effect of the neologism was to mark off the tea in which Masuda was engaged—that of industrialist—from what by default would be the tea practice of women, which his readers might infer was less a form of pleasure than of discipline. Less subtle was the scholar Takahashi Tatsuo, who would complain in a monograph advocating greater recognition of chanoyu's weight in the country's past that "though now women have become the people of leisure enjoying tea, from the perspective of Japanese history, [the tea ceremony] holds an extremely important position."[48]

## Modern Japan II: Women

This concern reacted to a second major change to the field of tea in the Meiji years, as the country was transformed into a modern nation-state. While references to "Nihon" were occasionally made prior to the Restoration, the meaning of the term was neither consistent nor consistently applied to the present-day country or a centralized political authority, let alone a unified people. Expressions like *kokoku*—"imperial land"—were more frequent. And the political system consisted of relatively autonomous domains, capped by the shogunate, in which the largest social unit was usually that of the "domainal people" or the "village people." While the scholars of the Native Learning (*kokugaku*) movement had begun to articulate ideas of cultural distinctiveness, and even formulate notions of the people as agents of government, these stopped short of conceptualizing them as constituting a nation.[49]

The political crisis that followed the arrival of Commodore Perry's squadron off Yokohama in 1853 abruptly altered the terms of earlier discourse, as the elites confronted the danger of foreign incursions and possible occupation. The contestation and competition that defined subsequent state- and nation-building processes centered on many of the axes of modern nationalism: territorial integrity, popular representation, cultural uniqueness, and political organization. Over the following decades, notions of Japaneseness were re-crafted to fit a national model, envisaged through the lens of familial metaphors. In the imaginary of the family-state (*kazoku kokka*), the country was headed by the newly emancipated emperor, and the populace incorporated through position-specific roles defined in relation to the head of the family. While the Tokugawa regime was content with merely the docile compliance of commoners, the new Meiji rulers sought to transform the population into a self-aware national community.[50]

Famously, an effective means of retooling a populace into national subjects is through state-run mass education, and the Meiji regime quickly adopted a modern education system with great success. The 1872 Fundamental Code of Education made compulsory four years of schooling for boys and girls and by 1878 over half of boys and about a quarter of girls attended primary school, which increased to almost all the youth by 1910.[51] Morality was given a preeminent place in this nationalizing endeavor, encapsulated in an 1881 Ministry of Education directive to elementary school teachers to teach that "loyalty to the Imperial House, love of country, filial piety toward parents, respect for superiors, faith in friends, charity toward inferiors, and respect for oneself constitute the Great Path of human morality."[52] Ideological debates toward the close of the 1880s centered on the role of morality in cultivating a "sense of the nation," leading to the promulgation of the Imperial Rescript on Education in 1890, which reinforced the connections between the school system, the state, and the national family, in a moralizing Confucian register.[53]

To this end, girls' education was reformulated to inculcate a new domestic ideal of femininity that would form middle- and upper-class women into "good wives and wise mothers" (*ryōsai kenbo*).[54] Mori Arinori (1847–1889), the first minister of education, explained that the purpose of this policy was "to nurture a disposition and train talents for the task of rearing children and of managing a household," and declared that "the basis of national wealth is education and the foundation of education is female education." For "the encouragement or discouragement of female education, we must remember, has a bearing on national tranquility or its absence."[55] Women, as household managers, carried a great responsibility to the state: it was their duty, in the words of Education Minister Kabayama Sukenori, not only to "nourish a warm and chaste character and the most beautiful and elevated temperament" but—and this was to be a crucial rider—to "furnish the knowledge of arts and crafts necessary for middle- to upper-class life."[56] Fukuzawa Yukichi (1835–1901), a leading thinker of the period and the founder of Keio University, drove the message home. "The arts," he maintained, "are the sole possession of feminine society, and in addition to music, training in the tea ceremony, flower arrangement, singing, poetry, and calligraphy, etc., should be made possible as far as family allowances can afford it."[57]

Fukuzawa's list of desirable accomplishments could, of course, have come from the repertoire required of any upper-class woman during the Tokugawa period, who took lessons in a range of aesthetic activities, including the koto, the incense ceremony, linked verse, flower arrangement, letter writing, sewing, singing, and rudiments of the tea ceremony as part of their training for service or participation in elite life. With the addition of cooking, this traditional cluster of activities now continued as skills in which girls educated beyond the compulsory four or six years of school were trained. Educators simply took the established package of arts and skills, added cooking and household management, and reframed these as a means to develop the ideal qualities of bourgeois domesticity rather than genteel femininity.

In this atmosphere, women's home economics and etiquette books proliferated, now read not only for private edification, as in the Tokugawa era, but also incorporated into the curricula at public schools. Commonly containing a section on artistic skills, these texts devoted anywhere from two to over fifty pages to the tea ceremony—the shortest offering only the most basic instruction in how to fulfill the role of a guest, the longest providing details on tea-room architecture, garden construction, and multicourse kaiseki meals, in addition to elaborate instructions about charcoal arrangement and thick and thin tea preparation. Significantly, the ceremony only rarely was included in boys' textbooks, usually under the heading of recreational skills or pastimes.[58] What was central to official renditions of femininity was only tangential to those of masculinity. If the aim of some texts for girls was simply to guard against potential embarrassments when attending a tea gathering, others provided much of the detailed knowledge covered in the first several years of tea training.[59] But in either case, such manuals played a defining role in establishing a commonsense view of the tea ceremony as distinctively Japanese in at least three ways: by including tea within a national framework, by inserting tea into a national narrative, and by promoting tea for its nationalizing effects.

Regarding the first of these, the textbooks established national grounds and goals for the lessons transmitted. In the early 1890s, their principal concern was preservation of a Japanese essence in the face of a threatening Westernization. Introductions to the manuals commonly offered descriptions of Japan as a "country of proper manners" that had recently become almost overwhelmed by an "influx of Western things" or "things from abroad that are unlike those in this country."[60] Invoking the long history of Japan, the texts encouraged readers to take pride in its customs, which were often feminized. "We should be proud of the qualities of our country's women and of the ways of our people in the past."[61] Thus it was up to girls' education "to keep our country's particular manners from dying out."[62] Such injunctions formed part of the broad contemporary concern with "conservation of the national essence" (*kokusui hozon*).[63] By the 1900s, however, this had yielded to a new imperative, as the household began to appear as the foundation of the nation. In the words of one manual, "The household is the basis of society, and if order within it is lost, then society itself falters."[64] But who was liable for this? "Home maintenance is the basis of the nation. . . . Men work outside and women work inside the home."[65] Women were not only "responsible for everything inside the home," but should "think of the home as the same thing as the nation."[66] It was their duty to "improve the household and revolutionize society."[67] In the background of these instructions lay the Civil Code of 1898, which had written the "family state" into law, encouraging women to serve the nation by maintaining a proper household, headed by men who possessed preeminent legal powers within it.[68]

Within this framework, the tea ceremony found its place in a national narrative. Textbooks in the 1890s often provided elaborate descriptions of the pre-seventeenth-century "history of tea in our country,"[69] beginning with its importation from China, moving through its adoption at prominent Zen temples as an aid to meditation, highlighting the development of elaborate tea parties by the Ashikaga elite and the staging of tea by famous warlords such as Nobunaga and Hideyoshi, and concluding with the institutionalization of standards for tea preparation by Takeno Jō'ō and Sen Rikyū. These descriptions mapped the history of tea into a national narrative carried by key political figures, thereby establishing a unified Japanese history from at least the tenth century. In it, chanoyu becomes a thread running through the activities of otherwise disparate political, social, and cultural elites, before attaining its fullest form under Rikyū. Tea practice after the sixteenth century is entirely eliminated from these narratives, leaving the impression that the ceremony ceased to change after Rikyū and that contemporary preparation procedures formed a direct link to this noble past. The same story can be found in history textbooks of the period as well.

Finally, the manuals—sporadically in the 1890s, regularly in the early twentieth century—contain definitions of the tea ceremony that imply nationalizing effects.[70] Tea was variously depicted as an ancient pastime of the elite, a method of social exchange, a form of manners, or a spiritual endeavor, whose benefits included the cultivation of morals, good conduct, ties of friendship, and aesthetic sensibility, and training in the practice bore on the duties of a good wife and wise mother. One text explained that "learning tea manners is useful for learning how to handle things in the kitchen"; another that what was learned in the tea room should be "applied naturally in everyday life"; a third that "if you learn the tea ceremony, you will, when drinking tea at home, naturally take [the cup] with two

Toyohara Chikanobu, "Edo Brocades: Tea Ceremony," 1904. Ink on Paper. 8¾ in. × 12¹¹⁄₁₆ in. (22.23 cm × 32.23 cm). Scripps College, Claremont, California, USA. Purchased by the Aoki Endowment for Japanese Arts and Cultures.

hands instead of one. You will always reply to an invitation. You will always see people off at the door."[71] Although not always explicitly marked as such, the proposed benefits of tea study could readily be understood as distinctively national. The Confucian ethics often mentioned were enshrined in the Imperial Rescript on Education as the basis of national pedagogy. Aesthetic sensibilities acquired through tea, such as the notions of poetic elegance encapsulated by concept of *fūga* or *fūryū*, were understood to be particularly Japanese.[72] Even the practices of everyday good behavior, such as the example of holding a teacup with two hands mentioned above, were often explicitly contrasted with Western customs—holding a teacup with one hand—in other sections of etiquette books. Presented as cultivating particular values defined as supporting the nation or particularly national characteristics, the tea ceremony was advanced as a nationalizing practice.

The reasons the tea ceremony featured so insistently in these manuals can be deduced from the few records that remain of the motives of educators for introducing tea instruction at their schools. The head of the Atomi School, one of the first girls' schools in Japan and the first to include tea ceremony classes, contended that tea was a more effective way of cultivating manners and morality than teaching them directly. By learning it, pupils would naturally come to refine their physical and spiritual comportment.[73] Such skills were now implicitly associated with women's roles in service of the nation, explicit references to which were more commonly articulated in schools at the geographic or cultural margins, where Japaneseness could not be taken for granted. For example, when the Seiporo Girls' School, a Christian outpost in the recently colonized Hokkaido, was due to be reviewed for accreditation by the Ministry of Education, tea classes were adopted in order to demonstrate that the girls were being trained in a "Japanese lifestyle," and were dropped immediately after accreditation was granted.[74] Even in the more central city of Kobe, a mission school instituted classes in the tea ceremony and flower arrangement, held in a purpose-built room, in order to reassure accreditors that, despite its Christian principles, it was still preparing "good wives and wise mothers."[75] In Taiwan, annexed in 1895, where schools were required to provide classes in which students could develop the "morality expected for leading a good, happy everyday life based on the essence of our country's morals, paying particular attention to general manners, beauty, and morality,"[76] Japanese-style rooms were either incorporated into the architecture of schools or, more frequently, erected in separate buildings on their grounds, where Taiwanese girls obtained regular instruction on how to open and close doors, walk on tatami mats, bow, and offer formal greetings. At some schools, the girls even wore the kimono they had stitched together in their sewing classes. But if learning Japanese behavior was as important as learning the Japanese language for "cultivating the national spirit," instruction was not only more basic, it was also far more detailed than in Japan, where more might be taken for granted. Here, where tea instruction was tinged with the exotic, pictures and depictions of tea classes—rarer in graduation albums at schools in Japan—were very common, tokens of their memorability as something noteworthy, or projections of an air of authenticity according to the standards of the metropole.[77]

In mainland Japan, few records remain of how tea training at schools actually proceeded in this period, but the evidence indicates that instruction was generally an extracurricular activity, taught once or twice a week on school grounds or in the dorms, where much of home economics education took place. While some girls' schools began to incorporate tea training as an extracurricular activity from the 1880s, most growth occurred around the turn of the century. If classes were large, the students could be broken down into smaller groups of five or so to facilitate direct instruction. Tea performances were also featured at some school festivals. In general, however, tea education for girls remained basic and did not probe the philosophical or artistic depths of the practice. As an employee of the Ministry of the Interior explained in a 1918 tract, though such training is useful for girls—even "rural women"—"as social graces, there is no need to learn the tea ceremony and flower arrangement very deeply. Only a familiarity with the parts dealing with manners of giving objects and receiving guests is essential. This is what is needed for future wives" and therefore "[tea and flower] instruction should promote manners."[78]

As the tea ceremony cemented its position in the package of skills that girls were expected to learn, it began to appear in other venues propagating images of the ideal woman. The popular magazine *Fujin Gahō* (Ladies' Graphic) began to carry articles on the activity shortly after the turn of the twentieth century, reinforcing many of the themes found in the etiquette books. Pitched to readers personally interested in (rather than institutionally required to learn) tea, these offered guidance in reshaping them in the romantic image of a distinctively Japanese middle- to upper-class life.[79] Early coverage consisted mainly of photographs of tea lessons or tea gatherings of elite women, placed toward the beginning of the magazine, together with shots of other aesthetic pursuits, such as flower arrangement, or prominent socialites. As magazines extended their circulation from the upper to the middle classes from the 1920s, images of the practice took on more pragmatic overtones: practical instructions and tips for performing tea began to appear with occasional written accounts of particularly memorable tea gatherings, and even pieces on Rikyū's teachings. By the 1930s, *Fujin Gahō* was carrying articles going beyond simply the mechanics of tea training to its deeper benefits and meanings, and in keeping with the heightened nationalism of the decade, on occasion presenting it as a means to improve the national spirit.[80] A 1935 article comparing Japanese and Chinese tea practices to illustrate distinctive cultural essences even employed an image of matcha to represent the quintessence of Japanese tea.[81]

Advertisements in the magazine latched onto such national associations as a selling point. In 1932, a prominent tea company featured a picture of a woman in a kimono making tea above a statement that "modern people are now removed from the Japanese tea ceremony. . . . While coffee shops abound, it is questionable whether tea in Western rooms, on tables and chairs, tastes good." Reminding readers that "tea has long been a skill of the elite in the East" and "in Japan, was valued for spiritual cultivation and social exchange," the company's founder enjoined them, "We need to bring tea into everyday life in new ways." An accompanying box regretted that "the tea ceremony is still not everyday knowledge among Japanese women."[82] Meanwhile newer media were also disseminating nationalized visions of tea across the country. In 1927, two years after the inaugural radio broadcast in Japan, the first program on tea was put out by—significantly—the women's section of the Tokyo Central Broadcasting Company. Over thirteen installments, the audience, presumably of female listeners, was instructed in "Tea Ceremony Manners"—the first of these presenting the practice as something "once passed down secretly, but that now would be brought openly to the people"—which formed part of "the matters of this country from which all things began."[83] Radiating across the territory, the tea ceremony was treated at once as—henceforward—a common national value, and tacitly as if it were now a typically feminine practice.

## Modern Japan III: Intellectuals

But neither the flamboyant activities of the sukisha above nor the mundane manuals for girls below were the cutting edge in the ideological reconfiguration of tea in post-feudal Japan. That role fell to the writers and thinkers who provided the intellectual elaboration that transformed tea into a touchstone of Japanese nationalism. The pioneer of this trend was an upstart young teacher, Tanaka Senshō (1875–1960), who split away from the Urasenke school to establish his own organization, Dainihon Sadō Gakkai, in 1898, which he called not a "school" but an "association," of which he was the "president" rather than "iemoto."[84] Setting out to modernize the institutional underpinnings of tea by consciously running his organization as a business, he abolished secret teachings, promoted independent learning through correspondence courses and detailed texts, and started the first tea ceremony periodical, *Chadō Gakushi*, in 1900—a medium soon copied by the Sen schools. But as its name made clear, Tanaka's project was also expressly nationalist: tea was to be used to produce better political subjects. The founding document of the Dainihon Sadō Gakkai opens with the lines, "Originally the tea ceremony in our country began with [Murata] Jukō, was restored by [Takeno] Jō'ō, and perfected by [Sen] Rikyū, and finally it has become a form of learning the national essence. The deep meaning of the real tea ceremony derives from Zen, contributes to reason, and lays down proper behavior. . . . It is the basis for ruling the body, ruling the family, ruling the state, ruling the world (*shūshin seika kokka heitenka*)."[85] Reacting against sukisha claims that tea was just a pleasurable pastime and media images of tea as simply graceful comportment for women, Tanaka dwelt on its Zen and Confucian inspiration, insisting that it belonged to the core of national being.

Tanaka proselytized for this conception of the tea ceremony as a way to make good national subjects in numerous public lectures and private engagements with arts, women's, and other associations. In a wealth of essays, too, he stressed time and again the spiritual component of the practice and its elevating impact on morals, distancing it from mere vulgar entertainment.[86] As he explained his mission, "Tea is the basis of national morality, and I have been attempting to spread national manners. . . . The tea ceremony is not women's entertainment, as many people are still misunderstanding, but in reality this path is, I believe, the basis for ruling the body, ruling the family, ruling the state, ruling the world."[87] That did not mean women should be excluded from it—a position that would have sat uncomfortably with his growing body of female adherents. Tea, he proposed, was not merely a hobby for women: those who learned it underwent a physical transformation, developing proper posture and behavior that conferred on them merits beyond those of other women.[88] It thus not only cultivated people into well-mannered nationals by refining body and soul and diffusing an etiquette that even the upper classes seemed to have forgotten, but also made women into better women. The practice conveyed "national morals" and "national manners." Without evidence of these, Westerners might acquire the false impression that the Japanese lacked cultivation, lowering the status of the country.[89] As such, tea offered the means to cultivate the ethical and etiquette capacities that defined the nation, where Japaneseness was simultaneously innate and improvable.[90]

Altogether more sophisticated, if less immediately influential within Japan, was the work of the polymath Okakura Kakuzō (1862–1913), a leading figure in the definition and institutionalization of "Japanese art" from the time he was a student of Ernest Fenollosa at Tokyo Imperial University, and who was appointed to head the first fine arts academy in Japan in 1891. Schooled by American missionaries in Yokohama, Okakura was effectively bilingual—indeed, his English was better than his Japanese in his youth—and well traveled in Asia, with sojourns in China and India, and later in Europe and America, where he played a key role in creating the exceptional East Asian collection at the Boston Museum of Fine Arts.[91] After dismissal from his position at the Academy of Fine Arts in Tokyo in 1898, Okakura lived for a year in Calcutta, where he developed a friendship with Rabindranath Tagore, and composed a blistering attack on Western imperialism, *The Awakening of the East*, calling for Asian resistance to European and American aggression in the region. Not the Yellow Peril, but the "White Disaster" was a danger to the world, its social system based on capital and the machine threatening to crush ancient Asian civilizations based on land and labor. Salvation lay only in the sword.[92] Unpublished at the time, *Awakening* was followed by a further volume, *The Ideals of the East*, published in 1903, whose message was scarcely less militant, opening with the ringing words "Asia is One," and closing with the rousing call, "Victory from within, or a mighty death without."[93] In it, he developed a fully rounded theory of the unity of Asian civilization and the special position of Japan within it, as the transcendent values of Indian spirituality and the immanent values of Chinese humanism fused in Japanese culture, where Buddhism and Confucianism had come together in a unique synthesis. Since Japan, unlike India and China, was never conquered,

> the rock of our race-pride and organic union has stood firm throughout the ages, notwithstanding the mighty billows that surged upon it from the two great poles of Asiatic civilization. The national genius has never been overwhelmed. Imitation has never taken the place of creativity. There has always

been abundant energy for the acceptance and reapplication of the influence received, however massive. It is the glory of Continental Asia that her touch upon Japan has made always for new life and inspiration: it is the most sacred honor of the race of Amaterasu to hold itself invincible, not in some mere political sense alone, but still more and more profoundly as a living spirit of Freedom, in life, and thought, and art.

Thus Japan became "the real repository of the trust of Asiatic thought and culture."[94]

Three years later, *The Book of Tea* appeared on the heels of Japan's triumph over Tsarism in the Russo-Japanese War. Based on a series of lectures Okakura gave in New York and written in English, *The Book of Tea* was the first work to elaborate an analysis of the Japanese culture to which he continuously referred in *Ideals* and its 1904 companion volume, *The Awakening of Japan*, a call to arms against the "White Disaster." In taking tea as a lens through which to read and present Japan, Okakura had as an example the book *Bushido* by Nitobe Inazō, published in 1899 and already in its tenth edition by 1906.[95] Although a eulogy to the ethics of the samurai, Nitobe's book was far from martial in tone and pallid in comparison with *The Book of Tea*. Defiant against the arrogance of the West and its ignorance of Asia, Okakura painted in vivid colors the development of the Japanese culture he had lauded as the savior of the East in his prior works. Historically, its pivotal moment had come in the thirteenth century, when Japan had repelled the Mongols to whom China had fallen, and in doing so preserved the continuity of the best of Song civilization, cut off on the mainland but safeguarded in the archipelago—not least of which was powdered tea, which disappeared under the Yuan and Ming but survived to produce chanoyu in Japan. In the efflorescence of the Ashikaga period (1336–1573), culture triumphed over raw military power, and its supreme expression became the tea ceremony, "our Art of Life."[96]

Since then, Okakura went on, tea had come to represent far more than a mere ritual or etiquette. As the book's opening pages explained, "Our home and habits, costume and cuisine, porcelain, lacquer, painting—our very literature—all have been subject to ["Teaism's"] influence. No student of Japanese culture could ever ignore its presence"[97]—an inversion in which it is not Japanese culture that generates tea, but tea that generates Japanese culture. In contrast to the West, Okakura declared, Japan revered the relative and not the absolute, and celebrated the spiritual over the material. Nature, on the archipelago, was respected rather than wantonly wasted as it was by Europeans. Western architecture, its symmetry yielding simply "useless reiteration," was "devoid of originality, [and] so replete with the repetitions of obsolete styles," whereas Western homes were filled with "bric-a-brac" in a "confusion of color and form." In contrast, the vaunted Japanese aesthetic—encapsulated in the practice of tea—was marked by emptiness, asymmetry, simplicity, and the ephemeral. These distinctions drawn against the West provided the fulcrum for elaborating the exacting aesthetic sense that, for Okakura, defined the core of Japanese culture.

> The Philosophy of Tea is not mere aestheticism in the ordinary acceptance of the term, for it expresses conjointly with ethics and religion our whole point of view about man and nature. It is hygiene, for it enforces cleanliness; it is economics, for it shows comfort in simplicity rather than in the complex and costly; it is moral geometry, inasmuch as it defines our sense of proportion to the universe. It represents the true spirit of Eastern democracy by making all its votaries aristocrats in taste.[98]

Far from disconcerting its foreign readers, this dithyramb enchanted them. Written in a style readily understandable in the West, and highly attractive to those taken with the "old Japan" of *japoniste* enthusiasm, *The Book of Tea* was a raging success in the United States, gaining a further international reputation with quick-fire French and German translations. Nor was this popularity confined to a middle-brow public. Among the writers and thinkers influenced by the book were not only Tagore but Ezra Pound, Martin Heidegger, Frank Lloyd Wright, and Wallace Stevens.[99] Laurels conferred on his tea opus and other work, Okakura was eventually awarded an honorary doctorate by Harvard University.

Okakura died in 1913, and it was another sixteen years before a Japanese edition of *The Book of Tea* appeared. But when it was published by Iwanami Shōten in 1929, it was an instant hit at home. Already familiar with the English original of Okakura's tract, Takahashi Tatsuo, prominent literary scholar at the prestigious Keio University, published the monograph *Chadō* a few months later, whose stated purpose was to "outline the place of the tea ceremony in Japanese cultural history." Adopting Western notions of aesthetic singularity, Takahashi argued that tea utensils should be regarded as objects of art in their own right, to be understood individually rather than through their coordination with other utensils—a constitutive element in the aesthetics of tea preparation. Echoing one of Okakura's refrains, connoisseurs of tea, he maintained, had the ability to judge the essential qualities that make the individual utensils art. But while "the best wabi objects of art were produced in the East, that is, China, Korea, and Japan, the very best remain only in Japan, thanks to this country and to the imperial family."[100] Positioning Japan as the first among peers within East Asia, Takahashi contended that it had preserved the most treasured cultural objects of the region—a claim following Okakura in *Ideals of the East*. But Takahashi departed from his predecessor by attributing this supremacy in part to Japan's imperial system, in a bow to the emperor worship coloring so much of the nationalist literature of the early Showa period (1926–1989). The depth of meaning to be found in the Japanese tea ceremony was comparable to the profundities of the most renowned Western philosophers. "Tea, as deep learning, exists only in Japan," he proclaimed. "The population of the world need not know of the spirit of tea, but Japan should be proud that it is unique in possessing the only tea ceremony that strengthens the spirit of the people at a time when the deep learning of the West, such as [that of] Kant, Hegel, Socrates, Tolstoy, Nietzsche, and Marx comes leaping at us across the ocean."[101]

Another writer swayed by Okakura's portrayal of the tea ceremony as a supremely Japanese art was Yanagi Sōetsu, the central figure behind the influential Mingei movement that celebrated the native crafts of his homeland, and critic of the Japanese occupation of Korea.[102] Part of the intellectual milieu of the growing urban middle class, Yanagi took aim at the decadence of the sukisha and their domination of cultural fields by championing Japanese and Korean "simple folkware." To pinpoint the profundity of humble ceramics for daily use, he mobilized the great wabi tea masters of the past and their eye for the beauty in everyday life to legitimate his aesthetic choices. Yanagi summarized his 1935 essay *Chadō o Omou*, published in the leading arts journal *Kōgei*, by announcing, "Cultivation of our incomparable Japanese beauty can be developed through many years of training in the tea ceremony."[103] Simultaneously claiming that a peculiarly Japanese vision (*mitate*) could transform a Korean tea bowl into a Japanese thing— a position in line with the imperialist notion of Japan as the first among equals in Asia—and that the forms of beauty unique to an ethnic group can only be understood by that group, he pronounced the wabi aesthetic informing the tea ceremony to be not only distinctively, but exclusively, Japanese. Yet the Japanese were in danger of losing touch with the essence of the nation's culture. So while Yanagi reproduced the now familiar image of Japan as the cultural leader of Asia, he combined it with the nostalgic yet mobilizing view that its historic being must at all costs be preserved, akin to the *kokusui hozon* concerns of the Meiji period.[104] But unlike Okakura's Western-oriented efforts, Yanagi's text elucidated the essence of Japanese culture to a Japanese audience, among whom the explicit contrasts with the West could be taken for granted, and which innately possessed the sensibilities that could be refined into a connoisseur's eye.

Meanwhile, spurred by an interest in the scientific study of what was, in the process, defined as Japanese culture, several scholars and sukisha began the *Chadō Zenshū* collection in the early 1930s. This encyclopedic set of writings on the tea ceremony explored the practice as an element of Japanese civilization that must be understood through historical research and carefully recorded utensil measurements. But its contributors also had no hesitation in treating tea as an expression of the national essence, its twelfth volume in 1935 projecting tea as nothing less than the "apex of Japanese culture,"[105] concentrating the essence of the Japanese, evinced in a respect for others and a distinctively Japanese taste. Echoing Okakura, its authors declared, "The tea ceremony stands at the top within our culture—the customs, traditions, and character of our Japanese people. Since the Middle Ages, the tea ceremony has been the greatest originating power behind Japanese culture." Lauding the contribution of the great tea masters of the past to the architecture, pottery, lacquerware, weaving, and other arts of the country, they were careful not to reduce tea to its aesthetic role alone: "The tea ceremony is not just an art, but also a way of refining character, a religion, and even contains science."[106] Connecting the ceremony both to a national populace and its heroic leaders of the past, prominent philosopher Tanikawa Tetsuzō offered chapters with populist depictions of tea as historically a cross-class practice in which anyone could participate on an equal footing, and one that had been a motivating force in the decisiveness of the great men of old. In another contribution to the volume, the intellectual Takamatsu Sadaichi described tea gatherings as a synthesis of the arts, in which the host was a creator who could express his individuality by producing a masterpiece. But wary of reducing the complexity of the ceremony to European categories, Takamatsu argued that Western art separated beauty from practical use, as the tea ceremony in Japan did not. Chanoyu, for him, was simultaneously high art and an everyday practice expressive of the nation, defined in contradistinction to the West by the refined aesthetic sensitivity that permeated society.

Thus, by the mid-1930s, the understanding of tea as the quintessentially Japanese art, first advanced by Okakura, had become commonsense knowledge. In these years, volumes by literary critics and philosophers such as Komiya Toyotaka and Hisamatsu Shin'ichi followed Okakura's lead in using tea to explain Japanese culture and tradition, though now to a domestic rather than international audience. Still, Okakura's example continued to provide a popular model for explicating Japan to foreign publics. When the Tourist Board of the Japanese Government Railways began a series of short books on Japanese culture written in English for foreigners, the first volume was on the tea ceremony.[107] According to the author, "Visitors from overseas in increasing numbers now take a deeper interest in the Japanese entertainment of serving powdered tea." Though his primary object is to furnish them with a handy work of reference, the author also hopes it may be of use to his compatriots in the explanation of this element of their "national culture." Headed by an epigraph from *The Book of Tea*, the main text came straight to the point. "Nothing is more closely associated with the arts and crafts of Japan than *Cha-no-yu*, an aesthetic pastime in which powdered green tea is served in a refined atmosphere."[108]

Such presentations of Japanese culture to those from abroad were not new. Performances of the tea ceremony for foreign audiences were staged at the Kyoto Exposition of 1872 and the World Exposition in St. Louis of 1904.[109] Likewise, when the Queen of England visited Japan in 1906, she was escorted to a formal ceremony at the Omotesenke family compound. Photographs showing foreign visitors attending tea performances appeared in women's magazines and national newspapers around this time as well. But few detailed records of these occasions survive, complicating analysis of how they were presented to foreigners as Japanese. More information is available about the tea performance staged by two women at the World Exposition in Chicago of 1933, portrayed in *Fujin Gahō* as "bringing understanding abroad about Japanese beautiful customs" and "showing the beauty of pure Japanese women."[110] Tacitly assuming the penetration of tea into the middle classes, the two practitioners gave voice, by contrast, to a peculiarly elite vision of Japaneseness that they hoped to convey to the audience, explaining, "We want to show not an everyday version, but the tea ceremony of the upper classes." As for those watching it, one of the women told the national *Asahi* newspaper, "I don't think Americans will understand its depth. But even if they don't, enjoying it is enough."[111]

Within Japan, concern for the image of national Japanese culture at this time was not limited to its reflection in the eyes of foreigners. The 1930s was a time in which objects, practices, and sensibilities defined as traditional were increasingly taken up as topics for study by Japanese academics—among them the aesthetician Kuki Shūzō, the cultural historian Watsuji Tetsurō, the writer Tanizaki Junichirō, and the Kyoto school's founding philosopher Nishida Kitarō. There was a pronounced growth of publications on the tea ceremony in this decade that addressed it from educational, cultural, and scholarly viewpoints, explicating the practice as an art, often in distinctively nationalistic tones.[112] As intellectuals vested with legitimacy as arbiters of knowledge, the authors of these works sealed the now commonsense understanding, not only of the tea ceremony as self-evidently Japanese, but of its status as a symbol of the country.

## Conclusion

If the tea ceremony today is often seen as emblematically Japanese, this is a relatively recent development, absent for those who practiced it in the 1500s and for most of the following three centuries. Initially a site where dominant warlords brokered deals and wealthy merchants enhanced their status, chanoyu in its early years moderated the rawness of social division, power politics, and military conflict, intertwining aesthetic pleasures and spiritual precepts in a striking new form. The originating association of the ceremony with the first unifiers of the country, at the summit of rule, stamped it with a political prestige it would never thereafter lose. But the openness and fluidity of tea gatherings in the Momoyama period soon rigidified, during the Tokugawa peace, into a vehicle for the self-cultivation of the warrior class in a caste-divided society in which mastery of its protocols of comportment was conceived as training in social responsibility, respect for hierarchy, and skills of governance. Below the samurai level, merchants continued their own practice of tea, and amid growing urban prosperity, even well-off women of commoner status started to acquire the rudiments of tea knowledge, as an introduction to gracious bearing. But the social function of tea remained essentially that of sustaining class distinctions, namely crafting better members of a closed elite, rather than better incumbents of a generalizing and widely embracing national identity.

With the overthrow of the shogunate in 1868, the foundations of the neo-feudal order over which it had presided were swept away—the domains of the daimyo abolished, the samurai de-classed, industry and citizenry introduced. The ensuing turmoil altered the position of tea in three fateful ways. Its prestige as an accoutrement of power and wealth migrated from warriors to captains of industry, collecting utensils and preparing the beverage in styles deliberately recalling the daimyo tea of the Tokugawa period, or even the gala displays reminiscent of lordly shows in the Momoyama or Ashikaga epochs. The activities of these sukisha magnates ensured tea against demotion, as at mass levels training in it changed gender, becoming for the first time a predominantly feminine affair. The basic reasons for this switch lay in the requirements of a modern industrial society that had done away with the leisured class of male aristocrats who had been its traditional patrons. Men of all ranks were now expected to work, and mostly work very hard, leaving them little time or space for aesthetic pursuits. Industrialists who had accumulated huge fortunes could allow themselves the pleasures of the collector and tea host, but these were the exceptions. Women, on the other hand, were now being universally educated, but—as in the West—if from middle- or upper-class families, they were certainly not expected to enter the labor force, becoming the principal reservoirs of domestic leisure in the new order.

In these conditions, educators in the new state-managed school system promoted the tea ceremony as a vehicle for refining girls into good wives and wise mothers, repackaging once desirable graces of the Tokugawa era into common fare in women's etiquette and home economics textbooks. By this time the focus of cultivation had shifted toward creating not simply Japanese defined vis-à-vis external others, but *good* Japanese, differentiated from their peers by their refinement of national or nation-serving qualities. Yet these were not private virtues, for by instructing girls in how to make tea, the manuals also taught them how to make a good household, the foundation of the nation. Under the Meiji dispensation, the object of cultivation through tea—the range of what practitioners were purportedly turned into—shifted from the refining of elites to the making of good imperial subjects. Tea was still relevant in a modernizing Japan since it fostered national morality and national manners—a potent formulation, anchoring tea in the relationship between the individual and the state. Proper ethical orientation was an essential part of national membership, and for women, training in the practice was a means to that end. So much so that when tea appears in literature and film by the middle of the twentieth century—Kawabata's *A Thousand Cranes* or Mizoguchi's *Gion Bayashi*, for example—the image is in line with housewives', rather than businessmen's, tea practice: it is presented as an activity of bourgeois women.

More decisive, however, for the future of the practice as a national symbol was a third trend of the period: the development of a fully articulated ideology of tea by intellectuals, exalting it as the inmost core of Japanese-ness, an all but complete synthesis of the arts and ethics of the nation.[113] Okakura's *Book of Tea*, felicitously published in English at the conclusion of the Russo-Japanese War, when foreign audiences were eager to understand this new rival to the Great Powers, and again felicitously appearing in Japan at the end of the twenties, a time of growing interest in native Japanese arts, played a key role in the crystallization of this discourse. But in the intensifying nationalist mobilization of the thirties, an avalanche of publications—learned or less so—amplified these themes. This intellectual literature was less concerned with the material act of making tea than with the cultural and aesthetic meanings embodied in it. By theorizing and formalizing an inherent connection between the tea ceremony and Japaneseness, intellectuals offered reasons far more elaborate than anything that could be found in school manuals or etiquette books as to *why* tea was essentially Japanese. Indeed, they presented the practice as integral to the national culture in a way that set Japan apart from Korea or China, where tea never became a representative national art during the period of nation-state formation. Whereas instruction for women was largely instrumental—tea was a means to produce a positive national end—these ideologies, erecting it into a banner of national being, treated tea as an end in itself. If women doing tea had a responsibility for sustaining the national culture, men doing tea were alone equipped to identify and certify what that national culture was, whether as sukisha connoisseurs of historic or religious objects, or as philosophers or antiquaries of the country's whole cultural legacy.

This gendered division of labor facilitated the production and reproduction of tea as Japanese. A minimal but not insignificant amount of shared commonsense knowledge is necessary for a symbol to communicate meaning effectively, even if its interpretation is not always unitary—indeed, polyvalence is a condition of durable influence. Women's tea was central to the dissemination of a shared base that could be taken for granted. But feminization of the practice stood in obvious tension with the image that elite businessmen projected of tea, and both sukisha and intellectuals tended to advance their conceptions of chanoyu as a Japanese art or tradition in part by distancing themselves from women's everyday tea practice. Yet both sides of this latently antagonistic balance contributed to a national canonization of the tea ceremony: a commonsense association carrying feminine overtones proliferated through textbooks and the school system, while elaborated masculine discourses formalized and heightened the same essentializing connection in a more overtly political register.[114] Through these productive tensions, tea became both a medium for imagining the nation—a tool for definition and explanation—and a means to becoming national—a resource for embodiment and cultivation. The distinctions with the West that structured many of the initial elaborations of what was Japanese were then set as the goals of what national members should become—the moral valences of differentiation. By the mid-twentieth century, the symbolism of the art form assigned tea to the core meaning of Japaneseness, while the instruction in the practice promised to make better Japanese of those who performed it.

By the end of the thirties, a bronze statue of Okakura stood at the entrance to the Tokyo University of the Arts, with his dictum "Asia is One" inscribed in gold letters on its base, as a standing inspiration to builders of the Greater East Asian Co-Prosperity Sphere. The tea ceremony had become a potent emblem of the nation, in a time of virulent expansionist nationalism. In due course that expansionism would lead, through its catastrophic outcome, to a transformation of Japan nearly as dramatic as the Meiji Restoration itself, in which the ultimate beneficiaries of the nationalization of tea would be neither industrialists nor housewives nor intellectuals, but the iemoto who had historically preceded them.

## CHAPTER 3

# Selling Tea

## *An Anatomy of the Iemoto System*

Today, the iemoto are the living embodiment of the tea ceremony. Wrapped in kimonos, they serve tea to prime ministers, presidents, and popes. Practitioners passing the front gates of their magnificent compounds in Kyoto offer a silent bow to these monarchs of the tea world. When such sovereigns enter a room, their adherents snap to attention, rounded fists on the floor in a traditional position of fealty. An iemoto's signature on a tea utensil or inscription on its box can add thousands of dollars to its value, and very few practitioners would dare to make tea in a way not sanctioned by them. Even outside their tea room dominions, these figures hold wide public sway, representing the country at international events and making televised proclamations about the state of Japanese tradition. How did these potentates attain their lofty status as authorities over the tea world and Japanese culture?

### The Iemoto: Beginnings

The origins of the iemoto go back to the passage from the Momoyama to the Tokugawa era. Since medieval times, military men, following religious precedent, sought to legitimate their grasp on power by constructing genealogies to furnish themselves with noble pedigrees. But during the late sixteenth and early seventeenth centuries, warriors solidifying their hold over vast territories began writing the household (the *ie*) into law. Hereditary distinctions drawn through patrilines became the foundation of a status-defined society. Legal designations of family membership monitored through land surveys and temple registration were established to prevent peasants from taking up the sword and warriors from taking up the plough. At the summit of power, an ideological keystone of the Tokugawa shogunate's domination became deification of the first shogun in the family, Ieyasu, a practice that inspired others to base their authority on the glorification of heroic or martyred ancestors.[1]

It was in this setting that the innovations that had marked the aesthetic pursuits of the sixteenth century began to harden around authoritative precedents in the seventeenth, genealogy providing the axis of this consolidation. The results in the tea ceremony were striking. Although he had historically been one of a handful of influential tea masters taking the form in new aesthetic directions in the sixteenth century, Rikyū was by the end of the seventeenth century set apart from his peers as the "patron saint" of the practice (*chasei*). The hundredth anniversary of his death was celebrated by the Omotesenke branch with the erection of a statue of their ancestor at the famous Daitokuji Temple. The dubious discovery in the same year of a set of Rikyū's writings, *Nanpōroku*, and the subsequent composition of the collection *One Hundred Gatherings of Rikyū*, helped to codify doxic principles purportedly derived from the founding father of the practice. The concomitant rise of a mass-publishing industry facilitated the wide circulation of these myths encouraging the Rikyū revival. By the end of the seventeenth century, essays and instructions on the tea ceremony could gain wider diffusion and greater popularity if they were presented as "discovered" Rikyū originals. Through familial claims, the three Sen families—Omotesenke, Mushanokōjisenke, and Urasenke—benefited most from the elevation of their ancestor to the lofty position of "tea saint,"[2] but the leaders of daimyo tea, such as Katagiri Sekishū, also used connections to Rikyū to legitimate authority by asserting that they transmitted his core teachings in their purest form.

Innovation waned as "good tea" became "proper tea," or preparation conforming to precedent-based rules. As Rikyū's protocols became authoritative, claims of descent facilitated control over—and later almost entire monopolization of—the tea arena in two ways. First, genealogical connections are inherently limited. Even a century after Rikyū's death, direct ties established through intimate teaching or blood relations were already scarce, and would become still scarcer over time. Grounding authority in inheritance claims created natural limits that confined possibilities for new schools to arise.[3] Second, the genealogical form itself prefers a delimited, static, "thing-like" inheritance—a property in the objective sense. Such pedigrees were encased, in turn, within a general institutional form that became increasingly salient over the next century: the iemoto system. Fusing the characters *ie*, meaning house or family, and *moto*, meaning origin or root, the term *iemoto* refers to the person who simultaneously heads a school or style of an aesthetic activity and a family that has passed down for generations the authority to define this style. Many Japanese aesthetic practices, from incense enjoyment to flower arrangement, were organized through iemoto systems—according to one count there were over thirty of them in eighteenth-century Kyoto. And while their contours varied across fields,[4] they were all marked by a hierarchical structure of master-disciple relationships in a patriarchy based on the household, combining real and fictive familial relationships to control the preservation of cultural authority and the transmission of specialized knowledge.[5]

In the case of tea, the Sen iemoto succeeded not to Rikyū's innovative ingenuity or creative skill, but to a body of knowledge they defined and attributed to the master. Formalizing Rikyū's legacy and standardizing modes of preparation, the rival schools reconfigured the diversity of tea practices into a codified field. Charged with preserving and passing on this inherited expertise, iemoto rarely introduced novelties (and on the few occasions when they did so, they generally passed them off as within the tradition of Rikyū). Claiming his mantle, the iemoto gradually extended their authority over the three critical domains of tea practice—preparation techniques, the value of utensils, and standards of taste.

## Techniques: Extending Authority over Preparation Procedures

A hallmark of the tea ceremony is the refined motions carried out in the making of tea, known as *temae*. Iemoto could accumulate control over temae only if preparations were formalized and standardized into rule-defined bodies of knowledge. From the sixteenth to the early seventeenth centuries, tea masters ostensibly shared their tea practices and theories freely with their students, and, in varying degrees, passed on the right to transmit that knowledge to others. As the iemoto system took shape in the late seventeenth century, the once readily dispensed teachings were increasingly transmitted in their entirety only to the iemoto's successor, with other students gaining access to merely part of that knowledge. Reconstituted as an inheritance, knowledge became the birthright of the eldest son or family successor, whose exclusive ownership reinforced his privileged status. The mystery of sub rosa teachings served to further valorize the iemoto, as they were the only ones who could lay claim to such privileged expertise. Secrecy thus defined orthodoxy and served as a buffer against upstart disciples usurping their masters.[6]

In consolidating their expertise, the Sen iemoto in the 1740s developed formal curricula of procedures that could draw in new learners and sustain their interest. At their core stood the so-called seven exercises, in which students drew lots to determine which of the roles as hosts or guests they would assume while making tea, with lots redrawn and the roles changed during the course of play. A strict choreography of movement was institutionalized as procedures for making and drinking tea were disassociated from individuals and codified into roles that all participants had to be able to assume at the turn of a chip. The drills encouraged formalization and standardization, such that students in disparate places learned the same thing and that people who had never engaged in tea together could, at least ideally, participate smoothly in a highly coordinated activity.

The iemoto elaborated the exercises into a proficiency system with seven grades, arranged hierarchically, and with access gained through the purchase of permission certificates—a system soon extended to other temae. Received before a preparation procedure was taught rather than after it had been mastered, these certificates represented the express permission of the iemoto to acquire the knowledge in his keep, purportedly passed down from Rikyū. Grounding their command through genealogy resulted in a system in which the iemoto did not certify skill, but granted access to an inheritance, which enabled them to retain authority while selling expertise. The hierarchy of licenses not only ensured a steady income to the iemoto, but also ranked the students in distance from the apex of a pyramid they could strive to climb. Furthermore, the certificates themselves offered a rationalized means for maintaining the iemoto's authority over the tea preparations of a large community of practitioners, most of whom he would never meet. By objectifying oral permission, these certificates freed leaders from physical presence when granting access to the teachings. Serving as his emissary when conferring certificates, teachers channeled and thus became endowed with the iemoto's authority, a process from which they gained so long as they (and others) accepted his influence.

Of course, express permission from a distant iemoto was not necessary to teach or learn tea preparation procedures, and independent practices of tea persisted throughout the Tokugawa period. The late-seventeenth-century publishing boom made printed texts on tea practice widely available, and a person who had mastered all of the procedures could simply learn or start teaching on his own, independent of any school.[7] But to the extent that the authority of the iemoto was recognized, the certificates legitimized those who held them, setting them apart from dilettantes. Though potentially undermining iemoto control over tea expertise, the printed texts also reinforced the exalted lineages as they frequently claimed Rikyū or a given school as the basis of the teachings on the printed page. Dependence on the formal structures was sustained, in addition, by the mode of training. While instructions for basic tea preparation procedures could be found in printed texts, a longer tradition of "secret teachings" in a range of domains helped to ensure that the most "profound transmissions" were taught orally, both reinforcing dependence on the iemoto and sustaining a sense of privilege—real to the extent it was believed in—as practitioners gained access to the "sacred core" of Rikyū's tea.

## Taste and Value: Extending Authority over Utensils

The iemoto generated and extended authority not only over how people made tea, but also over the objects they used to make it. Central to the spirit of creativity characteristic of sixteenth-century tea preparation was the incorporation of found objects—the baskets, bowls, and containers from everyday life—as utensils in formal tea preparation. A well-water bucket placed beside the kettle as a water container or a fisherman's basket hung on the wall as a flower container produced interesting, aesthetically subtle juxtapositions. But as Rikyū and his closest disciples became the venerated sources of "proper tea," such innovations were increasingly classified—and thereby legitimated—as following the styles of these masters. During the seventeenth century, the label *konomi* came to be used to recognize that a tea utensil, garden, or architectural form reflecting the tastes of a particularly revered aesthete not only bolstered the iconic status of "great masters" but also further ensconced the division between the muted aesthetic of the Sen families' wabi tea and the ornate karasuki aesthetic of daimyo tea. Eventually, by the mid-nineteenth century, the "iemoto's gaze" grew so strong that iemoto increasingly named konomi directly.[8] Taking control of their own stylistic canons by designing and producing utensils themselves, they extended their aesthetic reach by supplying and promoting authorized tea objects.

Iemoto also asserted aesthetic authority by certifying utensils as suited for the tea ceremony by writing on or signing the boxes containing them, or even the utensils themselves (*hakogaki* and *kaō*, respectively). Tea utensils had long been revered objects, even given proper names, and possession of particular items of exalted provenance symbolically associated the owner with great men of the past. Because these implements served as a center point of tea gatherings—aesthetes since the sixteenth century meticulously recording in diaries the utensils used—significant associations added to their value. From around the 1720s, the Sen iemoto began ordering special tea bowls from prominent ceramicists—sometimes even carving bowls themselves—and signing the wooden boxes in which they were stored. Giving these bowls as commemorative gifts on special occasions, the iemoto grasped that their value increased though association with the family line. Proliferating from the eighteenth century, the hakogaki messages on boxes or the kaō ciphers on boxes or utensils became visual signs of the iemoto's authority, adding monetary value and prestige to the utensil. But this was not all. The iemoto's expertise in utensil appreciation provided an additional source of capital through authentication. Practitioners would bring a tea utensil of anonymous pedigree to an iemoto, who might decide that something in its construction indicated that Rikyū had carved it, inscribing in ink this revelation on its box, and contributing considerably to its worth.[9]

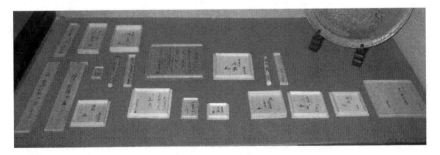

Signed utensil box lids on display at a contemporary tea gathering

## Consolidation of the Iemoto System

Naturally, utensil makers also prospered from association with iemoto, as official sponsorship could increase both the demand for and the value of their products. Iemoto benefited from such close relations as well, with intimately connected craftsmen producing, sometimes in large numbers, tea utensils conforming to the iemoto's taste that could be purchased by disciples. Indeed, the Raku pottery family, whose tea bowl style was supposedly developed in conjunction with Rikyū, enjoyed so much success that by the end of the eighteenth century production could not meet demand, a popular text revealing the family production "secrets" went through multiple prints, and dozens of kilns across the country were producing Raku-style ceramics. But if the parentage of a bowl was disputed, it could, of course, be taken to an iemoto or the Raku family for authentication. As this proliferation indicates, objects representative of an iemoto's style or bearing an iemoto's stamp of approval became models for extensive reproductions, encouraging practitioners to develop an aesthetic sense based on the iemoto's taste. Even when the actual objects were not available, the multiplication of printed catalogues with images of famous utensils, accompanied by descriptions of their construction and pedigree of ownership, helped to develop skills of connoisseurship in line with the aesthetic standards of tea leaders.[10]

Thus as the iemoto elaborated mechanisms for marketing their expertise to disciples during the eighteenth century, they intensified their authority over technique, taste, and value, regulating and routinizing tea practice as well as codifying hierarchies of utensil choice. Copies and mass-production aided in this endeavor as printed texts and utensil catalogues spread the "iemoto's gaze" beyond his immediate interlocutors. Utensil dealers became allies in this enterprise, producing replicas of favorite objects and benefiting from the vibrant market produced by iemoto adherents. The success of the genealogically grounded system of authority is observable at its delicate edges. On occasions when expert disciples split from the Sen families and began teaching their own styles of tea, they justified their rebellion by claiming to pass on the "true" spirit of Rikyū. And even if they were themselves critical of the iemoto system, the schools they created took on much the same trappings within a few generations.

## Elite Tea and the Limits of the Iemoto

Firmly entrenched by the eighteenth century though they had become, the influence of the iemoto was still circumscribed. The Sen families enjoyed the patronage of a handful of daimyo, but amateur disciples paying for certificates, kaō, and hakogaki were necessary for the development of the iemoto *system*, and these were for the most part supplied by well-heeled commoners—merchants, artisans, monks, and even some farm landlords— who enjoyed tea as one of several "elegant pastimes." While the legitimizing authority of formal certificates and the like was desirable for these types, the iemoto did not have the infrastructural capabilities to ensure that aficionados continued to practice tea as dictated from the center. Students of different schools, moreover, often mixed at tea gatherings, in a further centrifugal pull against homogeneity.

At higher social levels, the iemoto had still less presence. At the summit of power, tea continued to form an essential moment of the rituals of rule. Both the last effective reformer and the doomed final regent of the Tokugawa system—respectively, Matsudaira Sadanobu and Ii Naosuke— wrote manuals on the ceremony as an adjunct of statecraft. But this was in a stratosphere well above the iemoto. The Sen families had no access to the shogunate itself, where the Tokugawa elders (*rōjū*) practiced the aristocratic style of tea developed by Sekishū, and most daimyo followed suit. Initiated by a feudal lord, this form of tea had no need to petrify its aesthetic choices into a codified body of knowledge that could be appropriated and sold. From such heights, iemoto were surplus to requirements: throughout the Tokugawa era, daimyo tea remained free of any institutional corsetry. At somewhat lower levels, moreover, free-wheeling literati, inspired by the Chinese example, developed a subversive alternative to the tea ceremony— drinking not powdered tea (matcha) but infused tea (sencha) in bohemian settings, in which the small-minded rituals and mercenary undertows of the iemoto world were despised, and on occasion mocked.[11]

When the shogunate eventually collapsed in the 1860s, there was thus no guarantee that the iemoto would necessarily survive, let alone flourish, in the drastically altered conditions of Meiji Japan. The Restoration swept away the parcelization of power among the daimyo, who were finally dismantled with the abolition of the status system in 1871. For the iemoto, who lost their patrons and whose "traditional" aesthetic domains were discredited by the out-with-the-old, in-with-the-new fervor of the times, this marked the beginning of two decades of financial crisis. The Urasenke family sought to reassert itself by forging ties to the emperor, serving tea to the Chrysanthemum Throne in 1860 with a "rediscovered" procedure said to have been used by Rikyū, and claiming that tea training provided a means for cultivating the Confucian values all good imperial subjects should now possess.[12]

But no easy transition to a post-feudal society was within reach. The tea ceremony itself, as a tradition, remained too deeply associated with the exercise of power to be discarded, and the new capitalist elites sought to emulate aristocratic rather than more common forms of it. As discussed in Chapter 2, they spurred a thriving market for famous tea utensils, now redefined as objects of art and treasures of the nation, while their gala tea gatherings were attended by the powers-that-be and lavishly covered in the press. But their modes of tea preparation remained unregulated by the iemoto, and they were critical of the acquisition of certificates and indifferent to the kaō and hakogaki of the iemoto. And it was they who held the spotlight until the 1920s.

## New Domains

The emergence of these industrialists formed, as we have seen, part of a much wider reshuffling of the social deck in the Meiji period, as the new rulers of the country sought to build not only a powerful centralized state, capable of competing with the imperialist predators of the West, but also a modern nation in which every citizen-subject was educated to identify with the fate of the state. Victories in the Sino-Japanese (1894–1895) and Russo-Japanese (1904–1905) Wars gave a tremendous boost to a full-form nationalism, propagated at official and assimilated at popular levels. In this atmosphere, tea was for the first time promoted as a distillation of the essence of the nation, rather than, as more traditionally treated, a caparison of the state. In this conversion, women were not only increasingly liberated from status restrictions, but expected to contribute to the national polity of which they too were now, if still a lesser, part. In due course, the rising number of women able to afford tea lessons as part of marriage training supplied a profitable basis for expanding the iemoto's certifying and sanctifying authority. From the 1880s, educators at several girls' schools incorporated the tea ceremony as a part of the curriculum and extra-curriculum, and the Urasenke family quickly latched onto this trend, its iemoto not only donating utensils to girls' schools, but teaching classes at them as well. For the iemoto, young women were particularly well suited to become a lucrative pool of customers, as they could make use of the iemoto's certifying authority beyond the tea world. Included as part of a dowry, iemoto-issued certificates—some of them consecrating novel distinctions in expertise—imparted official assurance of a woman's worthiness as a wife. Following the Russo-Japanese War, the Sen iemoto began granting special licenses to war widows, certifying them to teach upper-level temae, and less than a decade later, they began certifying teachers who held tea classes at girls' schools.[13] Awarding the licenses after instructors attended a training course, the iemoto established a further opportunity to monitor the tea practice of their adherents.

Further enhancing control over temae was the spread of official texts. Though prior iemoto had been concerned about print technology's potential threat to their authority—earlier texts had been issued by dilettantes rather than the sanctifying centers—Tanaka Senshō was able to utilize the form in a way that reinforced institutional centralization by prescribing officially standardized movements. After founding the first tea ceremony periodical, *Chadō Gakushi*, in 1900 to keep in contact with his adherents, Tanaka was within a year printing detailed texts of all tea preparation procedures with the intention of encouraging the spread of tea to the widest extent possible. Though they initially condemned these publications, Urasenke and Omotesenke soon followed suit with the release of their own manuals and magazines, replete with images and descriptions of how tea was properly made.[14] This combination of developments strengthened the grip of the iemoto on the bodies and performances of their adherents: tea was to be done in a particular, officially sanctioned manner, and harmonized across the country. Deviations from the standard could be checked against the official manuals and corrected into a homogeneous end product.

Because women's tea participation concentrated around training and certificate acquisition, the rationalization and codification of tea procedures by the iemoto engendered normative standards and methods of control that disproportionately affected them. If elite men were largely uninterested in certificates, as they had little need for external validation of what was, in essence, simply entertainment, these paper proofs supplied women with an authoritative affirmation of the comportment and manners that formed the core of their training, which could strengthen their position on the marriage market, but simultaneously made them more reliant than men on the official stamp of approval. As the iemoto proffered their tea expertise to women, this new customer base provided fresh pools of not simply potential disciples, but dependent ones, in need of an iemoto's legitimation, which in turn buttressed his authority.[15]

Faced with difficult financial times and an uncertain future at the outset of the Meiji period, the iemoto were able to resuscitate themselves by expanding their institutional umbrella to include women, utilizing the school system to promote their tea and gather new practitioners, and by developing loose membership organizations that strengthened the demand for and their grip over tea technique, value, and taste. But women remained, of course, second-class citizens, and down to the end of the Taisho period (1912–1926), the iemoto could not compete in the scale of tea prestige with the millionaire sukisha, collecting priceless utensils for their own free-form ceremonies. It was not until the economic crash of 1928, followed by a depression, that this changed. The crisis severely damaged the public image of the sukisha (more than one was assassinated), and as the robber barons passed from the stage, their heirs took up more modern forms of entertainment.[16] The financial and geriatric decline of these Meiji plutocrats opened space for others to maneuver in a Showa Japan of escalating militarism and ultranationalism.

## From a State Tool to a National Tool

In the new decade, a rising tide of chauvinism saw official energies increasingly invested in defining the particularities of the Japanese. The Ministry of Education's *Kokutai no Hongi* (Cardinal Principles of the National Polity) of 1937, printed in an initial run of 300,000 and expanded to millions of copies circulating through Japan and its possessions, declared: "Our national Way appears strikingly in the arts that have come down to us from of old. Poetry, music, calligraphy, incense ceremony, tea ceremony, flower arrangement, architecture, sculpture, the industrial arts, and drama culminate in the entry of the Way, and find their source therein." This catechism of the jingoist ideology of the period extolled the wabi aesthetic of tea as a prime expression of the national spirit: "In the narrow tea room, sitting knee to knee, one enjoys the chance to meet as if for only once in one's lifetime. The host and guest become one and the same, and as such ranks of high and low merge, and without the individual self and without discrimination, a state of harmony is attained. This spirit in which an impartial concordance is created, reversing the time-honored discrimination of rank and occupation, accordingly nurtures the spirit of selfless duty."[17]

In this atmosphere, the iemoto were able to claim the limelight for themselves through two large tea events: the Showa Kitano Tea Gathering of 1936
commemorating the 350th anniversary of the spectacular mass tea ceremony
staged by Hideyoshi, and the memorial tea service of 1940 commemorating
the 350th anniversary of Rikyū's death. Use of grand gatherings to bolster
their image was not a new technique for the iemoto, who had, since the late
eighteenth century, employed tea events commemorating Rikyū for fund-
raising and publicity. Now, however, the accessible public was greater, and
new broadcast media facilitated the transmission and magnification of their
symbolic performances embodying the tea of their ancestor.[18]

Hosted by the three Sen schools, the Showa Gathering of 1936 was a
mega-event held at the Kitano Shrine and numerous other sites in Kyoto.
Notices touted the reenactment as a historical celebration and rare chance
to view an iemoto's temae. While a handful of sukisha participated, by this
time they assumed a subordinate position to the iemoto, who performed
a quasi-religious *kencha* tea service at the shrine in commemoration of
Hideyoshi's spirit. Pioneered by the Urasenke iemoto Gengensai, kencha
tea offerings to the gods at shrines and spirits at temples transformed the
practice into not only a sacrament offered to national deities,[19] but also a
spectacle placing the iemoto's tea performance on display for a public who
would otherwise have little or no chance of viewing the "most correct" way
of preparing tea. Advertised and covered widely in newspapers, the event
drew over ten thousand attendees—outstripping by ten times even the scale
of Hideyoshi's own assembly.

Four years later came a smaller yet grander gathering, as the iemoto of
the three Sen schools commemorated the 350th anniversary of Rikyū's death
by hosting tea performances at Daitokuji Temple, at which Rikyū's tea was
pronounced to contain the essence of the national spirit and ethical bearing
of good imperial subjects. Although participation in the event was limited
to seven hundred, the gala affair was amplified and radiated across the country though national newspaper coverage. The national radio broadcast of
the event projected the nationalized image of tea yet further, declaring that
"the 'harmony, respect, purity, and tranquility' expressed by Rikyū . . . is a
culture of wabi whose spiritual basis accords with the national essence of the
Japanese people."[20] The Mushanokōjisenke iemoto and several academics offered public lectures as a part of the activities, and the wider public interest
in Rikyū was evident in their packed audiences consisting largely of people
who were not tea practitioners.

Thus, while the sukisha had been engrossed with the daimyo tea of figures such as Sekishū and Enshū, around 1940 the spotlight had shifted to Rikyū's tea and the spiritual elements of his practice, thereby raising the public status of those connected to his tradition, namely, the iemoto of the three Sen schools. Rallying Rikyū's tea as a means to transmit a militaristic nationalism to the populace, the iemoto wove the practice into the imperial narrative, conveyed through extensive radio and press coverage, and abetted by a Rikyū book boom. A rash of titles on this "tea saint" helped raise Rikyū's tea into a practice "representative of Japanese culture" at a time when Prime Minister Konoe Fumimaro's 1938 promulgation of a "New Order" (*Shin Taisei*) moved the revival of tradition high up the political agenda. Looking toward the 350th anniversary, Takeuchi Yasu's 1939 book *Sen Rikyū* used the spiritual expression of a Japanese essence in Rikyū's tea ceremony as a fulcrum on which to elevate the servant above his master, Hideyoshi, claiming that "Rikyū's eternal achievement abides in the spiritual culture of the Japanese. . . . His spirit burns in all areas directly connected to Japanese life—food, clothing, and shelter."[21] In 1940, Nishibori Kazuzō's book *Rikyū* stressed "self-control" as a central part of the tea ceremony and of a distinctively Japanese national culture. A year later, Suzuki Keiichi's *Sen Rikyū Zenshū* recruited Rikyū for Japan's holy war to unify Asia.[22] As the war effort commandeered all facets of political, economic, and social life, the iemoto were serving the imperial mission in person, with the future Urasenke master Hōunsai (b. 1923) even recruited into a kamikaze squad, offering final tea services to his confederates who stepped before the inheritor of Rikyū in the line of duty.

## Ideological Escalation

Military collapse and occupation left the iemoto, as earlier at the fall of the shogunate, once more in a potentially precarious position, exposed to attack as remnants of a discredited patriarchal tradition that had become adjuncts of an authoritarian order. Over two centuries they had accumulated significant symbolic power, but had not yet secured it as a routine attribute of their calling. Under the Tokugawa, they had engineered and exploited genealogical connections to assert authority over the domains of practice and taste that define the tea ceremony. But even when they acted as tea advisors to a handful of daimyo, they remained social inferiors of the ruling elite, who might have employed objects or practices sanctified by iemoto, but did not depend

on them to legitimate their tea practice. Recovering from economic and social setbacks at the outset of the Meiji regime, they incorporated women
under their umbrella as a new layer of novitiates legitimizing their authority,
but still had to operate in the shadow of the showier and more powerful
sukisha. With the eclipse of the latter, the iemoto could finally move to the
front of the stage, as beneficiaries of the nationalizing undertones of women's
tea instruction, and the promoters of the tea ceremony as central to the national heritage. Magnified through media coverage, their efforts to rally tea
for the nation at the height of Japanese expansionism garnered broad public
attention. By the time of the Pacific War, the balance of prestige had shifted:
the iemoto were now able to claim an elite status for themselves as icons of
Japanese culture and embodiments of a venerated national tradition.

Imperial disintegration at the end of World War II put at risk all these
gains. Just as Meiji modernization had threatened to reduce the iemoto to
relics of an outdated past, so postwar democratization under SCAP brought
criticisms of their rigid hierarchies as an antithesis of the new patterns of
freedom and equality introduced by the victors. But as the Occupation regime came to rely increasingly on rehabilitated prewar elites, the ensuing
ideological adjustments allowed the iemoto not only to recover, but to enhance their position as guardians of what was inmost and best in the nation.
For following Prime Minister Katayama Tetsu's call in his first address to the
Diet under the postwar constitution, political leaders now aimed to redefine
a demilitarized Japan as a "cultured country." As early as 1948 the state instituted Culture Day as a national holiday, and began establishing cultural
affairs offices across the country. The iemoto lost no time in taking advan-
tage of this turn of events to reframe their practice of tea as the epitome of a
peace-loving Japanese civilization.

They were able to do so by refashioning their position in society in two
complementary directions. Economically, they would convert themselves
into modern business corporations, consonant with the high-speed Japanese capitalism of the post-Occupation period. Socially, they would ascend
to the status of cultural elites at a time when culture was one of the few
legitimate arenas for nationalist expression—a branding association that
could also serve as a pitch for marketing a new range of business endeavors.
Though often represented as disinterested cultural icons, iemoto remained
tea professionals living off their craft. Traditionally, they had reaped their
profits from the sale of tea certificates, classes, kaō, texts, seminars, and
publications—what might be termed "tea expertise." But from the mid-

twentieth century onward, the iemoto would enlarge their business interests in new directions by trading on the strategic potential of the tea ceremony as a presumptive synthesis of Japaneseness at large. In this process, symbolic escalation and market expansion went hand in hand.

Historically, emblems of nationhood in Japan—as elsewhere—had formed a variegated repertoire from which different groups or individuals could choose according to their commitments or interests. Since late Meiji times, the tea ceremony had always figured among them. Yet others were still more prominent in the high Showa period, when the cult of the warrior code, *bushidō*, was a more formidable expression of the national spirit. In the aftermath of defeat in World War II, this was no longer a contender for capturing it. Of the remaining possibilities in the palette of traditional symbols and practices, tea was now in many ways the best positioned. Other arts might be more ancient, and even today command a greater audience—sumo went back to the Heian age (794–1185), and would soon be a magnet on television. But wrestling is a spectator, not a participant, sport. Other possibilities—say, the composition of haiku, still widely practiced—lacked an inherent collective dimension. Nor, of course, could any compete with tea in the potency of its association with the summits of political power in the past. The postwar situation thus offered the iemoto an unprecedented opportunity to upgrade the status of tea in the national pantheon, which they seized by promoting it as not just one among other august manifestations of Japanese tradition, but as the veritable center of its web of aesthetic activities and objects. Tea was not only seen, but also explicitly advertised, as standing at the core of traditional Japanese culture. According to this new ideology, whose roots lay in Okakura's international best-seller on the practice, the tea ceremony was a "cultural synthesis" (*sōgō bunka*) of all the Japanese arts, combining within one form architecture, pottery, painting, calligraphy, cuisine, and flower arrangement, not to speak of corporeal grace.[23] These other arts were not slighted by this claim, but rather enhanced by it, as the tea schools soon formed mutually beneficial strategic alliances with others employed in the tradition industry. The density of these connections to other national traditions aided in sustaining the Japaneseness of the tea ceremony.

Its elevation to the rank of overarching cultural synthesis was accompanied, moreover, by its presentation as also a cure for specifically contemporary ills. Here the main strategies can be culled from the introductory greetings by the Urasenke iemoto Hōunsai in the monthly periodical *Tankō*, in which he addresses practitioners across the country with motifs that reappear in his public speeches, television appearances, and books. In these, a redundant theme—occurring in around a fifth of the greetings published during his tenure as iemoto (1965–2002)—was the role of tea as a salve for the putative crisis in Japanese culture in a period of rapid economic growth. The activity was regularly defined as a felicitous solution to the decline of human relationships and the loss of tradition associated with the rise of individualism and an excess of Westernization; tea practice cultivated precisely the fading qualities essential to, if not definitive of, Japaneseness. In his first address, Hōunsai declared, "Contemporary Japan is missing a foundational element, human interaction . . . as people think not about the country but only about themselves." Under these conditions, he went on, "all compatriots should turn to tea and the decorum of thinking about others, to spread a natural respect for humanity."[24] Two years later, he was reiterating that "traditional Japanese ways of life are withering." What was needed was a "Japanese attitude to life of which we can be proud," rather than "this confused society, in which the good taste of a Japanese life is being lost." The solution? "The tea ceremony can return society to its true abode."[25] Even an act as common as eating was under threat. In the 1980s, he explained that "in the past, Japanese table manners were ordered in detail," but now the sense of gratitude once expressed in salutations before and after a meal "has become completely lost" and even "Japaneseness has become forgotten." But here too "one can learn all those manners in the tea ceremony, in the serving of the kaiseki [meal]."[26] At work throughout these texts is the notion of an intrinsic Japaneseness that all Japanese have claims to and are even responsible for, but have failed to maintain. Consequently, it becomes the duty of every Japanese to learn the tea ceremony in order to recover the threatened essence of the nation.

Along a second ideological front, working in parallel with its domestic mission, Urasenke escalated promotion of the tea ceremony as a means of nurturing international understanding and building bridges to other countries by bringing the best of Japanese culture to them.[27] In 1975 the iemoto recounted to his readers how "in offering a bowl of tea to the Queen of England with all my heart, she was able to come in contact with our traditional culture, which I believe is the best way to obtain a good understanding of Japan."[28] A few years later, he was regaling them with details of his various tea performances to foreigners, and reporting with satisfaction that through these, "people from each country revised their views of Japan."[29] On occasion, the normal exaltation of the ceremony as particular to Japan could even be reversed, tea becoming a universal value capable of binding nations together. When a Chinese tea appreciation group on a study trip to Kyoto shared with him a bowl of matcha tea in a spirit of gratitude, he offered the thought that "this aspect of tea [the spirit of gratitude] that knows no country's borders can perhaps be planted in China as well," for "while languages and customs differ, people can understand each other through the tea ceremony."[30] But even as tea is offered as a means of crossing national frontiers, it reinforces national identity. Musing on the tea he has provided to so many foreign VIPs visiting Japan, Hōunsai asks himself, "What is a true international person?" and answers, "To be a real international person, one needs to know the history and culture of one's own country . . . and tea is a means to achieve that. If you offer a bowl of tea to foreigners, you can begin to teach them about Japanese culture."[31] More even than intercultural understanding was contained in teaware. In 1984, the Urasenke catchphrase, "peace through a bowl of tea" (an international flavor spicing up the Japanese version: *ichiwan kara "piisufurunesu"*) was coined, and its soothing interplay of the particular and the universal ceaselessly employed ever since. As Hōunsai characteristically put it, "Rikyū called for the spirit of harmony, respect, purity, and tranquility, and I have been continuing that through 'peace through a bowl of tea,' thereby helping the countries of the world to understand the Japanese form and Japanese heart. . . . Through that we can build world peace."[32] In this ideology, tea becomes not only a cure for the maladies of modernity at home, but also a prophylactic against strife and misunderstanding abroad—in both cases, though, it supplies a sovereignly Japanese remedy for the ills of the world.

## Economic Expansion

Ideological intensification was accompanied, and secured, by economic fortification, as the iemoto developed much stronger infrastructures than in the past. During the war, formal membership organizations were instituted at the most popular tea schools under a 1942 decree requiring large social groups to establish official organizations, thus enabling stricter government monitoring and possible future mobilization. At first run as small teachers' associations with only a few hundred members, these apparatuses were greatly expanded after the war. Hōunsai retooled his following along the lines of the Rotary Club system by founding a national network of regional associations and local branches managed by advisory boards—a pattern subsequently copied by other larger tea schools. Because the Urasenke membership organization, Tankōkai, is the largest and most elaborate, it can be taken as a template for general trends.[33]

Essentially a tool for creating a national tea presence, Tankōkai currently has over 160 branches in local communities, each required to hold several large public tea gatherings a year, in addition to arranging tea demonstrations at culture festivals or exhibitions. As volunteer associations, the local groups are a cost-efficient way for the headquarters not only to organize tea events across the country, but to staff the tea ceremony clubs it runs at over six thousand elementary, junior high, and high schools, in addition to colleges. Since participation in the organization is a requirement to move into the upper echelons of the tea hierarchy, Tankōkai also strengthens the iemoto's grip on practitioners' tea preparation techniques. At least twice a year, an emissary of the iemoto visits each association and conducts a public class with local students in a community center or concert hall. Instructed in the single, official way of carrying out the temae, audience members return to their tea groups to police the wayward gestures of others by invoking the "correct" way dem-

Tankōkai members attending a tea seminar in Tokyo watch a temae demonstration, mirrored on two screens magnifying the details of comportment

onstrated. In Tokyo, the disciplining gaze is drawn to the smallest details of movement by two large screens projecting simulcast images focusing on the hands, feet, and eyes of the participants on stage. Practitioners interested in more personal attention are encouraged to join the week-long seminars held at the headquarters twice a year to ensure they are making tea properly. And even when the minutiae of their own motions cannot be corrected by representatives of the center, they can self-adjust against the procedures narrated in dozens of photographs featured in Tankōkai's monthly magazine.

Tankōkai also boosts the market for iemoto-approved utensils. At the large gatherings the heads of local branches are required to hold several times a year, organizers are expected to stamp the iemoto's trusteeship onto the event by using utensils made by his hand or bearing his signature. These may be borrowed, but loaning expensive pieces that will be handled by strangers is a high-risk proposition even among friends, and therefore heads of local Tankōkai branches invest in a personal store of iemoto-approved utensils they can mix and match when called upon. For some practitioners, the large outlay needed may inhibit them from seeking leadership positions, but the proliferation of such norms is quite lucrative for the iemoto, who can rely on Tankōkai to organize a reliable consumer base. Advertisements or articles in periodicals and newsletters inform practitioners across the country about the products available, educating all to be able to recognize utensils consecrated by the iemoto.

In this new tea world, the Urasenke school, with around 70 percent of tea practitioners in Japan today, holds the upper hand. The Omotesenke school follows a distant second, encompassing around 20 percent of practitioners.[34] The remaining students of tea are members of one of around a dozen smaller schools, including the Mushanokōjisenke, Dainihon Sadō Gakkai, Edosenke, Yabunouchi, and Sōhen schools, along with the Sekishū and Enshū styles.[35] The public relationships among the various iemoto are congenial rather than competitive, but beyond annual celebratory tea gatherings and occasional meetings, interaction among them is minimal. Sharing the same form and similar content, the field of largely self-contained schools can be visualized as an array of identical, bounded units differing mainly in size. They draw their clientele from the 2.3 million Japanese who currently report engaging in the practice, a population discussed in greater detail in Chapter 4.

More ardently than other schools, Urasenke sells Japanese tradition, and its success has enabled it to expand its commercial endeavors into new arenas to become the most powerful, prominent, and profitable tea school. The combination of Japanese cultural iconicity with modern business interests is visible in the physical architecture of its headquarters. Located on prime real estate in Kyoto, its large, multistory modern office building houses not only the dozens of employees managing business operations but also a museum, library, and suite of reception rooms. On the street behind the modern structures, however, are the family compounds—elegant, well-preserved examples of traditional architecture containing the family tea rooms. Only a stone's throw away, the Omotesenke school stands in a similar arrangement.

A hallmark of these iemoto empires, their pyramid of certificates warrants a closer look. Beginners obtain a "membership" (*dōmon*) certificate enabling them to learn the most basic tea-making procedures, and they eventually progress through the hierarchy to more complicated and obscure procedures. The number of levels, types of tea preparation included, and cost of certificates vary across schools and over time within schools, but the same form holds.

The Omotesenke business headquarters

The Omotesenke family compound

Entry-level certificates are easily affordable, but prices increase dramatically with rank, and in addition to the cost of the permit, students typically pay gift money to their own teachers, which can range from a token sum of $50 to $100, to an adjusted amount of half or the same amount as the price of the certificate. After receiving permission to learn the most complicated procedures open to practitioners, students may apply for a "tea name" (*chamei*), signifying mastery of chanoyu. Although no new tea-making procedures are learned from the rank of chamei upwards, ceremonial titles such as "assistant professor," "professor," and "honored professor" can be bought for a few thousand dollars. The lengthy application time—sometimes a decade—encourages students to petition for these certificates as soon as the chance arises, while the extended wait provides insurance of their continued membership in the interim. The honorary titles afford entry into higher ranks within the organization: one must be at least an "assistant professor" to become an officer in a local chapter and a "professor" to become its head. But most dear to disciples are the invitations to major tea events held at the headquarters that high ranks guarantee, including the first tea preparation of the year and the thrice yearly memorial services for leading tea figures of the past. The elite of society, however, may have an easier time of it, and those with whom an iemoto wants to remain close—business owners or museum managers, for example—can purchase lofty ranks without the extended wait or time spent on their knees mastering arcane tea-making procedures. But such fast-tracks (and financial matters in general) are rarely mentioned, for in tea, as in many other fields of cultural production, its producers have an interest in appearing unconcerned with financial gain in order to sustain the impression that the value of their art inheres within itself.[36]

Nonetheless, the iemoto have leveraged their cultural authority to market products beyond the domain of the tea ceremony, with Urasenke, again, setting the model for others to follow. Here, the younger siblings in the family have stepped forward, establishing businesses dealing in Japanese culture that offer symbiotic support to the central tea enterprise. The first of these subsidiary companies is the Tankōsha publishing house, founded by the younger brother of Hōunsai in 1949. In addition to producing Urasenke staples, such as periodicals, manuals, reference books, trade journals, and instructional videos, Tankōsha also publishes titles—one thousand are currently available—on architecture, design, calligraphy, photography, religion,

Urasenke certificate system (1999)

| Level | Certificate/Temae | Price |
|---|---|---|
| Beginner | Nyūmon | ¥ 2,000 ($20) |
| | Konarai | ¥ 3,000 ($30) |
| | Chabako | ¥ 5,000 ($50) |
| Middle | Chatsūbako | ¥ 4,000 ($40) |
| | Karamono | ¥ 4,000 ($40) |
| | Diatenmoku | ¥ 4,000 ($40) |
| | Bonten | ¥ 4,000 ($40) |
| | Wakin | ¥ 5,000 ($50) |
| Upper | Gyō no Gyō Daisu | ¥ 12,000 ($120) |
| | Daien no Sō | ¥ 12,000 ($120) |
| | Hikitsugi | ¥ 25,000 ($250) |
| Teacher/lecturer* | Shin no Gyō Daisu | ¥ 20,000 ($200) |
| | Daien no Shin | ¥ 20,000 ($200) |
| | Seihikitsugi | ¥ 35,000 ($350) |
| Full-time instructor | Chamei, Monurushi | ¥ 150,000 ($1,500) |
| Associate professor | Junkyōjū | ¥ 170,000 ($1,700) |

NOTE: Prices are for applicants residing in Japan. Costs are lower overseas.

* Urasenke has an idiosyncratic system of naming levels after teaching ranks in higher education, but this bears no relationship to the state-recognized education system. A "tea name" is received at the level of full-time instructor.

history, culture, cuisine, travel, and other traditional arts. "Using the tea ceremony, the cultural synthesis of Japan, as an axis," the company describes its mission as "endeavoring day and night to develop Japanese culture through the management vision of 'an enterprise aimed at leading Japanese culture as a transmitter of information concerning traditional culture centered on the tea ceremony.'"[37] In the service of this ambition, Tankōsha also offers classes in Kyoto and Tokyo on pottery appreciation, flower arrangement, sweet making, and letter writing. Those looking to build their own tea room can turn to the conglomerate for the specialized parts needed, and their new tea space can be filled with wares from the utensil dealership Tankōsha manages, which offers both low-end utensils for tea lessons and high-end utensils, kimonos, powdered tea, sweets, and gifts.

In 1984, Hōunsai's second son began the business group Millieme to "promote modern living with Japanese culture" and "propagate the Japanese heart."[38] Merchandising a Japanese identity, the company presents "scenarios for modern lifestyles imbued with the traditional aesthetic consciousness cultivated in the tea ceremony." Its product lines focus on auxiliary needs: traditional sweets, often given as gifts at Urasenke events, advertised as not only "absolutely delicious" but "bringing together only things that do not forget the Japanese heart"; ceramic dishes intended for "a modern life instilled with the value of tradition and the beauty of authenticity"; and tables designed by the iemoto for performing tea in modern rooms.[39] Maintaining production within the family, the Sukiya Architecture group under Millieme builds the tea rooms that Urasenke donates to cultural centers, embassies, universities, and museums in Japan and abroad. The company also supplies over two thousand schools with utensils and other materials needed for their tea clubs. Visitors to the Millieme office building, a stone's throw from the Urasenke headquarters, may also purchase tea supplies from the associated utensil dealership occupying the ground floor—one-stop shopping for all tea ceremony needs.

In addition, Millieme runs the nonprofit organization Wa no Gakkō, or School of Wa—meaning both "harmony" and "Japaneseness"—whose goal is to "carry out activities in which anyone can easily participate" in order "to recover the goodness of Japan that is being lost and to make for a society rich in spirit."[40] Founded in 2003, the "school" is in fact a repository for information about elements commonly thought to compose Japanese culture. Its online network of over fifty traditional industries provides links to kimono dealers, manners experts, incense shops, and the like, which appear alongside essays about Japanese history and culture. Biographies—even family pedigrees—of the owners of these affiliates reassure customers that what they are purchasing is, indeed, authentic Japanese culture. Because the Wa no Gakkō is, at least by name, a school, occasional real-life lectures, classes, and performances are held, instructing participants about festivals, traditional practices, and the Japanese past.

Working in tandem "to further the progress and harmony of humanity by all citizens doing tea" is the Chadō Culture Promotion Foundation. With classes on making sweets and basic etiquette, the organization encourages parents and children "to learn about the cultural spirit that the Japanese are losing."[41] In recent years, the foundation instituted a national "Tea Ceremony Culture Expertise Examination"—an additional certification that practitioners may purchase, though one using the four-level format found in most skills-assessment tests in Japan. Urasenke provides not only the exam, but also the means to prepare, and registrants—over nine thousand the first year it was offered—can purchase a study guide or attend one of several preparation seminars to brush up on their tea knowledge. Those looking for greater specialization can enroll in an Urasenke junior college in Kyoto, whose program, "through the cultural synthesis of the tea ceremony," covers art, philosophy, sociability, morality, and religion. The tuition at this finishing school is comparable to that of other private colleges: a hardly trifling $50,000 for a three-year course. But here, where life "begins and ends with a bow cultivating the rich spirit that is being lost, a docile heart, proper manners, and a feeling of independence," potential students are promised they will learn not only "the true meaning of Japanese culture, but also become a true international person."[42]

This variant of cosmopolitanism is more pronounced at the International Chado Culture Foundation, established in 1947 to "use the tea ceremony, Japan's traditional culture, to contribute to world peace and international friendship." The foundation organizes tea experiences for foreigners in Japan—from elite gatherings for ambassadors' wives to brief demonstrations for tourists from abroad—as well as Japanese, who eagerly purchase package holidays on which they are flown abroad to learn about tea culture in other countries. But its main function is to train Japanese to demonstrate the tea ceremony in English through a spectrum of classes and workshops it offers. Recruitment stresses the importance of cultural ambassadorship, asking potential emissaries, "Would you like to learn about ourselves, the Japanese, and the essence of the tea ceremony, which stands at the core of Japanese culture and has flowed from the roots of the Japanese people? And while sharing mutual exchanges, would you like to introduce Japanese culture, centered on the tea ceremony, to the world?"[43] The foundation also manages the Aoyama Green Academy (AGA), which, in addition to lessons in the tea ceremony, offers expert lectures on tea-related topics, such as Zen, Noh theater, poetry, and calligraphy.

In combination, these subsidiaries establish a potentially self-contained tea world. From tea powder to tea rooms, all of the essential components of the ceremony are offered. From kimonos to gifts, all of the subsidiary elements are handled. From instructional texts to intensive teacher training courses, all of the requisite knowledge is sold. But as an enterprise, Urasenke has gone beyond the traditional economic mainstays of iemoto—certificates, lessons, utensils, and their authenticating signatures—not only to supply all of the basic needs of practitioners but to generate new ones as well. No longer is competence in temae sufficient to become a tea expert; one must also be knowledgeable in all the arts, able to concoct a full kaiseki meal, in possession of passing scores on expertise exams, and prepared to explain the tea ceremony in English—skills all presented as essential for anyone concerned with the recovery and promotion of Japanese culture.

## Social Ascent

As icons of Japanese culture heading wealthy corporations, the iemoto have been well positioned to cultivate new social networks in business and politics. The Japan Rotary Club offers a notable example. The iemoto of the Urasenke and Mushanokōjisenke schools have both been closely involved with the Rotarians (Hōunsai even serving as president of the national association), and have used these ties to establish tea clubs at many Rotary branches—a strategy Urasenke has deployed with the Junior Chamber of Commerce as well. The ostensible aims recall the sukisha of an earlier time—socializing and networking among business elite over tea—though these are now channeled through the tea schools, and even amplified through the membership organizations. Urasenke seeks out an elite man in the local community to head each Tankōkai branch. Rarely active practitioners themselves, these titular authorities can expect invitations from the iemoto to exclusive annual tea gatherings, attended by their counterparts from around the country—a networking opportunity of benefit both to them and to the tea school, which gains leverage in local power networks. The constellation

is mirrored at the national level, where an advisory board of wealthy businessmen, famous craftsmen, and powerful academics oversees the organization, allowing those involved to capitalize on their accumulated prestige.
Members of the upper crust more actively interested in tea—and with more
time and money to invest—may secure the opportunity to host elite annual
gatherings, like the Kōetsukai, held in tea houses owned by the iemoto. In
contrast to the sukisha, elites who dabble in tea today are likely to do so
under the iemoto's auspices—if on a separate track from others.

These networks are both product and producer of elite status for the
iemoto as well, securing their image as icons of the "cultured country of
Japan," en vogue following military defeat. In this period, the iemoto eagerly
plied their wares as carriers of peace and goodwill, preeminently capable of
rehabilitating the nation abroad. Urasenke was again in the vanguard of this
development. At the close of the American occupation in 1950, Hōunsai,
then crown prince, undertook a four-month "tea ceremony mission" to the
United States, which he followed with a twelve-month sojourn the next
year with the goals of sharing Japanese culture with Americans and changing their impressions of the Japanese. These two cultural tours marked the
beginning of a long career, initially as a self-appointed Japanese cultural emissary to the world at large, and later as an official Japanese cultural ambas-
sador to the United Nations. Within ten years, not only had he opened tea
chapters in Brazil, Argentina, Peru, and Mexico, but he had also given tea
lectures and demonstrations in Burma, Thailand, Malaysia, and the Philip-
pines, organized a tea demonstration at the Brussels World Fair, donated a
tea room to the Boston Art Museum, hosted tea for the Shah of Iran's visit
to Japan, and represented Japan at the request of the Ministry of Foreign
Affairs at the hundredth anniversary celebration of US–Japan friendship in
Washington, DC. These activities—international tea lectures and tea room
donations, tea services for foreign heads of state, and missions on behalf
of the Foreign Ministry—continued with increasing frequency in the following decades. Naturally, such performances received national newspaper
coverage, fostering widespread recognition of Hōunsai's role as a stellar figure among the nation's cultural elite. Other iemoto have since followed in
Urasenke's footsteps, arranging meetings with foreign heads of state and
hosting tea services at the request of the Ministry of Foreign Affairs.

The heightened profile of the iemoto as the bearers of Japanese refinement abroad has, in turn, assured their integration into the topmost levels
of society at home, most visible in postwar marriage patterns. The next-

in-line to the Dainihon Sadō Gakkai school has secured a match with the Tokugawa family—a prospect inconceivable under the shogunate—while the sixteenth-generation Urasenke iemoto has married a cousin of the emperor, an imperial connection the mention of which is rarely missed. With yet more publicity, the pinnacles of elective office invariably pay homage to the iemoto. In an annual New Year event, the prime minister and an entourage of top bureaucrats attend a celebratory tea preparation at the Urasenke complex in Tokyo. This spectacle, relayed to the public by press and television, stages the continuity of the role of Japanese rulers in the practice of the ceremony since the time of Nobunaga and Hideyoshi, and the novelty of the status of the iemoto in presiding over it. Little could better illustrate the passage of symbolic power from its accumulation to routine exercise.

## Conclusion

The Japaneseness of the tea ceremony, as a concentration of national meanings, has been captured and secured by the iemoto in a historical process of wider significance. In the first stage, they gradually accumulated the authority to define and certify authentic tea. Basing their claims on genealogical connections to Rikyū, the iemoto transformed a variety of innovative tea practices into a body of formalized knowledge that could be inherited and controlled, and they developed administrative mechanisms, including curricula, certificate systems, and utensil standards, to enforce this oversight. Print media aided in these endeavors by transmitting the aesthetic standards set by the iemoto beyond their arena of immediate contact. These first appeared as texts attributed to Rikyū and unofficial manuals and catalogues bearing the Sen family name, but then later would include official versions bearing detailed images of the iemoto-approved temae and utensils. Utensil artisans contributed as well by producing countless copies of favored implements that augmented the authority of the iemoto as they themselves gained from their sponsorship. And patrons and disciples alike benefited from association with these descendants of "tea saint" Rikyū, as well as from their proclaimed authority to certify the value of utensils. When early Meiji reforms left the iemoto on the brink, they came back even stronger by developing a customer base among middle- and upperclass women, who were not only more numerous, but more dependent than elite male dilettantes on the iemoto's authority, for this, objectified as permission certificates, held value outside the tea world in the marriage market. Later, the iemoto would fortify their command by building membership organizations that supplied a nationwide apparatus for policing tea preparation techniques and sustaining dependence on iemoto-defined standards of taste and the value of utensils.

Throughout these transformations, the tea ceremony—though not the tea of the iemoto—was wedded to the apex of political power, facilitating its later nationalization. In the first phase, the main competitor to the iemoto in the field of legitimate tea practice was the Sekishū-style of daimyo tea, which remained the variety of choice among the dominant classes through the Tokugawa, Meiji, and Taisho periods. The decline of its latter-day carriers, the sukisha business elite, in the 1920s, and the subsequent rise of nationalist fervor and the mobilization of cultural activities for the war effort, enabled the iemoto to annex associations between the tea ceremony and the Japanese nation diffused through etiquette and history textbooks in the school system, and to represent themselves as the living embodiment of this pediment of Japanese culture. But it was not until after the war that the political need for promoting Japan as a "cultured country" enabled the iemoto to become icons wielding symbolic power not simply over tea practice, but also over Japanese culture in general, and thereby to position themselves firmly among the country's elites. The iemoto could then employ a conflation of tea and Japanese culture to market new products beyond their traditional base of tea preparation certificates and utensil legitimization, and to diagnose problems of Japanese culture to which they could offer tea as a solution. Thus the tea ceremony remains such a stalwart symbol of Japan not simply because it was ideologically *imbued with* national associations, but because the organizational infrastructure sustaining the tea world has become economically *invested in* its Japaneseness.

The iemoto have been the great beneficiaries of these processes. Though merchandising and mass distribution might compromise the aura surrounding their products as emblems of an authentic traditional culture, they have done little damage in Japan, for the aristocratic bearing of the iemoto, projecting the image of an ancient lineage living *in* but not *off* the world of Japanese tradition, preserves the sanctifying halo. Their commodities offer not merely a distinctively Japanese option alongside other lifestyle variants, but also a way of becoming better members of the nation through them. Who these consumers are, we turn to next.

## CHAPTER 4

# Enacting Tea

## *Doing and Demonstrating Japaneseness*

Authority cannot simply be claimed, but must be acknowledged to be effective, for its power lies in the belief and submission of those over whom it is held. To decipher the workings of the tea world created by the iemoto, it is necessary to unravel how this power is recognized, validated, and reproduced by his following. These adherents not only activate the iemoto's authority over the ritual and their symbolic power over Japanese culture, but also enliven it through their own tea practice as they invoke and perform the historically produced national associations grafted onto the iemoto system. This vivification occurs both in their interactions in institutional structures, and in their commonplace tea activities. Indeed, they routinely invoke the Japaneseness peddled by the iemoto in venues far from his gaze. But to grasp how Japaneseness is enacted through tea requires first an examination of the relationship between the masters themselves and those who offer their unflagging allegiance.

### *Living the Lineage*

Genealogy—a crucial tool in the historic extension of the iemoto's symbolic power—continues today to anchor the tea practice of adepts. Signs of the

ancestral connections to Rikyū woven into the fabric of the tea world provide subtle yet recurrent reminders of the basis of the iemoto's authority,
while the kinship metaphors in common use project him as the head of a
great family.[1] Indeed, no membership meeting of the Urasenke school can
proceed without invoking the symbolic presence of the patriarch, as all participants chant in unison, "The iemoto is the parent, the members are siblings, and because we are thus of one body, we should not forget to embrace
when we meet." Symbolic adoption into the ménage—a practice of all tea
schools—adds weight to such pledges and positions the inductee within the
lineage. With several years of training and certificate acquisition, an initiate
may rise to the rank of "tea master." Baptized into the tea world, she receives
a "tea name," combining the character *sō* (宗), taken from Rikyū's sobriquet
*Sōeki*, and typically a character from her own name, that will henceforth
identify her as a member of the clan.[2] With the tea name comes permission
to emblazon one of the iemoto's family crests onto kimonos worn at tea
gatherings—a privilege not to be borne lightly. Teachers caution students
receiving the insignia to be always on their best behavior when wearing it,
as it marks them as representatives of the iemoto, and can be revoked for
inappropriate conduct.

In the Urasenke tradition, as in others, a ceremony tinged with the arcane consummates this rite of passage, which typically takes place in a tea
room. Dressed in a formal kimono, the inductee kneels humbly before her
teacher, who has positioned herself in front of the alcove, the apex in the
architectural hierarchy, to assume the role of the iemoto's emissary.[3] In his
stead, she carefully unfolds a statement on a long, horizontal piece of high-
quality paper, written in vertical calligraphy by the iemoto's hand (though
a laser copy, of course) conveying his regret that he cannot be present to
confer the name. In a solemn pronouncement welcoming the postulant into
the fold, she declaims the iemoto's words of congratulation to the student
and encouragement to pursue her studies further. An additional statement,
included in the packet dispatched from Kyoto, may be read as well, informing the initiate that she has become a full member of the Urasenke school
of tea and its historical legacy, but—bringing the family and the business
together—that she has also attained the status of teacher and its associated
benefits within the Tankōkai association.

But this is just the prelude to the ceremonial climax when the teacher
presents the iemoto's certificate bestowing the new "tea name" on the student. Printed on thick cotton paper and written in classical script utilizing a

Students kneel attentively at a name-giving ceremony

different word order from modern Japanese, the document is accompanied by computer-printed transliterations of the texts on a small sheet of office paper—visual and tactile contrasts between the antiquated and contemporary that further underscore the weight of history. These long-awaited prizes are handled with the same care as a treasured utensil. Housed in a cedar box and tied with a thick ribbon in the official Urasenke family colors, they are often afterward displayed in an alcove. As the student receives the documents with a bow, she demonstrates her mastery of etiquette that has brought her this far by immediately offering a token of her gratitude to the teacher: the equivalent of several hundred dollars in crisp new bills, amounting to a portion of, or in some cases, the same amount as, the fee for entering the iemoto's extended family.[4] Employing a box of sweets or an open fan as a presentation tray, she extends them to the teacher with the same flow of humbling motions as she would a bowl of tea.

The sacrosanct atmosphere invoking the iemoto's presence is replicated in the rituals that sanction progressing adherents to learn the most esoteric tea preparation procedures. Again, those attending don their most formal kimono, but the small corps of students is accompanied by an external instructor, invited to ensure that the procedure—taught mimetically and not to be found in any textbook—is carried out correctly. In a rare display of her own temae before students, the teacher performs the almost hour-long procedure before a hushed class, attentively setting the flow of movements to mind and body, for after the single viewing, the initiates will have to replicate it, relying as little as possible on their mentor verbally coaching them across any gaps in the somatic chain that putatively links them to the grand masters.[5] Practitioners sometimes talk excitedly about the yet more esoteric procedures that only the top-ranked assistants to the iemoto are allowed to learn. These "ur"-temae, supposedly simplified by Rikyū into the range of preparation procedures accessible to the masses today, lie at the apex of a hierarchy of procedures, whose receding peak ensures both continuous focus on the top and continuous effort to approach it.

In ascending this pyramid, disciples grant the iemoto authority over the entirety of their tea practice: from how it is done to what it is done with. Even after decades of training, few adherents innovate their own temae, and those who do quickly label it "outlaw tea." While the core procedures remain stable over time, the iemoto may develop one or two new preparation methods, inevitably variants of standard practices. And occasionally they may sanction small adjustments to canonical temae: changing, for example, whether a cord is straightened before tying it. The power of the past legitimates these amendments, with modifications accompanied by statements that recent historical research has revealed that they are indeed the original way the procedure was carried out. Though slight, such alterations spread quickly through the ranks of practitioners via the semiannual lectures and demonstrations by the top-level teachers, in direct service to the iemoto, at regional or local meetings of the national tea associations.

The material components of tea preparation provide conduits for the extension of the iemoto's command—and even presence—as well. Although practitioners are encouraged, "in the spirit of Rikyū," to employ as a tea utensil any object they deem appropriate, the styles of implements commonly used are remarkably limited, channeled by the aesthetic preferences of particular iemoto, the konomi discussed in Chapter 3 anchoring orthodox forms. Innovations are not unheard of—a plate picked up on a trip abroad might become a tray for sweets, for example—but most utensils employed at lessons and gatherings originate from the canon of iemoto-sanctioned styles. Acquiring an appreciation for the aesthetic taste of past tea virtuosi is, in part, an embodied accomplishment, aided by the regular rotation of utensils by season and type of temae. Students making tea with a *Rikyū-gonomi* ivory scoop—its smooth curves and cool touch contrasting with the natural variegations of the bamboo standard—learn that it is appropriate for use only with the somber colors and elegant lines of the most formal utensils. When using a *Hō'un dana*—a mahogany-colored wooden stand accented with a few swirling clouds of gold leaf—and told that it was designed by the fifteenth-generation Urasenke iemoto, students receive a lesson not only in genealogy, but also in aesthetic sensibility, as they encounter the stylistic preferences of this iemoto known for his opulent taste. This stands in contrast to the misshapen and worn utensils used in October as the summer withers to winter, when students preparing tea with a rusted brazier may be told—accurately or not—that its use began with the third-generation iemoto in the Sen schools, whose austere aesthetic sense earned him the moniker "Wabi Sōtan."

Branding utensils with an iemoto's approval, kaō ciphers and hakogaki messages ensure his omnipresence, and practitioners may hastily check underneath a lid or a bowl and "see if the iemoto is there" to assess its worth.[6] More than legitimating the tools they mark, these signs project the iemoto into the tea space, which even if only in symbolic form, still demands a respectful etiquette. Aficionados take pains to ensure that utensils made or signed by more recent iemoto do not usurp those by one further back in the lineage, a feeling that might be invoked, for example, if a scroll made by a sixteenth-generation iemoto is hung beside a bamboo flower container signed by his eleventh-generation forebear.[7] Viewing and discussing the inscriptions on utensils or boxes—a central activity of tea gatherings—extends the "iemoto's gaze" yet further. Signed wooden receptacles are typically displayed in the alcove of the waiting room, around which the guests crowd as they try to decipher the implement's name, maker, and geographical origin inscribed in flowing ink. This skill, enhanced by memorizing indexes of the signature styles of the iemoto, is prized, and those who can identify the lettering share their success with their neighbors, asking, for example, "Is that the new signature of the iemoto? I heard he changed it recently," or simply uttering a sigh of appreciation, "Ah, that must be the eighth-generation grand master." In discussing the boxes, the guests not only enact a respect for their contents, but also display their expertise in assessing the meanings and significance of what are, to the untrained eye, simply elegantly written hieroglyphics. For the host, the signed lids exhibit her taste and wealth while connecting her to the apex of the tea world. Hardly cheap—the brush strokes can add up to several thousand dollars to the utensil price—they are nonetheless a necessity on most formal tea occasions: those without such tokens will borrow them from friends, apologize profusely for their absence, or even decline to host gatherings.[8] What pieces have been endorsed by which iemoto is duly recorded on the "gathering record" (*kaiki*), handwritten in elegant brushstrokes on heavy-weight paper. As this document is passed around for examination before or during the tea preparation, guests with an extensive knowledge of the iemoto, along with the famous craftspeople, monks, and other historical figures associated with the imple-

Practitioners discuss the box lids on display at a large tea gathering

ments, are alerted to the most prized pieces, an aid in directing the utensil-dominated conversation with both the host and the other guests.

Yet the iemoto do more than authorize the rigid rules governing tea-making procedures and define a fuzzier set of aesthetic preferences in utensil combinations; they also serve as the standard in making practical decisions about uncodified matters. If the utensils are tightly arrayed on a narrow tatami mat, for example, a teacher may qualify the particular arrangement by saying, "This mat actually is the smaller 'Tokyo size,' but at the iemoto's they use the traditional, larger 'Kyoto size,' and so the distances [between the objects] should be greater." An expert practitioner at a New Year's tea gathering used a similar technique when she complemented the woman who owned the tea room on how fresh the new green bamboo fountain looked: "Before it was a bit crooked, but this one is absolutely straight. Though many people cut the bamboo diagonally, my *gyōtei* teacher [high-ranking assistant to the iemoto] says that it should be cut straight." The tea-room owner, both checking the rule and acknowledging her guest's connection to the top, promptly responded, "Is that how it's done at Urasenke headquarters?" The iemoto may serve as the guide in deciding not only that something is done, but also how it is done, with deviations from the standard justified by invoking his practice. At a lesson where a student followed the common procedure of placing sweets made of sugar pressed into a seasonal shape in the upper right-hand corner of a tray and round, cracker-style sweets impressed with a design in the lower left-hand corner, the teacher scolded her: "How you arrange the sweets depends not only on the rules of what they're made of, but also their shape. If it's a waterfall, it goes on top, even if it's a cracker-style sweet. If you go to the iemoto's, you see these things. They would never do it in an unnatural order there."

Correcting students might be common for most teachers, but correcting a fellow cognoscenti is a different matter, and the iemoto's practice can be used to assert authority among equals in such cases. This may occur at the large gatherings where teachers mix, and the host may employ unusual implements in an attempt to delight the visitors. A seasoned practitioner who tries to slice a runny sweet with a pick—the typical mode of consumption—might be cautioned by a fellow guest that "at the iemoto's" everyone uses a paper napkin to raise that particular style of delectable to the mouth. A woman who places a handkerchief on her lap before eating the meal—a commonly observed practice—can be corrected forthrightly by the host of the gathering: "No one uses a napkin at the iemoto's." Someone tempted to cool herself with the largely symbolic fan all guests carry might be warned that at the iemoto's she would be thrown out of the tea room for such behavior.[9] As such, the doyen's dictates do not simply confine as they define proper tea, but provide resources for extending a practitioner's own authority.

Though adherents most often acknowledge and enact the iemoto's authority at a distance, direct encounters provide rare yet treasured opportunities to legitimate his command in person. Ancestral memorial rites, part of the annual life of any Japanese family, are magnified into grand spectacles in

Invitees to a large tea gathering enjoy a modified kaiseki meal accompanying the tea preparation

the tea world, with over a thousand invitees from across the country travel-ing to Kyoto for the celebrations. Although a ticket to attend one of the main memorial services (or the New Year's celebration) at the headquarters costs upwards of $500—in addition to transportation and hotel fees, as well as the requisite gift money—even middle-class practitioners will squirrel away the funds to attend. These invitations are not easily declined, for it is otherwise difficult to gain admittance to—let alone be served tea in—the famous tea rooms constituting the heart of the family compound, imbued with the mystique of the past iemoto who built them. After years of reading about and viewing photos of these chambers in official publications, invitees are granted the opportunity not merely to tour past, but to experience in actual use the originals, often designated important cultural properties. At Urasenke, items such as the doors on which the eleventh-generation iemoto listed in elegant calligraphy the official temae or the old well used to draw water on New Year's day are pointed out by older, more experienced practi-tioners, who display as they convey their knowledge to younger ones. While imbibing tea in the rarefied atmosphere of these rooms is attractive, more alluring still is the chance to admire and even handle the original utensils that serve as blueprints for the replicas employed at lessons. The tea services are carried out with select antique bowls, tea caddies, and scrolls favored by time-honored iemoto, as well as tea scoops made by past masters, which are passed around and afterward placed on display, attended—and guarded— by the iemoto's retainers, who relate tales about their origin and history. These are conveyed yet further when practitioners return and recount their pilgrimage to those who remained at home, offering detailed descriptions of the implements that, in the anthropomorphic metaphor commonly used in comparing well-known pieces to stars, "appeared on stage" at the gathering.

While the experience of the rooms and utensils may be intimate, the events themselves are not. Wrapped in their most formal kimono, over a thousand practitioners arrive at appointed times, staggered by half hour intervals, at the headquarters to begin a day of waiting patiently in very crowded spaces. Divided into groups of about twenty and directed to vari-ous holding rooms, they sit knee-to-knee and shoulder-to-shoulder with a rigid discipline as they wait up to an hour for each of the half dozen tea services. Nonpractitioners with invitations in hand are nudged to close up the distances and sit efficiently, if uncomfortably, on their knees. The lax are prodded to attention by the top-ranked assistants to the iemoto who stand by to orient the lost and police behavior: folding fans are not to be unfurled

Practitioners wait to enter the tea room at a large gathering at a shrine in Tokyo

in the stuffy rooms, and the cameras that commemorate most tea gatherings must be tucked away.

The chance to witness the iemoto making tea is a coveted highlight, but this—like most encounters—is weighted by pro forma displays of deference and decorum. Those fortunate enough to gain entry to a service by the master will spend most of it snapped into the position traditionally indicating fealty to a lord: rounded hands, with the thumbs and index fingers curving into a circle, placed on the floor at the knees. The less lucky will still have the opportunity to encounter the iemoto as he makes periodic rounds of greetings, offering a wide smile and kind words as he blitzes through the flock bowing in return. Veneration is expressed a final time as the adherents leave the premises with a formal bow in the direction of the family compound after passing its main gate.

Yet such opportunities to encounter the iemoto in his own preserve are difficult to come by, and for many adherents the chance to see the iemoto in person is limited to public tea services at Buddhist temples or Shinto shrines, known as *kencha*. On such occasions, the top assistant teachers arrive far in advance of the iemoto's appearance to arrange the utensils for his just-in-time arrival, as he is escorted from a chauffeured car to the tea site, official photographers running by his side. Awaiting the grand master are hundreds of kimono-clad adherents, kneeling in straight lines several rows deep, on the broad deck projected from the front of the building. Most will have to crane their necks to view the priests performing a solemn service of Buddhist or Shinto rites that precede the dignified ritual tea performance by the iemoto, but they will still be able to follow along, guided by the a microphone-bearing emcee. Those who did not arrive early enough to get a seat within the building will stand outside, straining for a glimpse, and taking part in the unison bows.[10]

An iemoto performing a ritual tea service at a shrine with a cameraman capturing the event

Tea practitioners watching an iemoto perform a ritual tea service at a shrine

After the ritual tea offering, the iemoto changes from a kimono to a well-tailored three-piece suit to attend the accompanying tea services—usually three or four—organized by practitioners. Projecting the image of a gentleman rather than a "grand tea master," he shifts from a position of responsibility and instruction to that of a guest, though the most eminent one. Some iemoto attend the full tea preparation as would any other participant, examining the utensils in the waiting room and mingling with adherents before entering the tea room to assume the position of the main guest.[11] But if pressed for time, he may visit the accompanying tea services only briefly, in a strictly organized event where even the tea preparation itself is sidelined for photo opportunities—these yielding prized possessions for practitioners who may keep the shots in their wallet or display them in their living room beside pictures of family members. At a kencha service in Tokyo, an announcement came in the morning that the iemoto would attend an accompanying tea preparation at 8:30 am. Sent ahead to ensure that everything was organized, a handful of his representatives led a dry run-through of an abbreviated temae—the lengthy purification motions axed to save the iemoto's time. His appearance was heralded by several elderly men, large blue ribbons pinned to their suits alerting others to their VIP status, followed by the iemoto, who made a quick round of greetings to the practitioners in charge of the tea service before taking a seat. As the host explained the symbolic significance of the combination of utensils, the iemoto politely kept up the conversation, but without asking the typical follow-up questions that might prolong the narration. After the tea was served, he returned the bowl, and, truncating the closing procedures, immediately began to pose for pictures with various groupings of the participants. His jovial manner, friendly smile, and easy conversation, as well as the rare chance for a personal photo-op, overrode what might otherwise be seen as an abbreviated tea service, short-changing the audience. When he and his entourage left (a top teacher taking on the "bad cop" role, declaring that he was short of time), one of the people in charge said with audible relief that he was glad it went well. The woman beside him replied, "That was the easy part; from here on out you'll be judged by very strict eyes," referring to the far more stringent policing by the older tea teachers who would dominate the following tea services. Though such elders may scout for opportunities to display their own expertise though criticism—murmuring, for example, that a sliver of aromatic wood should not be hidden in the incense container on display if charcoal is not prepared before the guests—the iemoto need not concern himself with such direct injunctions, for the personage embodying the ultimate authority can rely on others drawing on his aura to do this work. Aided by a retinue assuming more unpleasant tasks, and supported by flocks of participants willfully cooperating to produce his lofty status, the iemoto can appear as at once rarefied and personable.[12]

## *Contours of Authority*

The concentration of authoritative power over the tea ceremony in the iemoto contributes to the comprehensiveness of his command over all elements of tea practice. Even if this singular figure comes in limited copies, with each school headed by a different master, the monopoly of authority ensures their independence. Though all traditions encompass more or less similar temae, the particulars of each vary—a bowl of tea that is passed among guests from hand to hand in one school, for example, may be set on the ground in between guests in another. Novices may pay little attention to whether a person enters the tea room on the left foot, the right foot, or the foot closest to the wall, but these differences become patterned into the body over time. Small variations in the utensils—a pentagonal versus hexagonal foot on a tea bowl, for instance—accumulated in the process of learning tea distinguish membership as well, and kaō, hakogaki, and ko-nomi venerating a particular branch of Rikyū's lineage see little light outside their own tea school. These physical and financial investments are written down as losses if schools are changed, providing insurance for lifelong adherence to one tradition.

Yet it is not the master above who is its direct producer. Because belief in the iemoto is sufficient to perform the social magic that authorizes him to define and certify tea practice and utensil taste, *actual* expertise is unnecessary: the iemoto is largely a symbolic centralizing feature. Although ultimately responsible for the rigid hierarchy of tea-making procedures, he himself performs only a limited number of temae and rarely teaches how to make tea. The assistants immediately beneath him are considered the real experts in this area. It is they who are pictured in textbooks, and it is they who instruct practitioners at official seminars. And, for the most part, they train each other in tea practice rather than taking lessons from the crown of the hierarchy. The iemoto's direct involvement in selecting utensils for authorization with kaō is probably greater, but even practitioners sometimes doubt that the insignias were written by the iemoto's own hand. Teachers may alert novices, handling a tea scoop made by an iemoto with beginner's excitement, that he simply carved the final bit on it rather than taking the pains to craft it entirely himself. Some practitioners even whisper that iemoto do not raise the brush to their own scrolls, or that the box and kaō signings are completed by office staff. Whether or not this is the case is secondary to the crucial point that even if adherents doubt the authenticity of such things, it matters little. Their preciousness flows from the symbolic worth assigned to the iemoto through an on-going process of collective appraisal by tea practitioners. If personal skepticism brings into question the bond between an individual and the leader, the group belief in his authority reinstates the value. Attesting to this power are the individual doubters who will invest thousands in authorized utensils and certificates because they know others will, nonetheless, recognize their worth, thereby witnessing and enacting the iemoto's symbolic power.

Given the VIP status of the iemoto, it is not surprising that outsiders may mock adherents for treating these figures "like gods or the emperor," or that insiders themselves can be heard grumbling to the same effect. One practitioner complained of the great lengths the local tea group went to in preparation for a visit by the iemoto, trying to cater to nitpicking demands. "Really," she said in exasperation, "it's like having the royal family come."[13] Those at the top are more than aware of their lofty status. In an interview held with the iemoto of a smaller school, the leader derided the followers of another, more popular, tradition for "doing or believing anything the iemoto tells them." He continued, "If the Urasenke iemoto says 'that crow is white' his followers will believe it, but if I say that," and he motioned toward the top-ranked teacher accompanying him in the interview, "He'd probably have me committed." But rather than laugh, the attendant simply smiled uncomfortably, caught between loyally concurring with the master's words and undermining his rank. Whether or not they agree, practitioners are often obliged to treat iemoto with exceptional respect and care—a demand garnering particular force as tea training itself invests so much in proper etiquette and interactions. Not upholding these standards would signal incompetence.

The implications of this enormous concentration of authority stand out by contrast with contemporary Sekishū practice, which lacks the iemoto organizational structure. Teachers issue their own certificates and pass on the right to their more advanced students, such that practitioners attaining a level of recognized mastery are able to branch off, instructing students in their new mode.[14] Thus, the Sekishū style of tea is marked by multiple variants of temae, rather than a strictly regulated standard—a variety considered a delightful part of gatherings that mix students of different teachers. Differences from one's own practice are pointed out as interesting innovations, rather than infractions of the rule. As a Sekishū practitioner remarked, "We don't have the KGB spying to see if you are doing things wrong. It's not like Urasenke. We're not nearly as critical." Sekishū members also comment on the almost mechanical recitation of greetings at the gatherings of other tea schools, where these nodal points of the conversation fall under the sweeping purview of temae strictures. To one Sekishū adherent, it appears as though "they don't just naturally converse. They seem to have a set phrase for everything." Indeed, such formulaic greetings would stand at odds with the role utensils play at Sekishū gatherings, where the value of the implements is not produced through symbols of an iemoto's approval. Importance is placed, rather, on the meanings attached to the objects. As a practitioner described it, "Most of the utensils are not worth a lot. If you can tell a good story, that's enough." Even at large gatherings, antiques passed down through the family or objects with an intriguing history are more commonly employed than those from a canon of utensils, and while boxes may be signed by highly respected tea connoisseurs, it is rare to leave such inscriptions on display for the guests. Without the dominating presence of a single iemoto, in the Sekishū style tea preparation procedures are less standardized and homogenized, policing is rare, and value issues from sources other than a stamp of approval from the top. But the commanding power of iemoto-based tea has even reached Sekishū practice in recent years—a marker of the twentieth-century ascent of the Sen traditions discussed in Chapter 3. Leading Sekishū teachers formed a national organization at the end of the millennium, which now issues a national newsletter, and hakogaki and kaō by Sen iemoto are appearing in increasing numbers at their gatherings. Even those outside the formal iemoto system have seen their tea practice bent by its gravitational pull.

Characteristic of the iemoto's monopolization of authority and its enactment by practitioners is the way that such performances are inflected with Japanese associations. Indeed, his command is expressed in a modality indivisible from tradition and sustained through juxtaposition with the quotidian. From the postures of fealty assumed in the iemoto's presence (otherwise now mostly witnessed only in costume dramas) to the assumption of family crests (now rare, but once commonly impressed on personal items) emblazoned on a kimono, the differentiations discussed in Chapter 1 can be seen again at work. The etiquette required to prove that practitioners are true tea adherents demands competence in a range of embodied postures and practices distinguished by their traditional hues. With them, the iemoto's investment in the national significations of the tea ceremony comes to life.

## Practitioners

But who is the body of tea adherents that activates the iemoto's authority? In 2006, tea practitioners numbered some 2.3 million people, or just under two percent of the population of Japan.[15] Women account for about ninety percent of practitioners—about one in every twenty-five in Japan participates in tea. What kind of women are they? From their distribution by age, traceable over the past twenty years, it is clear that while many learn tea in high school, probably as an extracurricular activity in a tea club, these numbers drop in college, though after graduation women are more likely to take up the practice. This does not last for long, for as marriage, job, and child-rearing duties increase for those in their thirties, the practice of tea declines.[16] But overall numbers are filled out again by women in their fifties and sixties, less burdened by the demands of infants and jobs. This generation of baby-boomers came of age during a time in Japan—uniquely in the OECD—when full-time female participation in the paid labor force dropped sharply under the Income Doubling Plan of the 1960s, producing a dramatic rise in the number of housewives who could afford training in hobbies like tea.[17]

Regionally, the practice of tea is spread evenly across the country, albeit at rates slightly below the national average in Okinawa and Kyushu in the south, and in Hokkaido and Tohoku in the north—differences that could, however, be an effect of the rural topography of these zones, as people in urban areas are somewhat more likely to take up the practice. Ishikawa and Kyoto prefectures, which historically have strong ties to the tea ceremony, possess somewhat higher concentrations of practitioners than other areas. Socially, it is clear that participation is also a function of income. The likelihood of men doing tea is the same whether they fall into lower, middle, or upper income brackets. But those at the very top, earning over $150,000 a year, are more than twice as likely to engage in the practice. For women, class differences are still more starkly drawn. Those from families with annual incomes above $100,000 per year are twice as likely to practice tea as those in middle-income brackets, and the latter in turn are more likely to be practitioners than women from families earning less than $30,000.[18]

Although still popular among the wealthy, participation in the tea ceremony has fallen in recent years. The somewhat more than 2 million practitioners of 2006 represented a drop by a fifth from the 2.8 million practitioners of 1986. A more detailed picture can be drawn from membership figures of the Omotesenke school, which has been losing an average of 2.7 percent of its membership every year since the turn of the twenty-first century, its numbers contracting steadily from 132,000 in 2002 to 114,000 in 2007.[19]

The decline in practitioners follows the passing of *hanayome shugyō*, or training in activities such as flower arrangement, koto, and Japanese dance, once thought to prepare women for marriage.[20] After reaching an apogee when the baby-boomers came of age, these pre-bridal lessons became less of an expectation for women born after 1960, when a driver's license and a college degree came to be regarded as better indices of a desirable partner. The overall decline in women's participation in the paid workforce in the immediate postwar decades produced a generation of housewives with more leisure time for hobbies.[21] In these years, the women who took up tea often did so more in response to social expectations than as a personal desire.[22] "All of my friends were learning it, so I did too," is an avowal I often heard in interviews, with even those more reluctant to learn tea acceding to parental pressure. One practitioner, born in the forties, explained she began lessons because "learning tea was a social requirement rather than an option," a description echoed in the remark of another, born in the fifties: "Tea and flower arrangement were just things you did when you reached a certain age. It was already decided." Instructors were typically found in the neighborhood, through personal networks, and lessons were attended casually. Those who enjoyed the practice carried on with it, while the less interested could use marriage as an excuse for quitting. Of these, a few return later in life, particularly if friends encourage them to join. As a retired entrepreneur said, "When I was young, I was completely against tea. I had to learn it before marriage, but protested hard. I never wanted to wear a kimono. When I

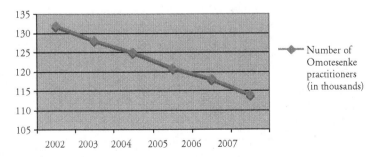

Membership in the Omotesenke Dōmonkai. Access to the data was granted to the author by Omotesenke in 2007.

got tired of working and retired, though, I decided I would take up a hobby. A friend recommended tea to me, and I thought, maybe I would try it. And now I'm really into it—and I love the kimono. I usually wear one to lessons, which makes the time feel much different."

Among later generations, familial expectations or friendship networks may still encourage tea study, but taking lessons is more often a personal choice, frequently prompted by an attraction to history or tradition, or simply the opportunity to wear a kimono. "I was interested in Japanese culture, and if it was going to be Japanese culture, then it was going to be tea," as one young women in her twenties explained. Or, in a commonly heard variant from another in her thirties, "I was interested in Japanese-y (*Nihonrashii*) things, traditional arts and the like, and so I majored in Japanese history in college. I wanted to try out the entertainment practices of the Japanese of old, and so I took up tea when I graduated." The shift in orientation from social expectation to concern with Japanese tradition could be made quite explicit. When I asked a group of students in a college tea club, two straightforwardly said they were interested in history and historical things, while one admitted she just wanted to eat the sweets that accompanied the tea—another motive commonly offered by the young. My question about whether they were learning tea with an eye toward preparation for marriage was met only with laughter.

The male practitioners I encountered presented a somewhat different picture. Many professed that familial or professional ties drew them into the practice. Their mothers might be prominent tea teachers, or they themselves—monks, art dealers, potters, shrine architects, or chefs—came from occupations related to traditional arts, though some were involved in more

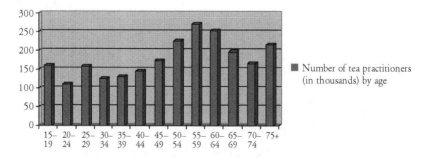

Number of tea ceremony practitioners in Japan (in thousands) by age, 2006. Data from Shakai Keizai Seisansei Honbu, *Reijaa Hakusho* (Time Use and Leisure Survey), 2006.

contemporary trades: middle managers, policemen, scientists, and the like. Those without such professional connections frequently confessed a curiosity about history or tea utensils as a motivation for taking up the practice. "I was always interested in museums," a fifty-year-old remarked, "visiting them on my way home from work. Looking at the objects I developed a pretty good eye for things, including utensils. Then someone said, 'Since you have a good feel for all this, why not do tea?'" A man in his thirties working as a real estate agent offered reasons similar to those spurring women of his age: "Japanese things are disappearing from everyday life, and Western, European things are increasingly taking over. I wanted to make kimonos, Japanese things, and the like, a part of my life. Maybe to do flower arrangement you have to have an eye for aesthetics, but I thought that with tea, all you have to do is learn the form, and so I started." Unsurprisingly, given the feminized image the practice has acquired over the course of the twentieth century, several men in interviews emphasized that the true foundation of tea lies in a noble samurai past. "Now tea is a woman's world, but it used to be men, true warriors at the center. That's been forgotten, but it's really a man's culture, and that needs to be recovered. I wanted to do that, so I took it up as a hobby," a forty-something worker related. The spiritual side entices some as well. As a man in his sixties told me, "You have to try to imagine what a Japanese business-man's life is like. You give everything to the company your whole working life and then you retire. You want to do something meaningful. I wanted to learn something that I could keep doing the rest of my time, so I chose the tea ceremony. The more you learn about it, the deeper it gets."[23]

## Lessons

While many outside and some within Japan assume that formal gatherings are the mainstay of tea practice, in fact it is lessons that occupy most of the time practitioners spend on tea. Full-dress gatherings—*chaji*—are rare, and most tea enthusiasts hold or attend these lavish events only a few times a year because of to the great cost in time, money, and effort required to stage them. In addition to a ritual preparation of thick tea and multiple rounds of thin tea, guests can expect an eleven-course kaiseki meal to be served, and the charcoal used to boil the water ceremonially arranged twice, with a break taken in the garden in between. Usually prepared for months in advance, these four-hour gatherings, as infrequent as they are, nonetheless serve as the ideal toward which practitioners strive in their lessons.

To lend a better sense of the training that is the principal experience of tea for most adherents, we may turn back to the Mushin'an complex described in Chapter 1 and examine a tea class there, focusing on the instruction. Mrs. Ebara, a widow in her seventies who began learning the practice as a teenager, has been holding classes at the complex for several years. Like most other teachers, she had taught out of her house for decades, but upon retiring to a smaller apartment, she traded her upscale tea room and garden for a much simpler and smaller washitsu, and shifted her instruction to Mushin'an. Typical of many instructors for whom tea is closer to a hobby than a full-time job, she holds a class for several hours two days a week. A few masters make a living from the practice, teaching all day and every day to maintain a student population of a hundred or more. With only ten students, Mrs. Ebara's group is on the smaller side, though not unusual. All are women, ranging in age from their early thirties to their mid-sixties; the younger ones typically are employed, while the older are mostly housewives. As is standard for lessons in traditional practices, students pay Mrs. Ebara not a fee for each class, but a set sum once a month whether or not they attend, providing her with a steady income, much of which is spent on the tea and sweets that will be consumed at lessons or on other tea accoutrements.

Once married to a successful doctor, Mrs. Ebara is well-off, and only faintly conceals her pride in a fine eye for purchasing exquisite utensils at good prices. Her teaching style is strict, much like that of the severe mother-in-law who initiated her into tea. While many tea classes serve as chances to meet and chat with friends, she discourages such socializing, seeking instead to replicate the thorough hand and unforgiving eye of the top-ranked instructors in service to the iemoto. This style is not for everyone, but many students whose teachers take a more casual approach to lessons—overlooking the small details like finger alignment that make for "sloppy" tea, or coaching students through preparation procedures rather than expecting these to be studied beforehand—long for such punctilious attention.[24]

Students begin to arrive forty-five minutes before class in order to prepare the tea space and implements for the day. Taking out utensils, sifting tea, preparing charcoal, arranging flowers, they bustle around to set up as much as possible before the teacher's arrival. As in many institutional settings in Japan, the students are positioned within junior-senior relationships, here determined by the length of time spent studying with Mrs. Ebara, and mediated to some degree by overall tea experience and age.[25] Junior students take care of the lowlier duties, such as arranging shoes or sprinkling water in the garden, while their superiors fill tea containers and arrange the delicate ash and charcoal. A hurried and anxious air often results as all of the preparations must be completed by the time the class officially begins, or Mrs. Ebara is likely to lecture the students on the central importance of timing and punctuality.[26]

The tea lesson proper commences and concludes with a formal greeting.[27] The students line up outside the guests' door to the tea room, and repeating the modest "no, please after you," they enact a etiquette of consideration while negotiating the order of entry, dependent on their time of arrival and rank on the junior–senior scale. Filing into the room, they position themselves evenly along the wall, kneeling compactly with hands folded in laps, backs absolutely straight, and a small folding fan to the side of each. Once the final student has come to a rest, Mrs. Ebara slides into the room from the host's door. Placing their folding fans in front of their knees, the students bow in unison and pronounce a formulaic request for the teacher's instruction. As they return their fans to their sides, Mrs. Ebara responds with a basic welcome, "I'm glad you could come today," and gives the day's announcements—often information concerning upcoming gatherings, student absences, and tea-related exhibitions. Many teachers take this opportunity to explain the meaning of the scroll selected for the session, providing an interpretation of the often cryptic Zen phrase that encourages a particular spiritual or seasonal awareness within the lesson. The greeting closes with another unison bow, dispersing the students who position themselves for the first tea preparation.

Such openings (and their matching closings) are common in other areas of life in Japan. Office parties and receptions, for example, typically begin and end with a greeting, compelling participants to assemble for the official start and disband in unison at the end. In most mundane cases, however, the expected behavior is not explicitly instructed—it is enough to look around and follow others—and the requirements are simple enough to remember after only one session. But in tea, these moments present more than a commonly employed ritualistic form of session initiation; they are an opportunity for students to enact and display—and have corrected—the etiquette of walking, sitting, and bowing, as well as the timing and consideration for others, that are taught in class.

The particular content of a day's lessons follows an annual cycle anchoring a curriculum of tea procedures. Not simply the decorations, but also the utensils change with seasons, and with them, the rules of their handling and the motions for preparing tea. From November through April, the colder half of the year, tea is made with a kettle set in a sunken hearth opened in the floor to the side of the host, while in the remaining warmer months a portable brazier is set on top of the tatami mats directly in front of the person whipping up the beverage. With the kettle's change in location, the position of the host and utensils shifts as well, and small adjustments in their handing—such as whether the lid of the water container is lifted with the left hand, adjusted with the right, and then set down with the left, or whether it is picked up with the right hand and then set down directly with the left—must not only be remembered, but seamlessly incorporated, so that the motions flow smoothly from the body. Many months carry thematic associations as well. In January, a time linked to the freshness and formality of the New Year—one of the central holidays in Japan—ornate utensils carrying seasonal motifs, such as pines, plums, or battledores, make appearances as students learn the procedures for preparing tea on very large and ceremonious lacquered stands. In April, the iron trivets on which the kettle rests in the sunken hearth are removed in preparation for the portable brazier of the summer months, and students prepare tea using a kettle suspended from the ceiling, teachers typically commenting that the pot's gentle swaying suggests a spring breeze.[28] In August, one of the hottest months, small portable tea sets make an appearance, and students are told these might be taken on a summer hike in the mountains. If they were to do so, they might encounter others, since their peers will be practicing the same procedure. Securing this standardization is not only the calendar, but also the official periodicals, which feature the tea-making procedures associated with the given month, and thus most teachers across the country teach the same temae at the same time.

In some cases, seasonal knowledge is explicitly taught, as when Mrs. Ebara names the flowers arranged in the alcove at each lesson, gradually imparting an understanding of what buds bloom in which months (and, concomitantly, of what months are symbolized by which flowers). Such direct instruction is most apparent when selecting "poetic names" for utensils, which the guests inquire about after the tea is prepared. While high-quality tea scoops have names inscribed on their bamboo cases, the anonymous "practice" dippers used at lessons provide an opportunity for students to choose an appellation appropriate to the occasion. The less experienced typically turn to the teacher, who suggests a few possibilities and explains the implied reference. In early autumn, Mrs. Ebara might offer "deer's call" (*shikanokoe*), and clarify that this term appears in a passage of the fourteenth-century poetry classic *Essays in Idleness.* Such prompting is not necessary for the more advanced students, who come to lessons armed with a few alternatives found in tea books or taken from their own lists of poetic phrases amassed over the years. Not one, but a selection must be on the tongue's tip, as the appropriateness of their choice for the occasion and utensils will be judged—and corrected—by the teacher.[29] When, for example, an advanced student proposed *kagura*—a Shinto dance for the gods—as the name of the tea scoop, Mrs. Ebara immediately interjected, "That's not a good selection. It's a name for August or the New Year's; it's one for festival times." The aging student explained that it was November 23, the ancient day of harvest celebration, with which she associates *kagura*. The attempt at novelty, however, was quickly suppressed: "If you are going to make that sort of strained reference, then there should be something else in the utensils that suggests it. If you pull *kagura* out of the blue, no one will get it. *Hatsuho* [referring to the first offering of rice ears at the temple] is better for fall."

These interludes take place within the lesson proper, during which each student has a turn preparing tea while the others look on as guests. Though they may be merely observing, this is hardly downtime, for with only one opportunity per session to practice the ritual, the students are expected to absorb temae by diligently watching their colleagues' attempts.[30] In this active learning, as Mrs. Ebara instructed a young new arrival to her class, "You need to learn the steps not behind, behind, behind, but in front, in front, in front. You need to see what the person [making tea] is doing and think about what comes next."[31] When the teacher corrects a posture or the host stumbles on an unusually difficult move, those observing may mime the gesture as well, patterning into their body the proper way they will be expected to demonstrate when their turn in front of the boiling kettle comes.[32] Nonetheless, observing similar—sometimes the same—temae for an hour or two can be numbing, and those whose minds or mouths wander may be sharply reminded, "You must learn with the eyes." Pauses between sessions can help to revive, allowing students to move to the back areas to arrange the utensils for the next tea preparation, and as the day wanes, talk about tea more frequently slides into casual conversation.

Like all teachers, Mrs. Ebara kneels facing the student making tea and talks her through the procedure. "Pick up the bowl. Right hand, left hand, right hand. Place it in front of your knees." These more detailed instructions for beginners are, over time, pared down to a mantra—"right, left, right"—that may echo in the student's head even when the teacher remains silent and the motions flow from the body. When words do not suffice to explain complicated or subtle maneuvers, Mrs. Ebara mimes gestures or uses her fan to illustrate. "Don't bend your wrist when you hold the water scoop," she corrects, perching her fan in her hand. "It should be like an extension of the arm. You hold it with your index finger at the side and your other fingers lined up at an angle, like this." With absolute beginners, these visual guides carry them through an almost half-hour procedure—sticking points repeated two or three times—while the teacher's gestures convey a sense of the overall flow. With several years of training, the more advanced students have less need for an escort, and their movements take on a tranquil rhythm, disturbances in which can alert the teacher to mistakes even when out of view. When sensing something amiss, Mrs. Ebara may mime the gestures to herself, observing what has become thoughtlessly embodied knowledge to aid in their verbal articulation.

The greater part of lessons is taken up with learning how to handle objects elegantly and with proper timing, while showing an attentiveness to guests—that is, the three loci of Japaneseness, discussed in Chapter 1. Mrs. Ebara, like many other instructors, selects a few details each lesson and hones these over time. At one session she may point out how the bowl should be picked up with the right hand, the thumb completely straight, resting on the lip of the bowl. In the next lesson she corrects the student again, telling her not to extend the thumb inside the bowl. Later she may advise the novice to curve her fingers toward the bottom of the bowl, and finally work with the student until her fingertips line up at an angle and her hand and arm are lightly rounded. Observing the teacher's rhythm as she mimes gestures provides an opportunity to absorb a sense of *ma*, but this may be explicitly instructed as well. When training initiates in how to pour water into the kettle, Mrs. Ebara takes the ladle in hand herself: "You need to pay attention to the sound, it can't be changing all over the place. It's an inner, spiritual thing. You scoop deeply and then pour ever more slowly, until the final drop releases." Drawing attention to the impact of actions on others cultivates consideration, and Mrs. Ebara cautions newer students not to hold tea bowls too high off the ground when examining them—not because they might drop them (less of a concern with lower-quality practice bowls), but because they might worry others that they could drop them. Interspersed between these instructions on the steps and style of tea making are explanations about tea history, utensil meanings, and other domains of what might be termed "cultural knowledge" of a distinctly Japanese variety, their associations with the nation sustained by a broader cultural matrix instantiated in books, schools, and the media, as discussed in Chapter 1.

As such, the structure and content of the classes make way for Japanese valances, yet it should be emphasized that not everything that goes on at tea lessons is about the nation. Many students attend the sessions for the chance to socialize with friends, get out of the house, or relax after work. Tea is not always whisked with the solemnity of a formal gathering, but sometimes whipped up rather carelessly as practitioners chat about recent life events or ask for advice, such conversations sometimes spilling over into a coffee or a meal after class. Novices are more often focused on trying to remember the convoluted temae than on any self-conscious vivification of tradition. Nonetheless, adherents may at times call on the Japanese inflections carried by the practice, and move such national associations from background to foreground, transforming them into an interactional resource.

The addition of a new student to a class offers an opportunity to examine how this is accomplished, for little can be taken for granted with entrants, encouraging teachers to clearly articulate what later may become common sense. A close analysis of an interaction that took place when a novice, hoping to begin lessons, came to observe Mrs. Ebara's class can provide insight into how the tea ceremony is presented as Japanese through the modalities of categorization, presented in the Introduction, that operate in nation-work.

One morning when the students were bustling about to prepare the next temae, the front door opened with a *garagaragara* clatter, and Mrs. Ebara, wrapped in her customary kimono, hurried to greet the expected visitor in the entrance area. She guided a Japanese woman in her thirties, hair neatly pulled back and fitting with the conservative brown tweed suit and skirt she had chosen for the day, to the small waiting room, where they knelt on the tatami mat floor, facing each other at a slight angle.[33] After a short greeting, Mrs. Ebara explained her goals and expectations to the new student:

> Is this the first time you've come to a lesson? If so, you need to know what to wear and what to prepare. Please take a look around you. See here? After taking off your socks, you need to change them before stepping on the tatami. When you walk on top of the tatami, you should always have new socks. Even me. I drive here, so I don't get them dirty, but I wear tabi covers.[34] When Westerners come, they feel strange walking around without their shoes. But I want to teach the spirit and rules of Japan. That's why you need to wear white socks.

In conveying the basic etiquette of entering the lesson space, Mrs. Ebara defines such behavior as also Japanese—the national inflections invoked through a distinction drawn across a we–they boundary between Westerners, who putatively feel uncomfortable walking around in socks, and Japanese, who by implication do not. With the instructions ultimately preparing the student for proper participation in lessons, her explanation encourages the cultivation of Japanese behavioral orientations expected of students. Mrs. Ebara proceeded:

> If you think tea is eating sweets, drinking tea, washing up, and just having a good time, that's not what goes on in these lessons. There are places out in the city with those sorts of lessons. But here the architecture is truly Japanese. It's really expensive—such a luxurious, beautiful place. *Everything* is authentic. Just look closely at any part of it. [She refers to the prints on the sliding doors.] Each one of those is made by hand. There is that much skill. [She references the paper on the sliding windows.] Each seam is in a different place. You see how they line up perfectly? Artisans of that level of skill built this tea room. If you aren't extremely careful, something bad might happen. If you go to a tea room out in the city, and something happens, you just say "Oh, sorry." But here, everything, all the paper, must then be changed. This is a place of that sort of standing. That's why study here is authentic.

As she continued her introduction to the class, Mrs. Ebara employed a second modality—specification—to identify what is authentically Japanese through a comparison with what is out "in the city." This set-phrase, commonly used in tea circles, contrasts the mass of middle-class housewives who teach the tea ceremony as a hobby in their homes with a small number of highly ranked teachers and wealthy practitioners possessing tea rooms and antique utensils worth hundreds of thousands of dollars. As such, it marks a class or status divide rather than an urban–rural one.[35] Mrs. Ebara stresses the difference by emphasizing the great expense and sophistication of the tea room, pointing to the fine craft skills and attention to detail that make it "real Japanese architecture." Employing a nonnational category—class—to specify the content of the national category, she intimates in the same breath that such costly objects need to be treated with care. She continued:

> The other day there was a TV program on [a kabuki actor] performing in Paris that showed the strictness of his training, his preparations from the first day to the time he left, and how he carried things out. Then he had to perform formal greetings, sitting properly. That sort of thing, much more

than in tea, is cultivating Japanese tradition. I think it is incredible that they [kabuki actors] make it a part of themselves. So the Japanese tea ceremony, if you practice it properly from the start, is not that difficult.

Again Mrs. Ebara's explanation encourages the cultivation of a particularly Japanese mode of behavior, but now established in a third way: differentiation within a national category. She avows the Japaneseness of tea training by contrasting it with the asserted far *greater* Japaneseness of kabuki instruction. The variation includes a moral component as well. Lauding kabuki actors for such strict training, she suggests they are not only more Japanese, they are also better. In such subtle ways, even the brief introduction of a prospective student to tea practice can invoke and encourage a distinctively Japanese understanding of the practice and of the sensibilities cultivated at lessons.

## Demonstrations

Lessons, though, are not the only locus of nation-work. Tea demonstrations offer adherents valued outreach opportunities where they apply their knowledge of chanoyu. At these spectacles, initiates typically elucidate the practice to an audience of novices, who witness a formal tea preparation and taste a bowl of whipped matcha tea. Such explanations can shade into injunctions for cultivation when the tea ceremony is staged as an archetypal expression of Japanese culture for which the audience, as Japanese, is also responsible. Demonstrations for children offer particularly rich opportunities for observing how the practice can be used to cultivate participants for this purpose.

At a tea gathering in 2007, the members of a baton club at an elementary school in Tokyo were assembled at a tea room by their coach, Mrs. Maegawa, who had been holding such occasions since 2004. The principal and two teachers from the school joined the demonstration and sat as the main guests, followed by a neat line of eleven girls, ranging in age from seven to twelve, each done up smartly in dresses or skirts. Before the event began, I asked Mrs. Maegawa why she had decided to host these gatherings, and she replied:

> I want them to learn things they will use later. It's almost New Year's now, and so soon they will visit shrines. Here they can learn how to wash their hands properly beforehand—they wouldn't know how to do it otherwise.[36] They can learn "Japanese traditional manners" [said in English]. You know, these days bullying is becoming such a big problem. People don't really think about others any longer, and so I want to teach the children that.

If we have that as a foundation, then bullying will end. Do you know *Edo shigusa*?[37] People in the Edo period carried umbrellas, and when they passed each other in the street, they shifted them so others could pass smoothly. It was a basic, unwritten rule—everyone's shared understanding. But now most people don't know those sorts of things, which is why I want to teach them to the children. And then when they become mothers, they will teach their own children, who will pass it on as well.

Mrs. Maegawa's reasoning presents tea as a means to cultivate proper comportment and interpersonal understanding, both here logged as a part of the traditional manners in need of revival and transmission—duties presented as distinctively feminine.[38] She calls forth national valences both directly—these reinforced by a switch to English that embeds a distinction between self and other into the expressive form itself—and indirectly, by reference to "people," an indexical expression implicitly identified with the nation in this context.[39]

Extending these justifications further, a handout distributed to the girls a few days before the demonstration described the tea performance as "offering something that will be useful not only when you go to other tea ceremonies, but also when you invite important guests over to your house"—domestic skills recalling the use of tea in the etiquette training of "good wives and wise mothers" a century before. Dwelling on the details of the extensive behind-the-scenes preparations of a formal tea ceremony, the handout enjoined the girls not to wear difficult-to-remove shoes as part of the "important thoughtfulness of guests," thereby encouraging consideration for others. The pamphlet concluded by presenting the injunctions as part of the traditions and customs of Japan, which the girls, as good nationals and good mothers, are to transmit to future generations: "I would be very happy if you all think about the importance of Japan's wonderful traditions and customs through this tea ceremony and use it as a beginning for passing these on."

During the demonstration, Mrs. Maegawa and her husband explained the symbolic significances of the utensils used and how to drink the tea, while the girls sat quietly for the most part, with only a few, unused to kneeling for long periods, occasionally fidgeting. Later, one of the teachers praised the physical discipline required for such stoic fortitude. "There are so few chances for kids to practice self-restraint and patience these days. Everything is so easy for them. But it's good to practice putting up with things sometimes." Even after the tea preparation concluded, the cultivation of proper comportment continued as one girl asked Mrs. Maegawa about the correct way to open sliding doors, and three others eagerly practiced how to bow, emulating the model of grace on display during the demonstration.

The event ended with the children taken to enjoy some drinks and snacks in an adjacent room, where, as is common at such parties in Japan, the principal of the school offered a few closing words:

> When I was a child I really liked Japanese things, and so I joined the tea ceremony club in high school where I learned just how deep Japanese culture is. It was 1964 when I first began learning tea—the year of the Tokyo Olympics. I went to a high school near here, and at the school's Culture Festival we put on a tea performance outside, under a broad umbrella, with everyone in kimonos. And now, when you think about what you will become [when you grow up], I hope that you will learn more about your own country. Our school is 135 years old, and when it was founded there was tea. Hideyoshi did tea as well—during his time there was tea. It has been around for ages, this part of ancient Japanese culture. In just one bowl of tea, you can think about a lot of things.

Claiming chanoyu as a thread connecting members of the school and the foundational figures of the past, the principal reinforced a historical understanding of Japanese identity, continuous through time, in which tea plays a crucial role. He not only directly marked the national associations, but also evoked them through distinctions with external others, these elicited by the Tokyo Olympics—the first major international splash-out following World War II—and by the other countries implied in the reference to "your own." The definitions here are minimal, and the specific qualities of Japaneseness are hardly elaborated, but even such epigrammatic expressions perpetuate a tight coupling of the practice and the essence of the nation.

Mrs. Maegawa then wrapped up the occasion, touched to the point of tears:

> Your teachers have a very important message for each one of you, and I hope you pay attention to what they say. And, when you become adults, I hope you pass that on as well. [She starts to cry.] When you become mothers, please become wonderful mothers and create a bright world for us. I'm sorry, my tears are just an expression of my feeling of gratitude.

Afterward Mrs. Maegawa explained that she had been overcome with emotion when she saw that a girl who frequently acted up was sitting properly and listening to her teachers for the first time—the embodiment of a successful lesson in how to become a good Japanese had moved her greatly. Yet, as an exercise in cultivating the children, the demonstration was designed to mold the girls as not just Japanese, but a specific type of Japanese. In a contemporary reworking of the "good wives and wise mothers" creed, they were to both improve household management and become future disseminators of Japanese culture to their own children. Though national specificity was, on occasion, located through the external contrasts of distinction, the overarching purpose of the day invoked a differentiation between the "good Japanese" the girls could become and those who did not—or not yet—possess the requisite national characteristics.

A pair of demonstrations at a Tokyo junior high school the same year offers a somewhat contrasting agenda. As a part of the Ministry of Education's Ibashozukuri Program,[40] four female volunteers, headed by the 60-year-old Mrs. Suzuki, presented a two-hour demonstration of the tea ceremony to a class of eighth graders. The students' homeroom teachers had decided to split the pupils into gender-segregated groups, as one explained, to prevent the boys from dominating matters and to give the girls a greater chance to participate. Thus a demonstration was held for forty-six boys the first week, and another for forty girls the following. With the school's own washitsu too small to hold the groups, the volunteers erected a tea space in

Junior high school students watch volunteers from their community perform a tea ceremony demonstration

front of a science classroom by spreading plastic judo tatami mats and hanging a scroll from a movie screen. After the students piled into the room, the first hour of the presentation consisted of watching a five-minute video by the Urasenke iemoto, followed by a live demonstration of making tea and the opportunity for everyone to sample the beverage.

A homeroom teacher launched the event with a brief introduction, which for the boys was terse: "Today, we welcome guest teachers and will get to know the tea ceremony, the spirit of Japaneseness." The girls, in contrast, were presented with far greater goals. "You know the term 'Japanese woman' (*Nihon no josei*), and your teacher mentioned that you will be learning about proper manners today, as well as Japanese culture. We have just a short time for Japanese culture and its long history, but I would like you to get a taste of it." Going beyond the simple connection between the tea ceremony and a generic Japanese spirit offered to the boys, the presentation for the girls portrayed tea as an element of a specifically Japanese femininity and proper manners, as well as the long history of Japanese culture. Though perhaps not foremost in the teacher's mind, these introductions laid the groundwork for a difference that would later emerge in what the students were expected to experience through the demonstration—spiritual elements of Japanese culture and proper feminine manners.

Next, the pupils watched a video in which the former Urasenke iemoto told them:

> Tea is a composite cultural experience of Japan. I would like you all to understand that first and foremost. We live in a time of international exchange, of internationalization. Yet in this era, the Japanese—the people of Japan—don't know a thing about traditional culture. I think that's quite embarrassing. Yet now foreigners are studying about it very hard. Bearing that in mind, you should know that, although it's just a bowl of tea, with that bowl you can get in touch with Japaneseness. The spirit of thinking about others is deeply aroused. It's about thinking of others. When you make tea, you come to see that. I hope you learn that.

Invoking both a distinction from national others to bring home the importance of knowing things Japanese, and a differentiation from "embarrassing" Japanese who fail to live up to this expectation, the video primed two topics: tea imparts knowledge of Japanese culture, and tea is thinking about others. The latter, defined as a Japanese spiritual orientation, is presented as critical for Japan's position in an internationalizing world. These themes, however, were not immediately integrated into the performance that followed, which focused largely on the mechanics of tea making. After the video, an assistant prepared tea while Mrs. Suzuki explained the practice, covering topics such as thin tea and thick tea, and the meaning of the words on the scroll, with no difference in the presentation to the boys and girls until the time to drink the tea approached. At that point, Mrs. Suzuki told the girls of a friend who had taken up tea after a trip to Canada.

> She was asked by a lot of people about various Japanese things, and when she started to answer, she found she couldn't. Someone said to her, "What? Why doesn't a Japanese know about the tea ceremony?" And after that she took up study. So, in the future, you'll probably have the chance to go abroad. When you do, people will think that every Japanese knows about their own culture, about Japanese things. Therefore, if you can say, "Ah, I've done tea before," I think it would be wonderful.

Framing the girls as future emissaries of Japanese culture, Mrs. Suzuki proffered their experience of the tea ceremony as a means to cultivate the abilities to fulfill this role. As in the grand master's speech, the move was dual, with distinction and differentiation in play. Accountability for Japanese things to national others grounded the necessity for self-improvement, difference encouraging cultivation that would differentiate them from less worthy members. When talking to the boys, however, she simply mentioned that more foreigners are interested in Japanese culture than the Japanese themselves, without projecting upon them the duties of cultural ambassadorship.

But they too would become the target of cultivation efforts. When bowls of tea were brought out for the boys to taste, they became rowdy. Against the jostling and teasing, Mrs. Suzuki raised her voice and began to scold them:

> Why are manners important? Is all of your talking a part of manners? [The boys begin to quiet down.] Good manners mean putting yourself in the position of others. If you can't do that, then you don't have any manners. Understand? I want you all to learn that tea contains that sort of spirit. In the previous video the iemoto said so, didn't he? You are going against the Japanese spirit. You are going against manners. Do you understand?

Claiming thoughtful consideration of others as a hallmark of both the spirit of tea and the spirit of Japan, Mrs. Suzuki railed at the boys for their deficient conduct, differentiating them from those true to the "Japanese spirit." They were not merely bad members of the school, but bad members of the nation.

For the girls, the problem addressed was not classroom but bodily discipline. Though no boy was shown how to bow correctly, the girls were not only guided step-by-step in how to bow with formality and grace, but also instructed in how to move when in a kimono. Mrs. Suzuki asked for a volunteer from the class to come up to the front of the room, and a girl in a sweatshirt emulated her movements while she pointed out to the others what to look for to distinguish a good bow from a bad one. Afterward, she showed them how to walk in a kimono, with their toes straight or pointed slightly inward. Taking a few steps forward, her body swaying side to side and her feet splayed outwards at a ninety-degree angle, Mrs. Suzuki demonstrated what not to do to the girl's giggles. "It doesn't look good at all. In a kimono, your feet should be straight or if anything pointed a bit inward." Walking with smaller, more controlled leg movements, her upper torso hardly moving, she demonstrated again. "So now, if you keep that in mind, when you wear a cotton kimono this summer, the boys will think you're really cute." As in the boys' session, she employed the tea ceremony and its elements to normalize behavior or correct failings, but with the girls, specification (a feminine Japanese way of walking) and differentiation (contrast with ungainly women) were both at play in the attempt to cultivate a particularly Japanese ideal of feminine movement and manners. In this and other demonstrations, the tea ceremony rarely appears without the Japanese trappings, vibrant or faded, acquired over the preceding century. Yet at stake on such occasions may be not only the national symbol, enlivened for the audience, but the national members responsible for it as well, with tea used to craft them into better incumbents of this role.

## Essays

While moments of instruction and infraction can encourage explicit evocations of national significances that may otherwise blend in with the furniture of the practice, texts are another venue that favor articulation of what may be implicit, but not necessarily involved in the immediate task at hand, when making tea. Since 1978 the Urasenke tea ceremony association, Tankōkai, has held an essay competition for the members of tea ceremony clubs at secondary schools and colleges, in which students describe why they began lessons and what they have learned from them. While there is no reason to doubt the sincerity of the submissions, they are inevitably guided by an understanding of Tankōkai's educational programs, which concentrate on the promotion of Japanese culture through the tea ceremony, as discussed in Chapter 3. Thus caution should be applied in reading these as a testament of the continuous tangible experience of Japaneseness for tea ceremony participants. Yet because the essay contest favors such national expressions, the texts supply copious material for examining the mechanics of how Japaneseness is presented, experienced, and naturalized through the tea ceremony. Out of over six hundred submissions in 2002, ten grand prize and twenty first-place winners were published in that year's *Collected Essays of School Tea Ceremony Club Experiences* (*Gakkō Chadō Takien Ronbunshū*), discussed here.

Most of the essays report what the pupils had gained through the practice of tea, with personal transformations the predominant leitmotif. In these descriptions of how a better self is cultivated, Japaneseness is consistently established through differentiation. Yamane Mayuko, a student at Kyoto Women's College, explained that before studying tea, she was only dimly aware of seasons, registering little more than whether it was hot or cold or if the flowers were blooming. But by attending tea lessons, she began to shift from an unrefined, geographically unspecific seasonal awareness to a sensitivity grounded in a distinctively Japanese climate. In the tea room, she started "to appreciate, feel—and want to feel more—Japan's beautiful seasons" through the "cherry blossoms in spring, the scent of new green leaves, the light in summer, the autumn trees preparing for winter, the snow dancing on the ground with suspense."[41] She describes how this appreciation for nature has followed her out of the tea room and into everyday life—an experience shared by Wada Sakiko, a senior in high school. Wada recounted how she first noticed the artificial flowers on permanent display at the entrance to her home only after joining the tea club. "Seasonless artificial flowers ignore Japanese seasons, and I realized that to have them in a Japanese-style hall was out of place." Training in tea alerted her to jarring disruptions in what should have been a harmonious coordination of Japanese elements. Taking the flowers used in the tea class home afterward, she began arranging them in the entrance at home to create an atmosphere in which "the spirit could be soothed."[42] Orthography underscores the Japanese inflections of her awakening, as she elected to write "soothe" (*nagomu*, なごむ, 和む) not with the phonetic hiragana script commonly used to transcribe the word, but with the character *wa* (和), which conveys a sense of both "harmony" and "Japaneseness." In cultivating a heightened "Japanese" awareness of seasonality, differentiation appears through a refinement that separates the author not from others who are less Japanese, but from her pre-tea, implicitly less Japanese self as well.

Fundamentally, Japanese membership across all of these cases is never thrown into doubt—national identity is treated as an internal essence, even if one that needs to be recovered. As Ogawa Maiko described it, the tea ceremony "provides a place where a Japanese identity can be confirmed." In everyday life, she explained, "people are anonymous and unconcerned. They generally feel anxious about people they don't know. But the tea ceremony relaxes these anxieties. When I enter the tea room, I think, 'Of course I am Japanese.' Through the tea preparation and the accompanying manners, the tea ceremony enables the Japanese heart to be seen." She stresses that "the tea ceremony has been one path through which I have been able to become aware that I am Japanese"—a latent identity ("of course" she was Japanese) coaxed out by the practice.[43] Suzuki Mami described a similar realization. After encountering the tea ceremony, she "became aware of the importance of learning about the culture of [her] country, which has been passed down over time," encouraging her to take on the civilizing mission to spread this knowledge among her peers. "Because I was born Japanese, I want to maintain the importance of the culture that has been transmitted from the past. To do that, it is necessary to feel closer to the tea ceremony and know the spirit of Japaneseness. If other students can try tea, they can also get to know the spirit of Japaneseness."[44]

Some cases, however, require a concerted rehabilitation. Lamenting the decline of a Japanese sense of self, a high school senior in Gifu declared, "Many people are now very disorderly, and an increasing number don't respect others," but "the thing that the Japanese are supposed to hold as important—a concern for others—can be revived through tea."[45] Ueda Riko also confessed that "an open spirit has been lost in contemporary Japanese society, and I, unfortunately, had lost it too." But seeing the flowers in the tea room, reading the powerful message of the scroll, and hearing the sound of the tea being whisked, she felt the depth of the tea ceremony and a purification of her spirit. Though, she admits, "I had forgotten the obvious fact that I am Japanese," through contact with "Japanese ancient culture" she could reclaim "the free spirit that contemporary Japanese are lacking" and discover "the joyful pride of being Japanese."[46]

If cultivating Japaneseness relies on making a differentiation between better or worse members (or selves), the explanations of it in the texts hinge more frequently on distinctions drawn across national boundaries. Indeed, such borders can supply a spur to action: pupils commonly state that they took up tea in anticipation of moments of being held accountable for explaining Japanese culture in their encounters with foreigners. Yanagita Eriko joined a tea club because "the world has become international, and exchange with foreign countries has increased, so when I tell foreigners about Japan, I want to know about at least one item of Japanese traditional culture."[47] Ogawa Maiko encountered such a situation herself. Only after having spent several years abroad did she become interested in "Japanese culture" because when asked about her home country, she often did not know how to respond. Wanting to learn about something "unique to Japan," she took up the tea ceremony "to be able to explain Japanese culture with confidence."[48]

Even if aimed at domestic readers, explanations still frequently invoke foreign contrasts. Noguchi Aya, for example, reported a debate at her school on the differences between Japanese and Western cultures. One of the participants audaciously claimed that "Japanese culture, after all, is only form. Inside the tea ceremony there is nothing at the core." Noguchi could not agree, but was unable to rebut the charge at the time. Only later did clarification come, through distinction. On a trip to Canada, she introduced the tea ceremony to her host-mother, who began making matcha tea every day by just mixing it in her mug without further ado. Noguchi noted that she wasn't doing "the tea ceremony I had shown her, but simply an odd form of drinking 'green tea.'" The experience enabled her to distill what was essential to the spirit of tea: that everything has rules, and if people can embody those rules, they enter the spiritual path.[49] For her, the contrast with foreign crudity clarified the meaning of the Japanese sense of exquisite form.

Students also portrayed the tea ceremony as a concentrate of universal values capable of overcoming national boundaries, but claims of this kind were typically couched in a distinctively Japanese style. One pupil, who had provided a tea demonstration to a foreigner interested in Japanese history, felt responsible for representing Japan through her performance. Happily, the foreigner had told her that "while the tea is bitter, it communicates the beautiful Japanese heart," and that samurai and monks in the past had probably shared the same feeling. Although conversation between the two was in a halting combination of pidgin Japanese and pidgin English, the author proclaims that through tea they were able to communicate heart-to-heart.[50] Yet if the tea ceremony is held up as a means of lowering national boundaries and recognizing a common humanity, the terms of the encounter remain Japanese. The stock phrase in tea circles, that "tea is heart-to-heart communication," promotes the practice as a means for understanding others without words—a highly valued skill in Japanese society, but one that reduces communication to only a minimal emotional expression. Such empathy does not lend itself to detail or clarification, let alone disagreement, yielding little more than pleasantries. Indeed, the practice may be so charged with national valences in such situations that any attempt to overcome them may fall flat.

## Conclusion

The Japaneseness of tea practice comes to life through the actions and interactions of its carriers. Even if not motivated to take up the hobby out of an interest in Japanese culture—though this is an increasingly powerful spur—practitioners animate national associations as they do tea, from the seasonal structuring of tea classes to the required etiquette channeling interactions. With time spent at lessons and demonstrations far outweighing that at formal tea gatherings, the dominance of pedagogy over practice brings to the fore explanation and cultivation. In the everyday activities of the hobby—sometimes so banal they go largely unnoticed, as in Mrs. Ebara's injunctions to an initiate—practitioners invoke Japaneseness both to elucidate the broader cultural significance of what they are doing and to inculcate in others, as they themselves have come to embody, the higher justifications that enabled tea to weather the difficult transition from the premodern to the modern era.

These national associations that vaulted the tea ceremony to the apex of Japanese traditional culture, as the synthesis of everything at its base, have not lost their resonance as the glare of originating nationalism's fireworks faded. With a vested interest in their perpetuation, the contemporary iemoto system encourages the practitioners who sustain both the business and the tradition to continue not only to invoke national grounds expressly for explaining what they do, but to more quietly enact national associations when practicing tea. Even outside direct interaction with the iemoto, these continue to pulse through the actions of their adherents, whether they are bowing in the formal greeting that opens a lesson, or encouraging an audience of children to become better national members through tea practice. Within the tea world, the iemoto system thus provides a powerful link between the nationalist charge of the tea ceremony and the everyday invocations of nationness evoked in tea practice. These, however, would hardly reverberate far if the Japaneseness of the practice were not sustained by powerful wider circuits in society, to which we now turn.

## CHAPTER 5

# Beyond the Tea Room

*Toward a Praxeology of Cultural Nationalism*

Although the overall number of practitioners has fallen since the eighties, this has not yet resulted in a diminution of the salience of the tea ceremony in Japan. Almost all in the country recognize chanoyu as a constitutive element of traditional Japanese culture, possess some sense of what it involves, and can name Rikyū as its founder. The practice is even identified by a gesture, intelligible across the country, of waving the right hand over a cupped left in a motion resembling beating eggs. Though most Japanese have never participated in a four-hour formal gathering, they have at least some notion of what the tea ceremony is about—a commonsensical, thin knowledge that is diffused and reproduced through educational and informational institutions, including schools, museums, and the media.[1]

## Diffusion

Foremost among these are the secondary schools, where all Japanese learn about the development of the tea ceremony during the Momoyama period and its role in elite culture. Even if he or she has never tasted matcha, anyone who has passed through the ranks of the school system thinks of Rikyū as the father of the tea ceremony. Since the turn of the twentieth century, history textbooks have, as a matter of course, discussed the development of chanoyu and the wabi aesthetic under headings such as "Arts Development in the Momoyama Period," and have emphasized Nobunaga's and Hideyoshi's connection to the practice, including the Grand Kitano Gathering, along with the accomplishments of Rikyū—a name set off in bold in more recent editions.[2] The rote memorization of entire textbook passages encouraged by the college entrance exam system is a powerful means for inscribing the practice into the national memory. But more than a basic historical awareness of the tea ceremony is gained in secondary schools, for its standard inclusion as an after-school club activity provides opportunities for direct experience of it as well. Over six thousand schools today—many boasting their own tea rooms and small collection of utensils—host clubs in which local tea teachers instruct teenagers in the basics of tea preparation and etiquette. Even nonmembers are exposed to the practice when the club is mustered for performances at annual Culture Day celebrations, a festival at which initiates, usually donning a cotton summer kimono, serve tea to their peers and parents as they wander from exhibit to exhibit.

What is learned or experienced at schools is reinforced by trips to museums—instruments par excellence for consecrating national culture. When the Tokyo National Museum's collection was reorganized in 2001, curators created thematic rooms anchoring the main building's four corners—tributes to national treasures, painted screens, Noh and kabuki theater, and the tea ceremony. Here a plaque invites visitors to learn about chanoyu, "part of the traditional culture of which Japan is proud,"[3] as they wander past glass-enclosed tea scoops carved by Rikyū, famous tea bowls—some designated national treasures—and other tea utensils. Gazing out to the garden behind the museum, visitors are greeted by five tea rooms donated by prominent figures such as Hara Tomitaro, which can be toured or even rented by practitioners for tea gatherings. Kyoto offers a choice of several such sanctifying institutions dedicated to teaware that elevate and legitimate the historical value of their collections. Not only do the Urasenke and Omotesenke headquarters house galleries exhibiting their contents as treasures for the populace, but so do the Nomura and Raku Museums.[4] Even establishments that do not specialize in chanoyu, such as the Nezu, Gotoh, and Mitsui Museums in Tokyo and the Itsuo in Osaka, not only house tea rooms but hold special exhibitions around tea objects. Department stores too—long a home to small art galleries—occasionally organize

Shoppers attend a tea ceremony demonstration at a Tokyo department store

displays around past masters, such as Rikyū or Enshū, affording shoppers an edifying tea break. As one might expect, the museums and galleries present their trophies lined up in glass cases, with plaques proclaiming their cultural worth. But these are also typically accompanied by in situ arrays of utensils in scaled-down versions of tea rooms, missing a wall, that invite viewers to pause and consider not just the object, but the ritual that gives it meaning.

Such physical emplacement is extended by municipalities, which build basic tea rooms, rented by teachers, in their community centers. Weaving the tea ceremony into the local fabric, towns typically call on practitioners in the area to set up tea demonstrations for national Culture Day celebrations and other public events—sometimes with tea as their raison d'être. At the Youth Tea Experience, a five-day affair held in front of the Shibuya train station in Tokyo, local practitioners serve over a thousand bowls of tea to children and parents stopping by their tent. Begun originally, in the words of a public official, "to keep kids from loitering and getting into trouble, and to teach them about their Japanese spirit," a handout informs visitors of this goal above the hubbub of traffic at the world's busiest pedestrian crossing. "The tea ceremony is a cultural treasure to be proud of to the world. We would like to pass on to future generations the spirit of the Japanese that is firmly grounded in the tea ceremony. . . . So please, while drinking this tea, feel within your own heart the spirit of the Japanese that has been passed down through the ages." Yet larger is Niigata's annual Citizen Tea Gathering, which since 1951 has transformed great swathes of both public and commercial space into a fête of the practice. Though the number of sites was greater in the past, tea performances are still held today at over fifty locations, including temples, schools, department stores, and pedestrian zones. For about five dollars per service, locals and visitors guided by a map can stop by each spot, watch tea being prepared, and enjoy a bowl of the drink and a sweet.

The practice's exotic aura has also been exploited to lure tourists—both Japanese and foreign—to destinations invested in its historical image.[5] Kyoto, of course, is the central magnet. While the city's tourist board no longer organizes the tea-based package tours once popular among older practitioners that attracted at their peak ten thousand participants annually during a two-month run, it has, in recent years, expanded efforts to draw visitors through *taiken tsuurizumu* (experience tourism), in which they can try their hand at things they would never do at home. Along with Zen meditation, paper making, pottery throwing, and dressing in a kimono, the tea ceremony is a popular choice, and tourist offices provide a list in Japanese and English of over thirty places, temples and restaurants prominent among them, where matcha tea can be had or a ceremonial preparation experienced. Typical of these is the café Kanō Shōjuan, located in a grove of trees along the popular "Philosopher's Walk," where visitors paying about ten dollars are guided to a room, enclosed by papered windows and anchored by an alcove, to be served a sweet and a bowl of tea prepared by a kimono-clad woman. An assistant stands at her side to explain the procedure and symbolic significances of the fine utensils, donated by Urasenke. Those looking for further experiences can purchase the tea ceremony edition of the Rakutabi Bunkō series of booklets, which provides those wanting to "savor matcha and Japanese culture" with a list of places where they can enjoy modern delicacies prepared with powdered tea as an ingredient, along with the addresses of utensil stores and locations where they can be served a bowl of tea itself.

Tea demonstrations are not to be missed at several of the cultural capital's annual events. Every autumn the enormous Grand Citizens' Tea Gathering

A Kyoto café advertises a matcha tea tasting experience with a utensil display in a glass case

occupies Tokugawa Ieyasu's imposing Nijo Castle, while the plum blossom festival held every February at the Kitano Shrine greets its visitors with a series of tea demonstrations—the most popular staffed by young local geishas-in-training. Tourists unable to get a ticket for this event may view geishas performing tea as an accompaniment to spring or autumn dance festivals. And, if all else fails, the popular Gion Corner, which attracts about fifty thousand visitors annually, half of whom are Japanese, offers a tea demonstration along with performances of Japanese dance, flower arrangement, court music, and traditional puppetry—advertised in English as a chance to "experience traditional Kyoto," and in Japanese as a "collection of Japanese traditional arts." Those who want to try whisking up a bowl themselves can pay a supplement for a hands-on demonstration. Since the turn of the millennium, in more formal—if "relaxed"—occasions, Kōdaiji Temple has been aggressively marketing "special tea gatherings." For about sixty dollars per person, dozens of visitors are paraded through a 2.5-hour tea experience at this temple complex constructed by Hideyoshi's widow. With the chance to view outstanding utensils—some made by Living National Treasures—at one of Kyoto's main tourist draws, participants are herded through rooms that are usually off-limits before reaching the tea preparation. A light meal in an accompanying building follows, completing the "formal tea gathering" experience.⁶ The distinctively traditional associations of the practice are even used in marketing Kyoto as a city, with pictures of an austere tea setting on tourism posters touting the locale as the "home of the hearts of the Japanese" in large script, accompanied by smaller English, Korean, and Chinese translations. But even if just stopping over in Tokyo, tourists picking up a leaflet at the airport might be led to the Kyotokan, located conveniently across the street from Tokyo Station, where employees regularly provide brief temae demonstrations with the kettle and utensils kept on permanent display. Those staying a bit longer might attend one of the grander monthly performances narrated in English.⁷

The less mobile are no less exposed, for the tea ceremony also features prominently in television, movies, and manga. Incorporating chanoyu in its pedagogical programs, the national TV channel, NHK, works in conjunction with the main tea schools to produce an annual ten-week series on the ceremony in which viewers are led though the procedures for various types of tea preparation. Eager learners can even purchase a set of accompanying books to follow along with the series. But the presence of tea is perhaps even more pervasive as a prop in regular television programs. While

Tourists in Kyoto try their hand at whisking tea

chanoyu—and even Rikyū himself—make occasional appearances in long-running costume dramas, such as *Taiga Dorama* and *Ōoku*, the practice also is featured in contemporary programs, often when a sense of tradition or elite refinement is called for. *Tatta Hitotsu no Koi*, a romance between a working-class boy and the daughter of the wealthy owner of a chain of jewelry stores, gripped an audience of some ten percent of all television viewers in 2006. The opening episode contrasted the social origins of the two prospective lovers by introducing the boy fishing illegally off a pier by a power plant with some friends and the girl kneeling at a tea lesson. Wearing an impeccable kimono in the stilted atmosphere of the tea room, in which only the teacher's voice instructing the students in the philosophy of the practice could be heard, the girl displayed not only her good upbringing, but also her free spirit—giggling when one of the students yawned, and then gesticulating wildly when tormented by an errant bee. The immensely popular NHK morning drama *Don-Don Hare*, which ran in 2007 before upward of twenty percent of television viewers, featured a picaresque heroine who left the big city for the rigorous routine of a traditional inn in the countryside, where as a matter of course she was subjected to tea training. The much-awaited announcement of who would take over the inn on the retirement of the punctilious woman running the business was made at a solemn tea gathering attended by family members and employees. Continuing the association of tea practice with upper-class refinement, the manga series *Hana yori Dango*, which ran from 1992 to 2004 and was subsequently remade for television and the silver screen, followed the lives of four boys born into powerful families, one of whom was heir to a tea school.

The image of the tea ceremony as a maze of strict, impossible-to-master rules is also employed to garner laughs. In an episode of the 2005 drama *Taigā to Doragon*, about the lives of traditional rakugo comedians, two characters related a pair of farcical stories, standard in their repertoire, about a tea novice nervous about attending a tea gathering. In the first, the neophyte is so anxious that he imitates every gesture—even the most superfluous scratchings—of the tea master. In the second, he receives instruction from an elderly teacher who has forgotten the proper procedures and resorts to ludicrous substitutes for them, like soap to produce the froth on the beverage, and turning not just the bowl but himself three times around in a circle. Even an episode in the classic cartoon *Sazaesan* included the tea ceremony, the characters making predictable gaffes as they tried to consume the beverage correctly.

The role of tea in Japanese history and the political intrigues surrounding the practice have also provided much material for other areas of the entertainment industry. The immensely popular *Hyogei Mono* manga, now an anime series, narrates the adventures of Hideyoshi and Nobunaga, with Rikyū, Oribe, and other tea masters at their side. Several of the installments are based on staples in tea legend, such as the initial design of Raku tea bowls, or Hideyoshi's stupefaction when Rikyū cut all of the morning glories in his garden save one, displayed in the tea room.[8] Rikyū has also been the subject of several historical dramas crafted for the silver screen, including Kumai Kei's 1989 *Sen no Rikyū*, with acting great Mifune Toshirō as the title character; Tanaka Kinuyo's 1978 *Oginsama*; and Teshigahara Hiroshi's 1989 *Rikyū* and 1992 sequel *Go-hime*, which places Rikyū's protégé Oribe in the limelight. Even if not a narrative focal point, tea can appear as a natural accoutrement of Momoyama period power politics, as in the opening scene of the 2006 film *Ō'oku*, in which Hideyoshi's courtesans entertain themselves by preparing tea.

These historical associations are typically juxtaposed with the modern when the tea ceremony appears in advertisements. A 2008 commercial for flat-screen televisions contrasted a depiction of Katori Shingo, a popular musician and television personality, preparing a bowl of matcha tea in a kimono with an image of him drinking espresso in a more relaxed fashion—apparently to point out the flexibility of the entertainment to be enjoyed with the new device. An advertisement for a popular donut chain in the same year featured the actor Tamaki Hiroshi wearing a kimono in a portable tea room, enjoying an "old-fashioned" matcha-flavored donut in a traditional space erected within a modern chain store. On the Tokyo subways, a 2007 poster used a similar contrast to promote public transportation: one image of a woman showed her in workout clothes, stretching in yoga-like fashion, and the other in a kimono, kneeling and drinking a bowl of tea—two aspirational visions of a graceful femininity.

Not merely a vehicle for learning about Japanese culture, tea is also presented in the media as a means for making oneself into a better Japanese. Why this should be necessary is explained in the etiquette book *Shitte Tokusuru: Wa no Keiko* (Know and Benefit: Lessons on Japaneseness), which features the tea ceremony as the first among practices a good citizen should learn: "Contemporary Japanese stand before Japanese traditional culture with the same feeling as a foreigner."[9] As might be expected in a magazine industry focused on targeted consumer groups, the Japanese qualities its readers are supposed to acquire are frequently gender specific. In women's

A Tokyo subway poster featuring the tea ceremony

magazines today, as in the past, refined comportment and aesthetic sensibility make regular appearances in features on tea as part of an ideal, often upper-class, woman's life. A typical example can be found in the November 2006 issue of *Fujin Gahō*—a magazine with pieces on or photographs of the practice in nearly every issue—where an article by a cousin of the Urasenke iemoto declares, "If one is Japanese, one is supposed to have a close relationship to Japanese food (*washoku*) from childhood,"[10] and then uses the tea ceremony to instruct readers in the proper way of holding chopsticks and serving themselves from dishes, not to speak of taking off one's shoes when entering a building (complete with illustrations of do's and don'ts). Another series of articles explains the role of kaiseki cuisine in the full ceremony. Large pictures of asymmetrically arranged, succulent morsels dominate the page, as each course of the meal is introduced by women in kimonos kneeling on tatami, accompanied by snippets of interviews with chefs and tea masters, along with the contact information for restaurants serving these delights. Echoing the theme of personal improvement, *CREA*—a magazine for a younger generation—published an issue in November 2008 on different kinds of lessons for "refining women" that featured on the cover a kimono-clad beauty holding a tea bowl. The first of these tutorials—they included flower arrangement, putting on a kimono, calligraphy, and Japanese dance, as well as horseback riding—was the tea ceremony. "If you are a Japanese woman, at least once you long for a life in which the kimono and the tea ceremony are a common part."[11] This desire, projected onto—and potentially into—readers is encouraged by an interview with an actress who explains that training in tea has refined both her grace on the stage and her courtesy in everyday life. For those who have embraced this aspiration, a Q&A section on the practicalities of lessons for beginners follows, together with snippets from students and teachers on their experiences in the tea room.

Magazines aimed at men have also picked up the tea ceremony, though typically taking pains to overcome its feminized image by featuring the chanoyu of great men of the past—a technique evident in the historical bent of the boy's manga *Hyogei Mono*. While women's periodicals highlight comportment, men's dwell on connoisseurship and aesthetic taste as the accomplishments of a proper Japanese man. In recent years *PEN*, an architecture and design magazine aimed at a youthful jet-set crowd, has been running annual issues devoted to tea. The first, appearing in January 2007, blazoned across its cover "Tea Ceremony Design: Japanese Traditional Beauty You Want to Know About Now." Stressing that tea is not just for women, it explained that in the past, tea was a "pleasure in which men manifested a sense of beauty and showed guests a creative hospitality," and expressed the hope that readers would "learn through 'tea design' how to improve their sense of tradition." In one article, the star designer Satō Kashiwa, image-maker for the international clothing chain Uniqlo, is taken through a tea preparation by a young male master, to whom he declares, "The Japanese sense of selection is terrific. There is a meaning in each and every design." The flow of the gathering is illustrated by photos accompanying a text on the details of the utensil selection—choices declared "very artistic in this male world." The architectural selections of Rikyū and other past tea greats are described and illustrated with an eye to how they extended the architectural possibilities of the time, culminating in a series of modern tea rooms designed by prominent architects. An article on the next-in-line to the Mushanokōjisenke iemoto presents the young man as a modern master, creatively "transmitting Rikyū's spirit." Another extols "the power of the tea ceremony, the 'top mode' of Japanese culture, [which] lies in creating new styles one after another," as exemplified by the artistic innovations of Rikyū and Oribe, and today in significant interactions between tea practice and modern design. In this narrative, sukisha are, of course, not overlooked, and a section focuses on the collector Masuda Takashi—the sort of man of taste that burgeoning designers might strive to become, or at least hope would purchase their own creations.[12]

A year later, *PEN* produced "Chanoyu Design Two: For Those Who Want to Know More About the Composite Art of Which Japan Is Proud." Focusing this time on tea rooms, the special issue contemplated famous specimens from the past, along with modern designs by well-known architects, including imaginative creations resembling inflatable golf balls or enormous gossamer jellyfish. In keeping with the design-industry basis of the magazine, it praised tea containers of Chinese origin for their "brand power," offered readers tips for evaluating utensils, and provided a list of dealers that collectors might care to visit. The February 2009 issue on "The Merits and Demerits of Rikyū" extended these themes, presenting the "tea saint" as the ur-ancestor of the design industry—"Japan's first creative director," originator of "minimal design" in which "the Japanese are expert," and "producer" of such glamorous public spectacles as the Grand Kitano Tea Gathering—in a spread topped off by interviews with leading artists explaining the influence of tea aesthetics on their work.[13]

Popular magazine covers featuring the tea ceremony

The gendered presentation of tea is not ubiquitous. Periodicals aimed at both female and male readers can also use the practice to anchor special issues. In 2007 the food magazine *Ryōri Tsūshin* published a number on "the spirit of tea." Claiming that "the tea ceremony is undergoing a quiet boom as people want to know about Japanese culture and learn to embody Japanese manners," it informed its readers that "for those concerned with hospitality and a spirit of exchange with others, the tea ceremony cultivates an eye for beauty and a skill for living well. Indeed, as Okakura had written, 'tea is the Japanese art of life.'" One expert opines that the practice is rooted in the very environment and seasons of Japan, which gave rise to the Japanese way of life—so "tea can awaken our DNA for discovering beauty in all that is related to Japan's environment."[14] For those in pursuit of such an awakening, the magazine features several elegant restaurants that exemplify the chanoyu ideals of "moving with a sense of ease," "placing the seasons on a plate," "being grateful for the day," and "bringing out harmony." Interviews—interspersed with liberal references to Rikyū and Hideyoshi—explain how learning tea refines hospitality, while inset boxes provide overviews of tea history and the seasonal basics of the practice, along with diagrams introducing tea utensils and the way to pronounce their sometimes hard-to-read names. Reassuring readers, the magazine proclaims that even a one-dollar bowl picked up on a vacation can make a good tea utensil if appropriately chosen, and that a tea gathering is not a stilted event, but a "party."

Images on the screen, whether flat or silver, tend to have a less edifying tilt, working more often with the basic knowledge and stereotypes that can be assumed of a mass public exposed to the practice through schools, museums, and local performances. Varied in their form and purpose as these institutions may be, they unfailingly project the tea ceremony in ways that sustain its image as integral to the country's traditional culture, the basso continuo that anchors the leitmotifs—whether feminine etiquette or masculine connoisseurship, a noble history or mocked mannerisms—played above.

## Impressions

Yet commonly conveyed views of the practice range in their take on it. What may be fascinatingly esoteric procedures to some can appear stultifying mystifications to others. While practitioners may appear as elegant experts in a refined traditional culture, they may also seem haughty. A span of such reactions is audible if we turn from the credos within the tea world to the voices without. An exchange at a drinking establishment in Tokyo offers some commonly heard sentiments.[15] The owner opined, "Most people doing tea think they're better than others. It's like, 'Look at me, I know what to do, I know better than you.' It's all about status. I really hate that. But that's not what it's supposed to be. Tea is about having a thoughtful heart." A novelist sitting at the bar interjected that high-society manners are similar to those in the tea room: "There's a different physicality—you have to be careful about everything." More impressed by the philosophy of the practice, a businessman in the room remarked, "Tea teachers can read the hearts of others very well. That's one of the reasons why it has strong links to bushidō. Hideyoshi and Nobunaga and what's-his-name . . . Rikyū! They did tea to understand their opponents, as a form of warrior training. So much about it is spiritual."

More straightforwardly negative valences are common as well. At a Tokyo party three businessmen talked about the practice after hearing about my work. The first offered an often-heard response that though he had never attended a tea ceremony, he was interested in the practice. His neighbor was less intrigued, stating that the thought had never crossed his mind since he didn't know the elaborate rules expected of guests. The third had done so, but didn't enjoy it, finding the strict procedures too distracting to relax and savor the experience. One of their wives, who had never studied tea herself, entered the conversation, concurring that "the image of it is very strict. People used to learn tea to acquire manners, but if you mess up, you get sternly corrected." Another housewife, met at a jazz performance later that year, echoed the sentiment. Describing her two experiences at tea gatherings, she said, "It was very strict. You go in, you kneel on the floor. . . . My feet fell asleep immediately. It's like going to a funeral and having to sit for a long time." One reason why the practice is so insistently promoted as relaxed in the "experience tourism" industry is because, as a representative of the Kyoto Tourism Bureau put it, "tea is a hierarchical world, with a strict relationship between teachers and students. Most people nowadays don't want that. They just want to try it out easily, sitting in a tatami room and enjoying a bowl of tea."

The impression that tea has become too rule-bound can be found even among admirers. An Osaka-based calligraphy teacher once remarked to me, "The tea ceremony is really wonderful, but the problem is now that people have just confined it to the rules. They think it has to be like this or it has to be like that. But during Rikyū's time, it wasn't like that at all. It was much more about creativity." Such nostalgia for a more aesthetically liberated past is not uncommon. A woman working in a Tokyo tempura restaurant, who had learned tea in her youth, explained to me, "The tea ceremony has moved very far from the way Rikyū did it. There's too much focus on utensils now, when it really should be about opening one's heart and showing hospitality." She picked up a water glass and, gesturing to it, continued, "You should be able to do it with any sort of utensil, but no one does that now." Predictably, the great expense necessary to move into the higher ranks of the tea hierarchy is also a frequent target of barbs, evinced by a husband's complaint when his wife paid several thousand dollars for an upper-level certificate: "It's ridiculous to waste so much on a mere piece of paper." The fatuity of such extravagant expenditures, from the view of nonpractitioners, was echoed in a small-town conversation with a tea teacher and her elderly mother. The daughter lamented, "People who don't know tea just say 'ohh,' without any interest. When you tell them a bamboo scoop cost ten thousand dollars, they just say 'ohh, ten thousand dollars.'" To this her mother burst into laugher and said, "Yeah, for an oversized ear-pick—one for the Great Buddha [a statue in Nara], I suppose. Ridiculous."

The uninitiated can find not only the monetary but also the aesthetic value attached to specific utensils mystifying. A workman encountered in a hole-in-the-wall restaurant commented: "While I can understand flower arrangement, the tea ceremony I don't get at all. With flowers, you just look at them and enjoy the sight. Sure there are a lot of rules about how you put them together, but you don't have to think about that to take pleasure in them. But with tea, I don't get this 'wabi' thing at all. You're supposed to hold the bowl and praise it, right? 'Ohh, what a nice tea bowl,' or something like that. But how can you tell if one is good or not? It's completely obscure." The unjustified value of teaware is also a staple in rakugo comedy. In a standard skit, a tea teacher and a young acolyte wander into a utensil shop and admire two black bowls sitting beside each other. "They're both quite beautiful, but I don't see why one costs one hundred times the price of the other" says the student. The teacher replies, "Oh, but clearly the profundity lies in details. See the misshapen side, the small chip in one corner, the way the light glistens off the uneven glaze—that is what makes an excellent tea bowl." The shop owner then wanders out. Pausing in front of the display, he takes a look at his commodities, and realizing he has made a mistake, switches the price tags on the two bowls.

Integrated into advertisements and other venues of popular culture, the tea ceremony enjoys a standing far above that of a quaint invented tradition. Though its image is not monolithic, carrying as it does both positive and negative valences, its associations typically signal an intense and time-honored Japaneseness. Modern media not only disseminate these images of the tea ceremony across a wide social horizon, they also enable what might otherwise have remained an esoteric throwback to fuse with a contemporary imaginary, preserving its relevance. This was not foreordained. Incense appreciation, for example, as ancient as chanoyu, has not enjoyed any comparable projection in popular culture and occupies a far more marginal position on the cultural radar of nonpractitioners,[16] while sumo wrestling, by contrast, has maintained a high—if tainted—profile through media attention.[17] Yet assimilation by the mass media and use in marketing strategies are not in themselves enough to explain why tea has become such a central icon of even postmodern Japanese identity.

## Toward a Praxeology of Nationness and Nationalism

To understand the connection between chanoyu and Japaneseness, one must look to the connection between the four dimensions of the practice explored in this study, relationships that have a wider analytical purchase. In the late nineteenth century, the long and continuous history of intimate association of tea with the apex of political power made it prime material for reworking into a national symbol. In so doing, it weathered remarkably well the dramatic reorganization of the political system and, on its tail, the economic restructuring of Japan in the Meiji period, the new elite ensuring that the practice remained active at the pinnacle of society as a certificate of noble conduct. Industrialists and politicians were drawn to chanoyu for many of the same reasons as daimyo and warriors had once been—it offered a symbolic link to prior rulers for purposes of legitimating power, a social space for networking with other elites, and a means for displaying a superior refinement, alongside the pleasures of an afternoon of elegant entertainment. Meanwhile, beneath this oligarchy, the school system—always a central forge of national identity—transmitted to the population below a knowledge of tea woven into a distinctively national history. Girls were encouraged to take up tea as a hobby in training for their role as "good wives and wise mothers." The tea ceremony was not simply a flat symbol, but a lived practice, with bodies conveying its national dissemination. Whether by business leaders or classroom leaders, tea continued to be done. The variously gendered valences of the nationalized result stood in a productive tension: women's practice transmitted popular understanding of the tea ceremony to households across the nation, while men's tea—often reacting to women's practice—stamped such understandings with the higher legitimacy of status and power.

But as a means of embodying and cultivating Japaneseness at both elite and popular levels, the tea ceremony would not have presented such a prime site for articulating definitions of the nation without the accretion of a novel discourse around it, developed by intellectuals. Aimed at an international audience unschooled in the rich cultural heritage of a newcomer state, Okakura's best-selling *The Book of Tea* set the pattern for a wave of other writers targeting domestic audiences. Once a national "we" was established under the Meiji order, these intellectuals set about explaining and illustrating just who "we" were. Here the key move, first made by Okakura and then expanded over succeeding decades, was to position tea as a supreme "cultural synthesis" of the historic arts and manners, not to say morals, of the Japanese nation. Wedding words to deeds more than Okakura would ever do, the upstart iemoto Tanaka Senshō developed both a strong body of adherents to his modernized tea school and an explicitly nationalist ideology around the ceremony, setting the stage for its integration, in the following decades, into the symbology of Showa imperialism.

Military occupation after the Pacific War, just as the earlier downfall of the Tokugawa, led once again not to a relegation but a mutation of the tea ceremony, which rose from the ashes of defeat with yet greater strength as the iemoto, whose prewar organizations already commanded a growing female constituency, capitalized on the post-imperialist shift from political to cultural domains as the legitimate arena of nationalist expression. Parlaying vertical international recognition garnered on overseas missions to elevate their status at home and horizontal domestic networks to tighten their links to business and political elites, the tea masters were able to craft themselves into icons not simply of tea, but of Japanese culture at large. By the time of the postwar economic recovery, they were marketing their products both by way of explanatory distinctions of the sort pioneered by Okakura, defining the image of Japan to the West in an internationalizing world, and as markers of a differentiating cultivation, developing those better members of Japanese society who knew how to retain their heritage in the face of a potentially erasive modernity. With this, the Japanese inflections of the practice attained the ultimate security: they had become central to the business interests of the organizations sustaining it, engaged no longer in selling simply tea, but Japanese culture.

But what is the significance of these nationalist or nationalizing endeavors for ordinary Japanese? While at a conscious level, as historian Eric Hobsbawm has remarked, most people's concerns are "not necessarily national and still less nationalist,"[18] the nation may be embedded unconsciously in daily routines that sustain national imaginings, even when not registered as such at any given moment. If the relationship between unconscious lifeways and invented traditions has been little explored by scholars, who have tended to keep the two separate,[19] a phenomenological perspective serves to bridge them. What renders the tea ceremony a quintessentially "Japanese" experience is not its fixity or apartness from the ordinary routines of living, but rather the alternation between the everyday and the exceptional—differentiation and distinction—that is inscribed in the practice. Although chanoyu is, in many ways, grounded in discontinuities with everyday life (it is, after all, a ritual), it is the continuities with other ways of doing things in Japan, expressed in concentrated form in the tea room, that enable it to highlight, and heighten, what is diffusely lived beyond its walls. "Western" entrances, with level floors, stand in contrast with "Japanese" entryways and their change in elevation—a difference accentuated in the tea room by the additional step and call for seated greetings. Here, not only is cutlery eschewed, but chopsticks must be "properly" held, with the cadence of raising and lowering them periodically incorporated into the rhythm of the event itself. Not semiotics alone, but its combination with practice—one reaching out to a self-reinforcing matrix of other items defined as "Japanese culture"—sustains these resonances. For it takes far more than tea—typically ceramics, scrolls, lacquerware, kimonos, tatami, and even kaiseki cuisine—to make a tea ceremony. In the moment-to-moment unfolding of the ritual, the stage, props, and scripted roles conspire to create a seamless flow that not only naturalizes very unnatural conduct, but also momentarily veils the oddness, apartness, and distinctive Japaneseness of what is going on.

Yet if asked, practitioners and others will characteristically register it as such, many indeed—particularly those of a younger generation—avowing that it was an interest in "Japanese tradition" that spurred them to take up study in the first place. Such sentiments are not only verbalized in essays solicited by the iemoto organizations or in demonstrations aimed at educating audiences in this time-honored tradition, but often emerge as almost unnoticed asides in tea room conversations. They are enacted in the conventions that make good practitioners—those who bow properly to the iemoto or possess a sharpened seasonal sensitivity. In such quiet embedding, the nation continues to be reproduced at a quotidian level. Radiating these national associations outward, museums, marketing, movies, and manga not only secure tea on the cultural scene, but also ensure the banality with which this Japaneseness is conveyed.

A similar dialectic is widely observable across cases, though it may appear in a diminished form or less potent combination than in the tea ceremony. Why this is so can be gathered from counterparts that also synthesize embodied performance and nationalizing rhetoric. Of these, the closest perhaps is the German gymnastics club (*Turnverein*) movement founded by Friedrich Ludwig Jahn (1778–1862) during the Napoleonic Wars. Indignant at both the dynastic fragmentation of Germany and the French occupation of much of the land, Turnvater Jahn, as he came to be called—mockingly or admiringly—was an early liberal nationalist for whom strengthening the national body began with cleansing the national tongue of foreign locutions. For language, according to Jahn, stood at the core of the nation, and this could not be resuscitated and unified without linguistic purification. These ideas he set out in his manifesto, *Deutsches Volksthum* (1810), a hodgepodge of considerable influence if not intellectual quality, that gave the German language the term *Volkstum* (along with other neologisms) as a healthier Teutonic substitute for the latinate *Nation* connoting the "essence of the people." In nine chapters Jahn laid out his vision of ideal German life and social organization, defining the specific governmental forms, religious institutions, and household arrangements that should sustain national education, literature, and feelings. Even hiking was rallied for the cause, for "wandering across the Fatherland is necessary, as it widens one's perspective without creating distance from the Fatherland. The people must know itself as the people, or else it will die."[20] These ideas were elaborated in subsequent writings, including military songbooks and nationalist texts on gymnastics, and were expounded on in speeches he gave on national heritage for his following.

But more than simply defining the nation, Jahn sought to cultivate it, foremost through building a stalwart national body. Faced with the menace of Napoleon, the fragmented German people needed above all to develop responsibility, liberty, and the ability to defend themselves—qualities best acquired, he believed, through rigorous physical training. For this task, Jahn created in 1811 a gymnastics field on the outskirts of Berlin, complete with apparatuses (parallel bars, vaulting horse, balance beam), a changing room, and a meeting place, where members—largely students at the out-set, though also craftsmen and merchants—would don their uniforms for both regulated and improvised exercises, political discussions, and rounds of folk singing that, he held, would transform them into "real German men." Though ridiculed by some, within seven years over a hundred such groups, claiming twelve thousand members, had copied this *Ur-gymnasium* and were following Father Jahn. These "centers for the cultivation of German-ness" anchored a widening network organized under the banner "honor, freedom, country."[21] Students toughened by "patriotic gymnastics" would pave the way for the unity of Germany that was yet to be achieved in the political arena, each "thoroughly train[ing] his body to serve the Father-land." Heralding this brawny corps was the ringing motto of the bourgeois nationalist masculinity offered by Jahn: *frisch, frei, frölich, fromm* (fresh, free, joyous, pious).[22]

Yet the revolutionary implications of Jahn's liberalism and antiauthori-tarianism—anathema to the ruling dynasties in Germany, not to speak of Klemens von Metternich as architect of post-Napoleonic Europe—brought repression upon him and his following: the 1819 Carlsbad Decrees dissolved the Turnvereine, and Jahn was jailed for six years by the Prussian monarchy for subversion. By the time he emerged from prison, the political impetus of his movement was spent. Gymnastics became part of regular school cur-ricula, but in the safer version codified by Adolph Spieß, who did away with Jahn's patriotic songs and countryside rambles, and offered a pedagogical rather than political alternative to established instruction. The upheavals of 1848 issued in a diminutive revival in the German Gymnastics League (Deutscher Turnerbund), but until German unification in 1871, it offered its now largely artisan and merchant membership only the harmless exercises of what leaders termed an "unpolitical politics." This changed in the prelude to the Second Reich, when Ferdinand Goetz re-christened the outfit the German Gymnastics Association (Deutsche Turnerschaft), with the aim to "develop the gymnasts into a powerful, moral, strong-willed sex, which is adroit and resolute, filled with ardent love for the Fatherland, and ready to answer for its [the country's] united and free development with its entire manly power."[23] Mustering its members under the slogan "Gymnastics our way, Germanness our aim"—no small call for the country that counted over 170,000 gymnasts by 1880—the association attempted to cultivate a strong national character marked by "order and punctuality," "proper behavior," and "German industriousness," which were to be taken out of the gymnasium and put into practice in everyday life.[24]

This membership was attracted by far more than simply physical training. From early on, Jahn had recognized the value of rites and symbolism for enabling the *Volk* to see itself as such (he even invented a national costume for the German male: a black jacket with gold oak leaves). The folk dancing and singing that Jahn had embraced now frequently extended meetings into long evening sessions that were, in the words of one participant, to awaken the "old German virtues: love of the Fatherland, loyalty, and brotherliness."[25] From the 1870s, the drills and sing-alongs were accompanied by theatrical performances, concerts, marches, and festivals, tethering gymnastics ever more tightly to a growing matrix of national symbology and activities. In a search for more fitting accommodation, the exercises moved from the meadow and into the shade of national monuments, before being displaced into purpose-built gymnastics centers. The voluminous practice halls were typically adorned with portraits of national heroes—Goethe, Schiller, Gutenberg, GutsMuths, Freiherr vom Stein—flanking a great bust of Jahn, and contained libraries for the study of *Turner* texts, along with national classics.[26] For annual festivals, these arenas were draped in flags and symbols of the nation and the sporting events accompanied by the recitation of sagas and fairy tales, as well as full-blown plays with costumed women representing a captive Germania liberated by Jahn.[27] During this thickening of patriotic organizations, gymnasts performed at men's choir celebrations and choirs at gymnastics festivals, strengthening an interlocked matrix of *echt*-German pursuits sharing the same emblems and activities of marching, patriotic speeches, and nationalist poems.[28]

Yet friction with the state remained. The *Turner* had little reverence for the Kaiser, and festivals celebrating the national spirit were held in opposition to official Wilhelmine ceremonies. Although, in the spirit of Jahn, small groups were the preferred organizational unit, these events that increasingly punctuated the calendar grew so large that the Leipzig exhibition in 1913 welcomed 60,000 gymnasts and 250,000 onlookers, many of whom were *Turners* themselves, who by this time numbered over one million.[29] The Weimar regime offered little change to this uneasy relationship with the political order, and many gymnasts took up anti-republican agitation, eulogizing not the constitution, but Hermann the German.[30] But once German unity arrived, Jahn could take his place in the pantheon of precursors. In 1928, the 150th anniversary of his birth was marked by Jahn-tributes,

Jahn-festivals, Jahn-texts, and Jahn-devotionals, with celebrations extending to "spiritual gymnastics" at which participants recited old German sagas and sang and danced to folk music. When Hitler came to power, the Nazis—with the cooperation of the association's spokesman—appropriated for their ancestry this patriotic icon, who had expressed anti-Semitic sentiments in his time.[31] Yet National Socialism had no space for an autonomous gymnastic movement, and the Nazis dissolved the organization into its own variant. After 1945, the *Turners* in the East were enveloped by the national sports association, while those in the West returned as the German Gymnastics League, which by the fifties claimed nearly a million members. But the fervor has long subsided for what is now a more or less colorless association, without any significant role in the imaginary of the Bundesrepublik—one far removed from the burnished luster of the tea ceremony and the empires of the iemoto.

Though eight years of Nazi appropriation and the unsteady grounds for patriotic displays thereafter might have dampened nationalist expression in both Germanies, a desecrated past does not tell the whole story, for the international derivations from Jahn's movement—variants were established in almost all European countries by the turn of the twentieth century—also saw their nationalist charges dim.[32] Of these, the Bohemian Sokol (literally "falcon") gymnastics, begun in 1862 by Miroslav Tyrš (1832–1884), became the most powerful counterpoint to the Teutonic version.[33] Raised in a German-speaking family, Tyrš was politicized by the growing nationalism of the 1860s, and changing his name from Tirsch to a more Slavic variant, he dedicated himself to the preservation of the Czech language and national essence. Though he took his cues from Jahn, he did so in reaction to his role model's success: the solidification of a German consciousness in a mixed Bohemia. Proclaiming "every Czech is a Sokol," Tyrš called for "a strong body preserving a strong will, [that] would once more unite with the dovelike meekness of the Slav, the falcon-like boldness of more glorious times."[34] The Falcons were to be not simply strong but beautiful, arousing the latent artistic instincts of the nation. Trained in philosophy and later to become a professor of aesthetics at the University of Prague, Tyrš selected combinations of movements and postures with an eye to their beauty, symmetry, and suitability for the mass exercises, which evolved into great "symphonic" displays.[35] These were anchored in philosophic principles he gleaned from Renaissance ideals of simplicity, clarity, symmetry, and variations on a theme.

Hierarchically divided into clans, units, and branches, and overseen by a congress of delegates, the organization was headquartered at the Tyrš House in Prague (which, decorated with images of Hussite heroes, provided a template for other gymnasia). By the end of the century its network encompassed Czech communities in Bohemia and beyond, providing a robust infrastructure for the spread of nationalist ideologies among the masses.[36] From the 1880s, the Falcons gathered for periodic festivals, or *slety* ("flockings of birds"), where they would don their uniforms—for men, a red Garibaldi shirt under a Polish revolutionary jacket and topped by a Montenegrin cap—and participate in gymnastics competitions and mass performances, in addition to nationalist singing, speeches, and theatrical events. The 1907 Slet included a parade of twelve thousand, a performance of Smetana's nationalist opera *Libuše*, and a reenactment of a 1422 Hussite victory in the form of a human chess game accompanied by over four hundred performers in period costumes dancing and singing Hussite tunes—all this in addition to the main event: a men's calisthenic display featuring over seven thousand gymnasts. Attended by over two thousand foreign guests, the grand celebration contributed to a growing international awareness of the nationality issues unsettling the Habsburg empire, with nervous diplomats from Vienna even dissuading Edward VII of England, taking the waters in Marienbad at the time, from attending the grand affair.[37] The Sokol organization recognized early on that attendant activities were just as crucial to the awakening of the national body, and local units hosted patriotic sing-alongs and plays, while discussion sessions became a center point for planning a nationalist revival. As in Germany, the utility of texts in this endeavor was not overlooked, and reading rooms and libraries at nearly half of all local headquarters stocked the weekly newspaper and numerous periodicals produced by the Sokol publishing house that lent verbal definition to its nation-building program.[38] Indeed, these ancillary offerings eventually surpassed the calisthenics in importance, as only twenty-five percent of its adult membership of 350,000 in 1930 participated in the physical training (of these a third were women, taken with the fittingly "feminine" variant developed). In the exhilaration of independence after 1918, though no less for their service in organizing local patrols to maintain order in the fledgling republic, the Sokols became the largest voluntary organization in the young Czechoslovak republic, counting over 550,000 members (including children) in 1925, with the first two presidents of the republic among them.[39] This was a far higher proportion of the population—nearly one in ten Czechs was a member—

than German gymnastic associations ever achieved. The centrality of the Falcons to the new nation-state was such that no less fateful a figure than Konrad Henlein, a Turnverein trainer who went on to become the leader of Sudeten German fascism and Nazi Gauleiter of Bohemia during the Second World War, could observe in 1929: "The Sokol is the creator of the Czech state, and is still today the strongest support of the official government ideology."[40] German occupation put an end to this. The Nazis banned the Falcons, and their phoenix-like recovery after 1945 and adoption of an anti-communist program led to their suppression by the communist regime, which substituted its own tamer variant. By the time the Sokols reemerged in 1990, their shrunken membership counted many aging hangers-on.

For all its initially rousing appeal, gymnastics proved limited as a tool for nation-work over the long haul. This was partly for social reasons: those at the top of society did not take to tumbling in undignified postures or to Jahn's peasant wear, and his rustic exertions were the butt of jokes from the start. The paramilitary movements themselves—the stretching, leaping, flipping—were easily decoupled from the behavior expected of good national members, and the great gymnastics halls never took a place among the esteemed architecture of the nation. Teutonic legends or Slavic sagas could be conjured up from the remote past, but a conspicuous gap lay between their mythologies and attempts by gymnasiarchs to mobilize them for present purposes: the projection of historical continuity was lacking. Though an elaborated institutional structure lent wings to the movements, as the accompanying elements declined—the men's choirs and folksong evenings, the homespun Germania plays—so too did the overall resonance of national associations. Political developments also moved against them. The original Turnverein and its successors were attempts to unite the nation from below, by galvanizing the populace in revolt against the established order. But in the German case, national unification came from above, at the hands of Bismarck, neutralizing or crushing such movements, and the associations lost their primary impetus, chafing lightly against the state thereafter. In Czechoslovakia, the state response came later, but was more total, shattering the Sokol as a force for anti-communist nativism.

Though in some ways a measure of success, the international diffusion of the practice undermined the nationalizing ambitions that had first spurred it forward. Today gymnastics performances are one of the most watched events in any Olympics, whiz flips accompanied by waving flags expressing the pride of the populace. Yet though the international organization of the sport allows for a multiplication of nationalist sentiments around it, these are notably shallow. Even if excitement or anger is aroused, most participation in sporting events is vicarious, in what is more an effervescent spectacle than a lasting somatic transformation. Die-hard fans are greatly outnumbered by intermittent enthusiasts with flexible loyalties who rarely hesitate to root for teams from other nations, particularly when their own has been eliminated. The homogenizing structures of international regulation make performance itself far less amenable to distinctive nationalist content, now reduced to a "Russian style" or "Chinese style" relish that may flavor televised commentary or the sports pages of newspapers, but rarely with much elaboration beyond the clichés of "efficient Germans" or "feisty Americans." Indeed, the same could be said of most international sports today.[41] Even if soccer, the most dramatic example, can readily rouse a nation to its feet with cheers of pride or bring tears to the flag-painted faces of fans, in the end the somatic experience is fleeting, allegiances fluid, and definitional capacity weak.[42]

Thus the strongest contemporary analogies to the European gymnastics movements are perhaps to be located outside the uniformities of internationally organized sport. A revealing case can be found in the political brotherhood of the Rashtriya Swayamsevak Sangh (RSS) in India—a nationalist paramilitary group created in 1925 with the goal of reviving the Hindu community through rigorous physical discipline. Donning a uniform of white singlets and khaki shorts, yellow socks and black cap, groups of up to a hundred boys and young men meet daily in public places, under the shadow of a duly saluted saffron flag (declared the true national banner), for an hour of calisthenics, games, and training in combat with bamboo staves.[43] The drills are followed by a discussion of problems facing the nation and intonement of patriotic songs, and the sessions close with a prayer to the nation and a salute to the flag. Supplementing these daily meetings are training camps and annual festivals suffused with symbols and rituals of Hindu custom and legend, whose more episodic and exciting occurrence— marked by the traditional Hindu calendar—help guard against the banalization of the everyday exercise routines. Women's support associations, community volunteer-work, and cooperation with schools help to transmit the message beyond the drill ground. Girding a mass membership of between two and six million is an organizational hierarchy of local leagues, state boards and committees, and national councils.[44]

More than disciplined bodies and dedicated spirits are formed in these activities. The founder of the RSS, Keshav Baliram Hedgewar (1889–1940), and his successor, Madhav Sadashiv Golwalkar (1906–1973), penned and encouraged numerous theoretical texts and treatises—disseminated through a weekly journal and associated bookstores—that detail the ways physical training is to bring about a Hindu renaissance by purifying the nation of Muslim, Christian, or Western pollution.[45] Drawing on the Advaita Vedanta school of classical Hinduism, these typically rally somatic imagery to explain that the Hindu nation is "the living god," and the members of this organic body must contribute in an individually appropriate way to its well-being. "The ultimate vision of our work," Golwalkar explained, "is a perfectly organized state of our society wherein each individual has been molded into a model of ideal Hindu manhood and made into a living limb of the corporate personality of society," and "each cell feels its identity with the entire body and is ever ready to sacrifice itself for the sake of the health and growth of the body."[46]

Standing behind India's second largest party, the BJP, which has twice formed a government in New Delhi, the RSS is today one of the most powerful mass organizations in India. But it is also widely shunned and feared as dangerously chauvinist. Banned three times since independence, the organization was charged with the assassination of Gandhi in 1947 and the demolition of the Babri mosque in Ayodhya in 1992, and its antagonists readily denounce it as a native version of fascism. Unlike Jahn's Turnverein or Tyrš's Sokols, the RSS aims not to create a nation-state, but to transform an existing one. But since its Hindu-revivalist objectives clash with the officially secular ideology of the Indian republic, its nation-work is highly divisive, splitting rather than unifying the country. It must also compete with the orchestrated mainstream forms of the Indian state itself, celebrating the nation in a blaze of parades and pageants, as well as televised versions of Hindu epics and other patriotic fare.[47] With its partisan underpinnings, the RSS has remained a sectarian movement, whose bid to substitute a new round of nation-building for ongoing nation-maintenance has little chance of rallying the whole community around it.

With generally—though not invariably—less controversy than calisthenics, music offers another powerful locus for uniting linguistic and somatic modalities of nation-work. The most ubiquitous expression—the national anthem—is perhaps the shallowest, not only spare in form but, like the Pledge of Allegiance in the United States, risking easy banalization. More elaborate genres provide far stronger footholds for potential nation-work. Opera, combining the pull of both music and drama, was the stage for some of the greatest symbolic battles of nineteenth-century European nationalism. The impact of Verdi during the Italian Risorgimento, extending from the 1840s to the 1860s, is the best-known case: interpretation of his operas by political activists often exceeded the patriotic intentions of the composer himself, as when the *Va, pensiero* chorus in *Nabucco* became the rallying melody in the struggle against Austrian domination.[48] Altogether more programmatic than Verdi, Wagner conceived his operas as monumental expressions of the nation in music that defended the Teutonic identity against insidious Italian and French influences. In his words, "the German movement could only take the character of a reaction against the foreign, deformed and also deforming, Latin model."[49] Against the preference for virtuosic song to the south, and the mania for ballet to the west (let alone the Jewish "degeneracy" within), he defined a distinctive German variant, if diffusely, by qualities of beauty, nobility, and naturalness. By and large the German people were still unaware of this kernel of national being Wagner had isolated, but the essence of the nation lay within them—much more so than in a "Frenchified" aristocracy. It had only to be retrieved and purified. For this, musical institutes and theaters were needed, for "in drama transfigured by music will the people [*einst das Volk*] find both itself and every art ennobled and improved."[50] Foremost among these was Bayreuth, a place of pilgrimage, where stagings of Wagner's *Gesamtkunstwerke*—"which embodied the entire existence and content of the nation"[51]—followed a seasonal cycle, disconnecting opera-going from everyday life and its routines. These "total works of art" would, according to Wagner, "represent the actively realized receptivity of German feeling for the original demonstration of the German spirit, in the same areas which until now have been left to the neglect of the most un-German cultivation."[52] Wagner's project of awakening the nation musically soon found imitators. On his heels, Smetana in Bohemia and Grieg in Norway sought to craft a music out of folk traditions that would define the nation and cultivate its citizens. In adopting Wagner's complex instrumentation and treatment of harmony, however, they laid themselves open to the charge that their innovations were "too Germanic." In France, recently defeated by Prussia, Wagner had his admirers, but in the main provoked a strong national reaction. The 1891 performance of *Lohengrin* in Paris had to be cancelled owing to public outcry, critics denouncing it as a threat to the "essential qualities of the French genius, clarity, and precision."[53]

If the opera theaters that sprang up across nineteenth-century Europe, and even overseas, offered the loftiest forms of national definition and explanation through music, the most effective means of embodiment and cultivation were to be found in schools. From the Revolution onward, France saw successive attempts to harness music for its *utilité publique* in propagating civic virtues. At a time when beauty was still felt to be closely linked to morality, musical education and performance were promoted as ways to elevate the national character by developing independence, intelligence, and largeness of mind, as well as patriotism and solidarity. From the 1880s, republicans lobbied for the inclusion of music classes in schools, where songs would not only awaken national pride, but inculcate honesty, fraternity, duty, obedience, taste, and a collective spirit.[54] Germany, as might be expected, was not left behind. There, childhood training blossomed into adult male choirs that became a popular means of cultivating a distinctively national masculinity from the Second through the Third Reich. The German Choral Association—boasting half a million members by 1925—brought together local groups for festivals, ceremonies, competitions, and "patriotic evenings," while its newspaper publicized old and new songs celebrating the nation.[55] Not only did the lyrics and texts delineate and stimulate thought of the German *Volksgeist*, but the contours of the practice did as well. Uplifting rhythms putatively instilled discipline, sociability, and virility by uniting the singers and firing them with enthusiasm for the Fatherland. But like many other organizations born during the decades of nation-building, and whose nationalizing thrust remained sharp through subsequent periods of war, these patriotic effects dulled as nation-making shifted to nation-maintenance. Rousing songs were still learned in schools and sung by amateur choirs, but with less fervor as expressions of collective identity. With the rise of commercial popular music, this form of nation-work has everywhere gone into steep decline, remaining unwedded to business interests.

To these expressions, one might add others providing prime material for nation-work—not only further practices, aesthetic or athletic, but also places like monuments, heritage sites, and theme parks, and objects as common as flags and coins.[56] Yet these give force to the nation with unequal vigor. The efficacy of any will be a function of its position within three overlapping parameters: constitutive, institutional, and sociopolitical. At the most basic level, the modes and intensities of nation-work vary according to the cultural weight of the form itself. Symbols like stamps may offer ubiquitous reminders of the nation, but casually viewed and automatically affixed, are weak supports for its embodied expression. Spectacles of one kind or another trigger far more intense affective reactions, but bursts of national excitement at festivals or parades may fade quickly. More durable in their effect are practices or skills whose acquisition transforms their bearer. Typically, however, these demand an investment of time and money not available to all. Combining forms can circumvent these individual limitations, and indeed such complexity is common, grand examples including mass gymnastics festivals, whose fusions of symbol and spectacle set them apart from routine exercises. Such amalgamations are important for a second reason: they increase the opportunities to link to, or even incorporate, similar items also charged with national resonances. For nations are made tangible in any number of ways—by historical events, heroic persons, expressive landscapes, official monuments, signature buildings, public holidays, tics of character, and repertoires of gesture, in addition to local forms of music, literature, painting, or dance, or varieties of fashion, sports, and cuisine. A montage of such forms can multiply the effects of each. Wagner's conception of a *Gesamtkunstwerk* is a famous illustration. Bayreuth was constructed as supremely German by interweaving music, legend, costume, and architecture, though these threads have faded since the Third Reich.[57] Such connections enable nation-work to continue off-site as well, if not always as intended: Smetana and Grieg had to defend the heavy harmonies of their patriotic compositions against suspicion of lurking German influence.

Institutional structures too will determine the relative impact of any given form of nation-work. Organizations, by nature, impose a systematicity on what they organize—whether it is gymnastics, singing, or tea making—that facilitates not only control, but also intensification and dissemination of it. The network of Sokol branches allowed nationalist messages to radiate far beyond their headquarters. In such cases, the importance of the written word—charters, newsletters, pamphlets—in modern organizations encourages verbal articulation of nation-work. When national associations of this kind are wed to business interests, a drive to counter the risks of creeping banalization is built into them—the iemoto cannot let the Japaneseness of their product be taken for granted. No less significant, of course, are public institutions like schools, whose pedagogical mission always includes explicit inculcation of ideas of the nation, long after it has been consolidated as a collective fact. The reach of the media, in turn, extends deep into the adult population, though the images it projects are typically more schematic in form. Institutional encapsulation as such nearly always leaves diffuse effects, beyond the institutions themselves: patriotic songs learned in schools producing an audience humming along to men's choral performances, movements like the RSS piggy-backing on the school system, Olympic television coverage momentarily lending national colors to the exertions of the gym.

Sociopolitical configurations, finally, are a fundamental determinant of the shape and direction of nation-work at large. Historical timing matters enormously: epochs of nation-building and times of war—defensive or aggressive—inevitably generate more visible and vehement forms than periods of peaceful nation-maintenance. Likewise, differences in political power lead to varying outcomes: strong states will create or nurture powerful infrastructures—centralized school systems or ubiquitous media coverage—projecting national messages further than they would otherwise penetrate, although even in the weakest of states, advertising campaigns may construct a nation of consumers with some success.[58] Nation-building may require a call to arms against the ruling order, which can then become the nation-maintenance of a satisfied or ruthless establishment. Jahn's romantic liberalism was no obstacle to Nazi appropriation. Nor is nation-work socially neutral: it typically involves a gendered division of labor—men often projecting the nation into the future, women anchoring it in the past—with unequal outcomes in the great national family.[59] Class differences may leave an even deeper mark. Nation-work invoking descent from an aristocratic past can furnish legitimacy, yet risk remoteness, while appeal to popular traditions may require reinterpretation of once stigmatized lower orders to retrieve a prestige fitting the nation.[60] Tensions of this kind can equally help to conjure into being a community that is more than the sum of its constituent parts.

Within all three parameters—constitutive, institutional, and sociopolitical—the tea ceremony in Japan has been unusually favored. Long associated with the pinnacle of political power, the ritual's high cultural past had attracted much literary elaboration—a wealth of definition and explanation that averted the need to invent this tradition entirely from scratch and provided a trellis for national inflections to take hold. At the same time, the ceremony was an emphatically physical practice whose demanding etiquette required the cultivation of a refined self that could be worked into a means of exemplifying and inculcating the moral fiber of the new collectivity. The male elites—sukisha, iemoto, and Showa intellectuals—who gave its modern national imprint to the practice, and the schools and media who disseminated diluted versions of this across the archipelago, usually worked in concert with, rather than against, dominant state interests. That eased the way for middle-class housewives, cultivating Japaneseness within, to become a broad pedestal supporting the practice without detracting from its historic prestige. Since its arrival as a "cultural synthesis" of national architecture, ceramics, cuisine, costume, and other arts, the tea ceremony has lain calmly enmeshed in a largely uncontroversial matrix of traditional Japanese things. As extraordinary versions of the ordinary, the spaces, objects, and gestures of which the ritual is composed offer a shifting balance between the exotic and the mundane that has preserved its aura in the fraught move from nation-building to nation-maintenance. Superintending that transition was the organizational system of the iemoto, who, once they consolidated their grip over the practice, ensured that its national sheen—essential to their profitable expansion in the epoch of modern commerce—would not be dimmed. Radiating it beyond the confines of the tea world are, in turn, institutions of education and industries of entertainment that guarantee a broader—if also shallower—take-up.

Study of the linkages between culture and nation has mostly trained its sights on moments of nationalist ferment, and for good reason. Nation-state formation, and its frequently militarist trappings, rides upon explicit invocations of patriotic pride and national glory. A great analytic literature has arisen around such processes and their often fateful outcomes. On this terrain—the invention of tradition and the imagining of communities—little excavation is necessary: evidence is strewn across the ground, even if putting the shards together is another matter. Digging out the roots of garden-variety nationness is a project only just begun. The sociology of nations has rarely moved with much fluency between fiery nationalism and prosaic nationness—a stiffness tacitly criticized in Anthony Smith's call for a framework integrating historical and ethnographic approaches.[61] Yet a striking similarity in the pragmatics of nationalist projects and everyday nationness, spanning macro and micro fields alike, can be seen in nation-work. The characteristics of the nation are defined by distinctions drawn between the self and nonnational others—traits that often carry a specifically classed or gendered inflection—and these qualities are cultivated in a process that differentiates members into greater and lesser incumbents. Yet if the typical forms and modalities of nation-work are similar across contexts, their relative weight is not. Most originating nation-work defines the nation into existence by linguistic instruction designed to create nationally conscious subjects. This is a process in which ideology transforms dispersed scraps of myth, memory, and custom into fully fledged national traditions, in which appeals to a (largely legendary) past delimit who "we" are through implicit or explicit distinctions between "us" and "them." As a rule, the subjects interpellated by the ideology are initially unaware of the glorious history they will henceforward share and remain reliant upon its definitions and explanations for the "awakening" of their national consciousness. Its embodiment and cultivation normally arrive half a step behind definition and explanation, for these forms of nation-work require a prior signifying apparatus that constitutes them as national. But once they take hold as lived performances—at their most powerful, somatic transformations—they can be far more potent than verbal utterances. Patterning ordinary life, even as they differentiate some members into better incumbents than others, they become central to the everyday maintenance of the nation, long after the pyrotechnics of nationalism have faded.

*Reference Matter*

# Glossary

chadō (sadō), chanoyu　茶道, 茶の湯　the tea ceremony

daimyō　大名　the most powerful territorial rulers beneath the shogun in pre-modern Japan

gomei　ご銘　"poetic name" given to tea utensils, often taken from literary classics

hakogaki　箱書　inscription on the lid of a tea utensil box

hiroma　広間　tea room larger than 4.5 tatami mats

iemoto　家元　head of a school (or style) of a traditional aesthetic practice

kaiseki　懐石　traditional multicourse meal considered the equivalent of Japanese haute cuisine

kaō　花押　an iemoto's cipher on a utensil or its box

kencha　献茶　ritual preparation of tea, typically offered to the spirits at temples or shrines

konomi　好み　a characterization applied to utensils conforming to the aesthetic style or taste of a venerated tea master

ma　間　interval, interstice, or gap

matcha　抹茶　powdered green tea typically used in the tea ceremony

mizuya　水屋　the preparation area attached to a tea room

Nihonjinron　日本人論　theories of Japanese uniqueness

seiza　正座　kneeling; literally "correct sitting"

Sen Rikyū (1522–1591)　千利休　person considered the father of the tea ceremony

sencha　煎茶　steeped tea

sukisha　数寄者　business magnates turned tea ceremony connoisseurs in the late nineteenth and early twentieth centuries

tatami　畳　mats of woven rushes used for flooring

temae　手前, 点前　standardized motions for formally preparing tea

toriawase　取り合せ　the combination of utensils chosen for a given tea
　　performance

Urasenke　裏千家　the dominant school of tea since the twentieth century

wabi　侘び　an aesthetic of austere beauty

washitsu　和室　literally "Japanese room"; refers to rooms with tatami floors,
　　sliding doors, and an alcove

# Notes

## Preface

1. A white French "observing participant" of a largely black boxing club in Chicago, Loïc Wacquant describes a similar process in "Carnal Connections": "My whiteness receded as I climbed up the *gradus* of the trade and as my own organism absorbed and then displayed its distinctive practical skills and sensibilities" (452–53), enabling him to "*provisionally suspend* or significantly attenuate many differences" (450). But unlike the "racially indifferent" bodily dispositions of boxing, the properties I was in-corporating carried Japanese valences. See Kondo, *Crafting Selves* (12–14), on the utility of "Japanese behavior" for putting informants at ease.

2. Etsuko Kato's experience studying contemporary tea practice provides a sharp contrast, for as a Japanese, she was granted less access to private spaces. Kato, *Tea Ceremony and Women's Empowerment*, 19.

3. See Iguchi et al., *Nihon no Chake*, for descriptions and histories of the main schools and over a dozen smaller ones.

## Introduction

1. This term carries with it several misleading connotations. Okakura Kakuzo's 1906 international bestseller *The Book of Tea* popularized the phrase "tea ceremony" in the West, where *Teezeremonie*, *cérémonie de thé*, and *ceremonia del tè* are now in standard use. However, "tea *ceremony*" is a misnomer insofar as it suggests that the practice is simply a solemn ritual rather than a coordinated social interaction centered on hospitality. This evocation is avoided in the Japanese, Chinese, and Korean terms 茶道 (Japanese, *chadō, sadō*; Chinese, *chadao*; Korean, *chadu*), which are constructed from two characters, 茶 (*cha*), or "tea," and 道 (*dō, michi*) or "path, way." The "Way of Tea" is the English translation currently favored by the major tea schools in Japan, which emphasizes the continual learning, incorporation into daily life, and spiritual elements within the practice. In premodern Japan, *chanoyu* (hot water for tea) was the standard term and is still commonly used in the Japanese tea world. Neither of these native terms, however, invokes "ritual" or "ceremony." Contemporary practitioners themselves frequently refer to what they do as simply *ocha* (tea), allowing the context to establish the distinction between the practice and the common beverage. With the above caveats in mind, I use the term "tea ceremony"

for simplicity, and occasionally employ the practitioners' convention and refer to "tea" or "chanoyu."

2. In Etienne Balibar's strident terms, "A social formation only reproduces itself as a nation to the extent that, through a network of apparatuses and daily practices, the individual is instituted as *homo nationalis* from cradle to grave, at the same time as he or she is instituted as *homo oeconomicus, politicus, religious*" (Balibar, "Racism and Nationalism," 95).

3. At one extreme stands Scandinavian work scrutinizing even the most miniscule and mundane of everyday activities, including such texts as Löfgren, "The Nationalization of Culture"; Ehn, "National Feeling in Sport"; and Linde-Laursen, "The Nationalization of Trivialities."

4. See Billig, *Banal Nationalism*, on the national deixis, and Comaroff and Comaroff, *Ethnicity, Inc.*, for an incisive account of the commodification of national belonging.

5. This bifurcation applies to critical treatments of Japan as well. Here studies of nationalism have grown apace in recent years, with landmarks including Oguma Eiji's dissections of nation-state and empire formation in *Tan'itsu Minzoku, Nihonjin no Kyokai*, and *Minshū to Aikoku*; Kang Sang-jung's trenchant postcolonial disquisitions *Han-Nashonarizumu, Nashonarizumu Shikōno Furontia*, and *Orientarizumu no Kanata*; and Ueno Chizuko's relentless reminder that gender matters, *Nashonarizumu to Jendaa*. Books on nationness abound, but consist largely of contributions to the popular—in both senses—literature on *Nihonjinron*, or studies of Japanese uniqueness, that add more to the phenomenon of everyday cultural nationalism than they do to its analysis. Yoshino, *Bunka Nashonarizumu* and *Cultural Nationalism*; Dale, *Myth of Japanese Uniqueness*; Mouer and Sugimoto, *Images of Japanese Society*; Sugimoto and Mouer, *Nihonjinron no Hōteishiki*; and Befu, *Hegemony of Homogeneity*, map this field; and McVeigh, *Nationalisms of Japan*, situates *Nihonjinron* discourses within a broader typology of the nationalisms in Japan.

6. The most significant case is the exchange between the co-authors Jon Fox and Cynthia Miller-Idriss with Anthony Smith, representing respectively ethnographic and macro-historical standpoints. Fox and Miller-Idriss, "Everyday Nationhood"; Smith, "Limits of Everyday Nationhood."

7. The central argument in Brubaker et al., *Nationalist Politics*, for example, proceeds from a disconnection between the domains, as the authors set out to explain why nationalist calls to arms have not resonated with the populace in recent years.

8. Here I build on Handler, who proposes that to understand the production of nations, one must look to how they are objectified. See Handler, *Nationalism and the Politics of Culture*. Others examining similar processes have employed a terminology of national materialization (Mosse, *Nationalization of the Masses*; Foster, *Materializing the Nation*), visual domination (Fujitani, *Splendid Monarchy*), or fetishization (McClintock, "No Longer in a Future Heaven").

9. Brook and Schmid in *Nation Work* were the first to employ a morphological variant of this term, written without the hyphen, but attributed a somewhat different meaning to it. Their eponymous edited volume uses the phrase to draw atten-

tion to how Asian elites have produced and reproduced national identities not only in interaction with the West, but also by navigating divides within Asia. Though they recognize a number of activities that "nation work" may involve—"acts of interpretation, the careful scholarly study required for cultural inheritance and continuity, the creation of new symbols and their infusion with national meaning, the construction of representations, the appropriation of national forms and ideas from abroad, struggles against rivals—and always the effort to disseminate and instill the results of [elites'] work in as wide an audience as possible" (6)—the authors do not refine this laundry list into a rigorous conceptualization of what such labor entails. However, they do emphasize the importance of context in determining the sorts of "nation work" carried out, a theme returned to—along with materiality and organization—in Chapter 4.

10. A number of other authors have adopted the "-work" suffix, with early uses stretching as far back as Freud's 1899 *Interpretation of Dreams*, wherein he analyzes the "dream-work" that transforms latent thoughts into dream content. Goffman, *Interaction Ritual*, 5–45, examines the "face-work" that sustains everyday interaction; DeNora, *Music in Everyday Life*, 68–74, describes the "identity work" through which individuals construct the self through music; Gieryn, "Boundaries of Science," looks at the "boundary-work" of demarcating scientific disciplines—a notion expanded by Lamont and her students (Lamont and Molnár, "Study of Boundaries"; Pachucki et al., "Boundary Processes"); and Miller in *Beauty Up* follows the "beauty work" that creates an aesthetic Japanese body. Common across these cases, as with the nation-work analyzed here, is a focus on the often misrecognized effort needed to sustain the social world, for as numerous ethnomethodological studies have shown, even the taken-for-granted must be achieved. Maintaining the ordinary requires, in Harold Garfinkle's words, "serious and practical work" (*Studies on Ethnomethodology*, 34).

11. Anthony Smith's successive volumes on ethnosymbolism have been the touchstone in this line of inquiry. See, inter alia, Smith, *Ethnic Origins of Nations*, *Ethno-Symbolism and Nationalism*, and *National Identity*.

12. For prior work emphasizing the discursive production of national forms, see Wodak et al., *Discursive Construction of National Identity*; Verdery, *National Ideology*; Ries, *Russian Talk*; Yurchak, *Everything Was Forever*; and Calhoun, *Nationalism*; and for studies stressing the physical enactment of the nation in everyday life, see Jenkins, *Being Danish*; Edensor, *National Identity*; Borneman, *Belonging in the Two Berlins*; and Presner, *Muscular Judaism*. Studies sitting squarely astride the two can be found as well, such as Wedeen, *Peripheral Visions*; and Foster, *Materializing the Nation*, which illuminate the textual practices and bodily actions that invoke the nation.

13. Indeed, as Connerton, *How Societies Remember*, 102–3, describes it, bodily practices are often acquired in a way that hampers scrutiny. For an elaboration of the qualities of embodied competences, see Bourdieu, *Logic of Practice*, 66–79. For a discussion of how practice theories have formulated the differences and commonalities of embodiment and language, see Rouse, "Practice Theory," 511–23. Farnell,

"Moving Bodies, Acting Selves," also offers an overview of the alignments and re-alignments of studies of language and studies of the body.

14. Elaborating John L. Austin's work on speech acts, Bourdieu, *Language and Symbolic Power*, 107–16, stresses the importance of institutions in constituting the authority that enables speech acts to be performative. "To institute, to assign an essence, a competence, is to impose a right to be that is an obligation of being so (or to be so). It is to *signify* to someone what he is and how he should conduct himself as a consequence. In this case, the indicative is an imperative" (120).

15. On the ways dispute and dissent can vivify national ideologies, see Verdery, *National Ideology under Socialism*.

16. Ries, *Russian Talk*, for example, explicates the genres of everyday discourse that sustained national identities through the collapse of the Soviet Union.

17. For classic statements on the centrality of schools in producing national publics, see Weber, *Peasants into Frenchmen*, 303–38; and Gellner, *Nation and Nationalism*, 27–29.

18. For a discussion of national habituses, see Löfgren, "Nationalization of Culture," 15–17.

19. Drawing on James W. Fernandez, Herzfeld in *Poetics of Manhood* describes this nuanced move away from the conventional pace of things as "effective *movement*," that is, "a sense of shifting the ordinary and everyday into a context where the very change of context itself serves to invest it with sudden significance" (16).

20. The ordering of the world declaimed can normalize behaviors and suggest others as deviant or in need of discipline, shifting from definition to cultivation. See Foucault, *Discipline and Punish*, 177–84. At the limit, not only members but also nonmembers of the nation can be the subject of cultivation. In cases such as contemporary Japan that exhibit a high degree of social closure, guarded by mutually reinforcing ethnic and cultural boundaries, out-group members' successful incorporation of nationally inflected practices can deflate the perceived distance between members of separate national categories while simultaneously reaffirming a constitutive difference between them, as when foreigners learning the tea ceremony are praised as "more Japanese than the Japanese." Though non-Japanese may become "better than Japanese," they can never be "better Japanese."

21. Brubaker et al., "Ethnicity as Cognition"; and Brubaker, "Ethnicity Race, and Nationalism," chart the development of this analytic tack.

22. On the lingering effect of Johann Gottfried Herder's conceptualization of culture, see Wimmer, "Herder's Heritage."

23. For an overview of Barth's contribution to academic conceptualization of ethnicity, see Vermeulen and Govers, "Introduction."

24. Espiritu, "Intersection of Race, Ethnicity, and Class." Marx, *Making Race and Nation*, 18, 20, describes a similar process in Brazil where intra-group distinctions among races have been downplayed when consolidating resistance against dominant groups.

25. Notable treatments of internal differentiation include Weber, *Economy and*

*Society*, 390–91; Eriksen, *Ethnicity and Nationalism*, 66–67; and Brubaker et al., *Nationalist Politics*, 230–31.

26. The Japanese language offers a few naturally occurring possibilities. Qualifications expressing exemplariness are commonly used with specific instances of ethnic groups, including the adjectives *Nihonteki* (Japanese-y) and *Nihonrashii* (Japanese-y), and the noun *Nihonrashisa* (Japanese-y-ness).

27. Exemplary analyses include Collins, *Black Feminist Thought* and *Fighting Words*; McCall, "Complexity of Intersectionality"; and Glenn, "Social Construction and Institutionalization of Gender and Race." For an overview of the literature, see Davis, "Intersectionality as a Buzzword."

28. Key statements on the gendered nature of national belonging can be found in Yuval-Davis, *Gender and Nation*; Yuval-Davis and Anthias, "Introduction"; McClintock, *Imperial Leather*; Duara, "Regime of Authenticity"; and Mosse, *Nationalism and Sexuality*.

29. Hobsbawm, "Mass-Producing Traditions," 300–301, 305–6. Obviously, not all of these trickled very far—as illustrated by the particularly upper-class vision of Britishness represented by Ascot. See Huggins, *Flat Racing*.

30. On this, Elias, *Civilizing Process*, still provides the definitive account.

31. Respectively, Daniel, *Rumba*; and Savigliano, *Tango*.

32. In this sense, it differs from the reinscription of we–they oppositions at a subnational level. On this form of fractal replication, see Gal, "Bartok's Funeral."

33. Herzfeld, *Poetics of Manhood*, 57, offers a meta-national example: only on the premise that both are Europeans can Greeks view themselves as more European than Serbs (themselves naturally more European than the Turks).

34. Goffman approaches this process when describing how stigmas index social norms in his eponymous book. "For example, in an important sense there is only one complete unblushing male in America: a young, married, white, urban, northern, heterosexual Protestant father of college education, fully employed, of good complexion, weight and height and a recent record in sports. Every American male tends to look out upon the world from this perspective, this constituting one sense in which one can speak of a common value system in America. Any male who fails to qualify in any of these ways is likely to view himself—during moments at least—as unworthy, incomplete and inferior; at times he is likely to pass and at times he is likely to find himself being apologetic or aggressive concerning known-about aspects of himself he knows are probably seen as undesirable" (*Stigma*, 153).

35. See, for example, Verdery's analysis in *National Ideology* of the ways the lively debate over national meanings in Romania kept this frame vitally present even under Soviet-backed rule.

36. Yoshino, *Cultural Nationalism*, 5. Here one might note that even in long-established nation-states flamboyant nationalist claims can emerge particularly during times of war or other threats.

37. See, for example, the description of the practice offered by Jesuit missionaries visiting Japan in the sixteenth century discussed in Chapter 2.

38. The "myth of the homogeneous nation," as Oguma has shown, is a post-war construction. On the historical vicissitudes of Japanese national ideologies, see Oguma, *Tan'itsu Minzoku*, available in English, though in an incomplete translation, as Oguma, *Genealogy of "Japanese" Self-Images*.

39. For a global comparison, see Fearon, "Ethnic and Cultural Diversity by Country." Japan is home to some 25,000–300,000 Ainu, 1.6 million Okinawans, and 2.1 million registered foreigners. The three percent figure excludes the 2–3 million Burakumin stigmatized by association with the Meiji era outcaste groups, but whose minority status does not turn on the construction of a separate national identity.

40. Intellectual treatment goes back further, as will be discussed in Chapter 2. See Kumakura, *Kindai Chadōshi*, 1–47, for an overview.

41. Most of these historians have produced numerous lighter texts, whose glossy images and straightforward explanations are aimed at the audience of tea practitioners. These include Kumakura, *Mukashi no Chanoyu, Ima no Chanoyu*; Tanihata, *Yokuwakaru Chadō no Reikishi*; and Tani, *Chajintachi no Nihon Bunkashi*. In another vein, Nomura, *Sekishūryū: Reikishi to Keifu*, deserves mention as one of the rare extended histories of the Sekishū style of tea preparation; and Ōtsuki, *Sencha Bunkakō: Bunjincha no Keifu* offers a history of steeped tea rituals (*sencha*). The two volumes of Kumakura et al., *Shiryō ni yoru Chanoyu no Rekishi*, provide key primary sources with modern transliteration and commentary.

42. An exception is Kobayashi Yoshiho's successive articles that challenge many myths about tea ceremony and flower arrangement lessons at women's schools in the late nineteenth and early twentieth centuries.

43. Kondo, "The Way of Tea"; Plutschow, "An Anthropological Perspective"; and Cox, *Zen Arts*.

44. Mori, "The Tea Ceremony" and "Traditional Arts as Leisure." Mori also produced a book in 1992, *Americans Studying the Traditional Art of the Japanese Tea Ceremony*, on residents of Hawaii learning the practice.

45. A further discussion is in the April 1978 issue of the periodical *Reikishi Kōron*.

46. See Pitelka, "Introduction to Japanese Tea Culture," 8–10, on the influences and distortions the major tea schools—and the Urasenke Foundation in particular—have wrought on tea historiography.

47. It follows, but as an afterthought, semi-detached under a juridical heading, and unlike the others. "All these phenomena are at the same time juridical, economic, religious, and even aesthetic and morphological, etc. They are juridical because they concern private and public law, and a morality that is organized and diffused throughout society; they are strictly obligatory or merely an occasion for praise or blame; they are political and domestic at the same time, relating to social classes as well as clans and families. They are religious in the strict sense, concerning magic, animism, and a diffused religious mentality. They are economic. The idea of value, utility, self-interest, luxury, wealth, the acquisition and accumulation of goods—all these on the one hand—and on the other, that of consumption, even that of deliberate spending for its own sake, purely sumptuary: all these phenomena

are present everywhere, though we understand them differently today. Moreover, these institutions have an important aesthetic aspect that we have deliberately omitted from this study" (Mauss, *The Gift*, 79).

48. Weber, *Economy and Society*, 394–95, 922–26.

49. Brubaker, in "Ethnicity, Race, and Nationalism," emphatically makes this point in his overview of the literature (24–25). Empirical examples from other authors working in this mode include Laitin, *Identity in Formation*; Wimmer, *Nationalist Exclusion*; and Brubaker et al., *Nationalist Politics*.

*Chapter 1*

1. Edensor, *National Identity*, vii.

2. Barthes, *Mythologies*, 143.

3. Ibid., 148–49. As a myth, the nation "summons" the beholder of the Basque chalet in Paris "to see it as the very essence of *basquity*."

4. This chapter deals largely with understandings that often remain tacit or implicit during actual tea interactions. See Chapter 4 for an analysis of explicit engagement with Japaneseness in situ.

5. Barthes, *Mythologies*, 153.

6. "Mushin'an" and the names of the practitioners are pseudonyms.

7. The juxtaposition recalls a comparison made over seventy years ago by the literary figure Tanizaki Jun'ichirō in his nostalgic essay *In Praise of Shadows*:

> What incredible pains the fancier of traditional architecture must take when he sets out to build a house in pure Japanese style, striving somehow to make electric wires, gas pipes, and waterlines harmonize with the austerity of Japanese rooms—even someone who has never built a house for himself must sense this when he visits a teahouse, a restaurant, or an inn. For the self-satisfied tea master, and the like, it is another matter, he can ignore the blessings of scientific civilization and retreat to some forsaken corner of the countryside; but a man who has a family and lives in the city cannot turn his back on the necessities of modern life—heating, electric lights, sanitary facilities—merely for the sake of doing things the Japanese way. (Tanizaki, *In Praise of Shadows*, 1)

(I have replaced "solitary eccentric" in the Harper and Seidensticker translation with a more literal rendering of the original: "self-satisfied tea master, and the like." See Tanizaki, *In'ei Raisan*, 7–8.)

8. In rakugo comedy, a fading tradition now receiving government support, a single storyteller wearing a kimono kneels on a cushion and narrates a long and humorous story using only a fan and a handkerchief as props. Changes in pitch and intonation as well as onomatopoetic sounds are important tools for evoking an amusing scene for the audience.

9. In contemporary Japan, vertical writing is read from right to left, and horizontal writing is read from left to right. Before horizontal writing proliferated, with imperial defeat in 1945 lending a push, single lines of characters were sometimes written on horizontal spaces following the older practice of writing from right to left. Initially commonsense, this practice now appears as an irregularity, but one recalling older ways. Walking through the streets of Kyoto, one comes across signs

on old temples or shops selling traditional goods that are still written in the right-to-left horizontal style.

10. Most tea room names end with the character *an*, or hut. However, the polyvalent Zen term *mushin* is more difficult to translate. One possibility is "empty spirit," which could refer to a Zen-like unintentional, pre-reflexive state of just simply being.

11. Illustrating this hospitable posture, the cover of a book produced by the traditional inn Sumiya, entitled *Kyōto Sumiya: Omotenashi wa Ocha no Kokoro de* (Kyoto Sumiya: Hospitality in the Heart of Tea), features a kimono-clad hotelier smiling warmly while kneeling from a raised entrance area. The photo is taken from the point of view of a visitor standing outside the building, allowing for an evenly met gaze.

12. Sensitivity to ever-changing shadows is considered a key element of connoisseurship in several Japanese arts, captured most succinctly perhaps in a Noh actor's manipulation of the shadows on his mask to express emotions. The title of Tanizaki's essay *In Praise of Shadows* conveys this esteem.

13. For an eloquent analysis of how tea gardens were transformed into specimens of a distinctively Japanese gardening style, see Tagsold, *Spaces of Translation*, 133–35.

14. The size of rooms with tatami mat flooring is customarily measured in mats, with one tatami mat measuring approximately three feet by six feet. The term "4.5-mat room" is a direct translation of the Japanese *yojōhan*, or "four-and-a-half mat room." The term is so commonly used that it has become a referential noun rather than a measure emphasizing size. *Hiroma* refers to a room of six tatami mats or more.

15. As Sand, *House and Home*, notes, such postwar controversies helped embed alcoves as indispensable to a distinctively Japanese architectural style (376). Incorporated into the design of Shōin rooms in the Muromachi era, these recesses became requisite in dwellings of the upper strata during the Tokugawa period, but sumptuary laws limited their construction. When these were lifted under the Meiji dispensation, alcoves became standard in urban interiors, but in spaces set off as distinctively Japanese (123).

16. Combining a character for Japaneseness, *wa*, and the character for room, *shitsu*, the term stands in contrast to *yōshitsu*, which substitutes the character for "West," *yō*. In contemporary Japan the latter are typically run-of-the-mill modern rooms rather than those with a particularly European or Western inflection and are now the unmarked standard. Though rooms in a house may be conceivably categorized into yōshitsu and washitsu, an advertisement would list a residence as having "a living room, a dining room, a kitchen, two bedrooms, and a washitsu." These *wa* and *yō* varieties reappear in other areas—the clothes expected to be worn in the tea room are *wafuku*, not *yōfuku*; the sweets consumed are *wagashi*, not *yōgashi*; and the like—but it is now the "yō" variety that is most common in Japan.

17. Here I distinguish negotiated hierarchies, in which positionings are decided in situ, from those in which they are pre-given. Large offices, for example, are generally arranged with the boss at a single desk gazing down a row of tables paired fac-

ing each other, with the lowest on the ladder sitting the furthest away. In this case, a hierarchy is inscribed into space, but positions are not negotiated.

18. This statement was made by a teacher to a twenty-something Japanese woman attending tea classes for the first time. Her description establishes the altered sensation of a Japanese room by differentiating it from everyday flooring and a lifestyle using tables and chairs dominant in contemporary Japan, and by heightening it with a qualifier: "Nihon no washitsu," or "Japanese washitsu." While Japaneseness may be more or less inadvertently tagged by her word choice—since Japaneseness is constitutive of the term *washitsu*, the item cannot be named without flagging it—she explicitly underscores the Japanese frame by labeling it a "Japanese room of Japan" or, less awkwardly but still insufficiently phrased, a "*Japanese* Japanese room."

19. See, for example, Yatabe, *Utsukushii Nihon no Shintai*, 163–67; *Tatazumai no Bigaku*, 99–102; and Tei, *Seiza to Nihonjin* (Seiza and the Japanese), which bears a kimono-clad kneeling woman on the cover and purports to answer the question "Why is seiza the formal way for Japanese to sit?" While many countries have not produced extended self-reflexive engagements with national bodies, a sizeable literature can be found in Japanese.

20. Once I was told, while kneeling on the floor and conducting an interview with a tea practitioner, that sitting seiza was simply impossible for foreigners.

21. A frequent subject of light humor, the difficulty of seiza is amusingly captured in Itami Jūzō's 1984 film *The Funeral* with a camera shot that pans across the uncomfortable feet-twitching of the family kneeling before the Buddhist altar carrying the bones of the recently deceased member while a priest chants over the remains. When a phone rings, one of the party leaps up at the opportunity for increasing blood flow to his legs, but immediately falls over, his feet asleep.

22. Yet the elevation of seiza to the sole standard is recent, and historically samurai typically sat cross-legged, even in tea contexts.

23. See Sand, *House and Home*, for a meticulous history of the constitution of the washitsu, along with other interior elements, driven by imperatives to create a "national style" distinctive from Western forms, and molded by hygienic and family concerns.

24. Japanese inns (*ryokan*) and Japanese restaurants (*ryōtei*) are part of a service industry known for serving formal "Japanese" food, such as fine *kaiseki*, in "Japanese" settings, with tatamis and gardens, as distinct from their quotidian counterparts—*hoteru* and *resutoran*.

25. As such, it encourages the same informality as the kitchen in the Shetland hotel that Erving Goffman in *The Presentation of Self* uses to illustrate his discussion of region-specific behavior (118–20).

26. Sand, *House and Home*, 115–16.

27. On the history of tea rooms as representations of or influences on a distinctively Japanese architectural style, see Sand, *House and Home*, 115–16, 314–15; as well as Isozaki, *Japan-ness in Architecture*. In a recent contribution to the genre, leading designer Uchida Shigeru begins his monograph on Japaneseness and space, *Chashitsu to Interia* (Tea Rooms and Interiors), by declaring that removing one's

shoes and sitting on the floor is "the basic embodiment of Japanese culture" (13) and goes on to discuss elements of the national essence epitomized by tea architecture.

28. Like the rooms and the tea-making proper, such preliminaries are remarkably uniform across cases, though classes less formal than those at Mushin'an will invite more everyday conversation and casual action or distraction during the preparations.

29. Wagashi sweets, made from fine sugar molded into forms subtly evoking seasonal references and packaged with traditional patterns, are distinct from *yōgashi*, their typically unmarked quotidian counterpart. Shoppers, for example, will purchase either wagashi or "just normal" candy. For a penetrating analysis of a small business producing wagashi, see Kondo, *Crafting Selves*.

30. These are listed in books cataloguing the most common motifs and their historical sources, which practitioners purchase to study the canon.

31. For a critical history of this association, see Pitelka, *Handmade Culture*.

32. The additional care such wrapping demands is not always embraced by tea students, who may decry the inconvenience of tradition. At a group interview I held with work colleagues who had learned tea, though with different teachers, two practitioners talked about the extra hassle. "You always have to clean up before and after [the lesson]. That can take some time." Her neighbor agreed, and she continued, "You have to take everything out of all the boxes and then put them back. There's even a special way of tying the bows. It's such a pain." For this, her neighbor offered an explanation: "But you know, people use to do that all the time. When I was younger, my grandmother would always take out all the different dishes for the New Year's holidays, or even when guests came. And then we would have to put them back afterward. In the past, it was just assumed that's the way it was." "Yeah, but now it's a pain to do," came the reply. See Kumakura, "Reexamining Tea," on the historical importance of boxes in the tea ceremony (7–13).

33. Though taken to an extreme in the tea ceremony, a focus on boxes and proper storage is common in other areas of Japanese society. The original cardboard boxes for appliances or electronics are often retained, and the paper advertisement wrapped around many books carefully preserved. Wooden boxes are still used to encase exquisite objects even outside tea contexts, lending a sense of the exceptional to the objects inside. Although the practice was more widespread in the past, expensive kimono accessories and fine pieces of pottery, for example, may still be housed in cedar containers, similar to those encasing tea utensils.

34. In this matrix of Japanese space, a framed picture is as rarely found as a scroll affixed to a white plaster wall. Even in the early twentieth century, when department stores began selling Western-style paintings for interior decoration, these were hung above the alcove—between the lintel and the ceiling—rather than within it. See Sand, *House and Home*, 123.

35. Standardization is encouraged by the industry of tea utensil makers and dealers—shops can be found even in small towns—that supply a common range of implements used for practice, and a small number of unique, high-quality wares.

Urban centers host a select set of elite dealers, some without storefronts, who trade solely in rarities worth thousands of dollars.

36. Numerous tea utensil catalogues and books—images accompanied by historical explanations—provide further study opportunities for students and teachers, and the most dedicated will seek out the originals housed in museums.

37. As one practitioner explained, "If the guest doesn't know about history, then it's not interesting. If you see, for example, that the scroll is by [a famous historical leader], then you should know that he retired to Kumamoto and took up drawing. That is then referenced in the choice of the incense container using *higo* inlay, which Kumamoto is famous for. This is all just the assumed background knowledge. You need to have a deep understanding of Japanese history and art history to truly enjoy utensils."

38. *Kokoro no Nooto*, 124. This book, distributed for free by the government, was commissioned in response to what was seen as a decline in youth morality, but textbooks without such explicitly moral motivations typically contain passages about Japan's "unique" four seasons.

39. Ogasawara, *Utsukushii Furumai*, text edition, 176.

40. See Kondo, *Crafting Selves*, for a piquant description of how seasonal awareness is nonetheless interwoven into everyday life (241–44).

41. See Fujitani, *Splendid Monarchy*, on the Meiji era negotiations that established Kyoto as the symbol of the past and Tokyo as that of the present and future (31–92).

42. The focus on utensils increases with the exclusivity of a tea gathering, and some of the most elite are organized around the creative display of antiques so valuable they are not even used—guests simply enter the tea rooms to take in the discriminating arrangement. Tea is imbibed elsewhere, as an accessory to the implements.

43. Even common references can be dexterously manipulated for the delight of guests, as occurred at a large gathering in Tokyo, where the host had hung an image and poem from the *Tale of Genji* in the alcove, setting this as the theme of the gathering. As she read the scroll, she talked about the literary masterpiece, mentioning a key scene in which the lead character lands in the village of Suma during inclement weather. "Therefore I put the images of the gods of wind and thunder [a famous pair at shrines and in Rimpa design] in the waiting area," she explained, drawing an audible gasp from the practitioner beside me, moved by the subtlety of juxtaposition.

44. A designer I spoke to, who had begun tea lessons two years before, explained through national differences how this awareness sharpened: "The placement of utensils is very important. In the West, harmony is achieved when everything is the same. You use the same plates—maybe different sizes, but the same pattern. In Japan, harmony is derived through contrast. I first began to notice that as a fundamental difference when I started tea. The utensils come together through their differences, and by making sure they resonate together."

45. Holland, "Tea Records," provides a case study of how practitioners develop the toriawase for a gathering.

46. The following description is of the Urasenke school's procedures used in the warmer half of the year. Small details differ from school to school—whether a tatami is traversed lengthwise in four or six steps, for example—but the overall form and effect do not vary.

47. Though an economy of movement prevails, an overall economy of procedures does not, and the large number of actions required often seem like "too much work" to nonpractitioners, who may sarcastically query why the host can't just hurry up and make the tea.

48. Such seemingly superfluous convolutions are a frequent target of self-deprecating humor that picks at national stereotypes. This is witnessed in the video shorts *Nihon no Kata* (Japanese Forms) produced in 2006 for local consumption by the comedy team Japan Culture Lab. In a representative installment, viewers are instructed in how to eat sushi properly—grasped with three fingers, sloshed until drenched in the precise number of milligrams of soy sauce, and then tipped into the mouth with the head inclined at a 45-degree angle. Itami Jūzō's 1985 film *Tampopo* also plays on these associations in a scene in which a young, casually dressed man sits down to learn how to eat ramen from a wizened senior. When the ramen arrives, the youth hastily breaks apart his chopsticks, picks up the hot bowl, and utters "hot, hot, hot" as he prepares to dig into the soup. With great solemnity and decorum, the kimono-clad "ramen master" beside him proceeds to teach him the "proper" way to eat this dish employing abstruse rules, refined motions, and obscure aesthetic sensitivities. At the end of the instruction, the initiate pauses, then continues to slurp down the bowl.

49. See, for example, Ogasawara, *Utsukushii Furumai*, photo edition, 60–83.

50. Ibid., text edition, 130. The full chopstick discussion can be found on 130–34, and the images in the accompanying volume, Ogasawara, *Utsukushii Furumai*, photo edition, 62.

51. Less experienced men will often wear *hakama*, or a large, pants-like cover over the bottom of their kimono that enables them to spread their legs more widely. Men certified to teach usually wear a standard male kimono, whose shape closely resembles that of the more familiar women's kimono.

52. The *Kōjien* dictionary offers a similar definition as its fourth: "the pauses or interval between phrases that produce rhythm in Japanese music and dance, and the like."

53. Ogasawara, *Nihonjin no Reigi*, 218.

54. Others have written popular tracts on the way *ma* structures other practices, including calligraphy and Noh theater. On calligraphy, see Mukai, "Characters That Represent"; and on Noh theater, see Kenmochi, *Ma no Nihon Bunka*.

55. As one teacher explained, "*Ma* is very important in the tea ceremony, and in Japanese culture. It's the space between two actions. A pause, but not an empty time, not simply a pause. It's when you are preparing for the next action. In *kagetsu* [a training game typically involving five people] you learn to synchronize intervals.

When you replace the silk cloth in the kimono belt, everyone does it together." She demonstrated by taking out a silk cloth and folding it, pausing momentarily after running her hand down the middle of the straightened sides, before replacing it in her belt.

56. At one lesson where an esoteric temae was taught, the teacher corrected a student who handled the implements with swift efficiency: "This procedure is about the utensils. You must create a mood that makes the guest focus on them by projecting respect [for the utensils]. You need to think about how important that tea caddy is and let your body move in that way. As your hand moves close to it, you should immediately change due to its importance."

57. Later in the same lesson, the teacher corrected the student as she wiped the tea scoop: "You need to watch it when you take your hand away, otherwise the guests will feel uneasy. Not stopping, but doing it slowly is the most important." The teacher closed her eyes while she pointedly recited the steps to the student, whose gestures accompanied the words. In the course of the flow, eyelids suddenly flying open, she broke in, "Wait, you put that down too fast. Do it again."

58. See Befu, *Hegemony of Homogeneity*, 38–39; and Yoshino, *Cultural Nationalism*, 12–17, for discussions of nonverbal communication in Nihonjinron publications.

59. Fujiwara, *Kokka no Hinkaku*, 3. Over two million copies were sold in 2006.

60. See Yoshino, *Cultural Nationalism*, 9–38, for an analysis of the nationalist content—including the celebration of ambiguity—in business manuals. Ambiguity has a long history of distinctively Japanese associations, stretching as far back as the eighteenth century when scholars of the Native Learning school (*kokugaku*) drew contrasts between the logical, sharp distinctions of the Chinese and an embrace of the in-between and ambiguous as a distinctively Japanese sentiment. See Ikegami, *Bonds of Civility*, 221–22, 232–34.

61. This includes not only how things are expressed, but word choice as well. Tea practitioners in Tokyo will occasionally speak with a slight Kyoto lilt, with endings from the Kyoto dialect, such as *-te haru*, otherwise rarely heard in the capital.

62. A recent addition to this genre, for example, claims that this orientation to the local variant of hospitality is increasing as more people are "placing the utmost importance on Japanese things" (Chiba and Gotō, *Omotenashi no Genryū*, 7).

63. Some teachers regularly articulate such a concern, warning students overzealously tapping off the tea, "There should be no sound at all! The guests will notice if you're not careful—you must not make them feel anxious."

64. Even high school students may recognize this, as did one who explained that "thinking about others" was the most important thing she learned through tea lessons. Her classmate repeated the response and added, "It's not just about making tea and putting it out, but making tea in a way that will make the other person feel relaxed. I think about my movements now, and my mother has begun to notice it as well, like when I set things out with two hands." She immediately went on to indicate the success of the cultivation by attesting, "I feel like I've grown up a bit."

65. "Chanoyu Dezain," 8. Such images resonate outside the tea world, though sometimes with a more critical nuance, expressed by one cab driver who said, "I've never done the tea ceremony, but I like the idea behind it—serving tea with all of one's heart. That sort of hospitality is the Japanese spirit. But now it's been forced into a ceremony and turned into just a bunch of rules."

66. The presence of a foreigner can encourage the express articulation of these national associations, as was illustrated at an all-men's lesson. The youngest in the group began drinking the tea without offering the scripted apology to the next guest, and the teacher chided him, "You make tea by opening your heart to others, you know." The young man replied, "I have!" to which an older student responded with teasing that incorporated my presence as a foreign woman in the room: "But you don't have any love." The young man then forgot the next greeting as well, neglecting to offer the bowl of tea to the guest who had just drunk. "Want another cup [mō ippai]?" he asked, drawing the eyes of the other students to him as they let out a unison, "huuh?" The teacher immediately corrected, "You mean, 'another bowl' [mō ippuku], right?" employing the rather archaic term standard in tea practice. One of the students laughed, "He seems to be learning Japaneseness," but another chided, "He's really a bad Japanese." The young man responded cheerfully by embracing the joke, "I'm the champion of the bad Japanese!" eliciting a round of laughter from everyone. His inattentive behavior illustrates through infraction how someone Japanese can be projected as a better Japanese through mastery of the tea ceremony—one sensitive to the relational positioning of others, a collective morality of Japaneseness.

67. Yet more is at work than a simple opposition. Toilets can illustrate this complexity. In public spaces these often appear in two kinds, "Japanese style" and "Western style," though the latter are hardly identical to the range of variation found in the West. Indeed, many Westerners traveling to Japan for the first time are taken aback by the numerous buttons and options—even sinks—that are attached to the "Western" toilets they find. Over time, these variants have become creolized and normalized (almost all new houses have "Western" toilets), etiolating their sense of otherness. That sense was not yet lost when Tanizaki in *In Praise of Shadows* could extol the elegance of what would now be considered a traditional Japanese privy, in contrast to the Western varieties then beginning to enter Japan.

68. The choice of "she" is deliberate here. While all adult members of the nation might be held accountable for basic knowledge of what are defined as national traditions, women are more frequently charged with the actual task of reproducing national culture and therefore are more likely targets of actual questioning and may feel the actual burden more strongly, a theme addressed in Chapters 2 and 4.

*Chapter 2*

1. Evans in *Tea in China* provides an evocative account of tea consumption in Tang and Song China, on which this section draws (44–64).

2. According to a mid-fifteenth-century writer, a man of "tea discrimination" is one "who keeps tea utensils in beautiful condition, and who loves and possesses,

according to his own tastes, such objects as *tenmoku* [Chinese] tea bowls, kettles, and water buckets" (quotation in Murai, "Development of *Chanoyu*," 21). Here it is striking that the utensil handling and connoisseurship trumps any refinement of the palate. Other texts, such as Murata Shukō's "Letter of the Heart," devoted much attention to the taste for Chinese wares (*karamono*) and how they could be used in pleasing combination with Japanese wares (*wamono*). This and other primary material can be found in the valuable collection of transliterated documents in Kumakura et al., *Shiryō ni yoru*.

3. See Murai, "Development of *Chanoyu*," for an overview of the early history of tea in Japan, as well as Sen, *Japanese Way of Tea*, 47–115. See Kramer, "Tea Cult in History," on the Ashikaga (15–18).

4. On sixteenth-century tea practice, see Berry, *Culture of Civil War*, 259–85; Slusser, "Transformation of Tea Practice"; and Tanihata, *Kinsei Chadōshi*. This trend was part of the broader spread of aestheticized sociability beyond aristocratic circles in the upheavals following the Onin War (1467–1477). Professional artists who had served Kyoto's elite were driven outside the capital to find new audiences and enthusiasts. The subsequent economic prosperity of the late sixteenth and early seventeenth centuries led to an increased demand for training in "elegant pastimes" (*yūgei*) that cut across class boundaries, from samurai to peasants. Not only artistic practices but also aesthetic sensibilities and standards of refined comportment followed this path of transmission from aristocrats to warriors and down to commoners. On this transmission, see Ikegami, *Bonds of Civility*, 112–13; and Varley, "*Chanoyu*: From the Genroku Epoch," 163. Even outside formal gatherings, tea preparation was an essential element of hospitality in Japan, noticed by European travelers in the mid-fifteenth and early sixteenth centuries. Jesuits establishing forward bases on the archipelago and, as elsewhere, attentive to local customs even set up their own tea rooms and hired tea masters as standard etiquette when receiving guests.

5. Berry in *Culture of Civil War* provides a lively account of these gatherings, based on an analysis of the diaries tea connoisseurs kept (262, 269–79). See also Kumakura, "Reexamining Tea," 36–39; and Tanihata, *Kinsei Chadōshi*, 501.

6. The wabi aesthetic, first elaborated in treatises on poetry and Noh theater of the Muromachi era, valued restraint, imperfection, and simplicity. But it was in the tea ceremony that it achieved a practical form, enacted both in tea preparation itself and in the design of the tea room, of which precursors were to be found in ascetic hut-like retreats in the city that emerged in the wake of the Onin Wars. See Haga "*Wabi* Aesthetic," 201; Murai "The Development of *Chanoyu*," 26. Contemporaneous progress in other crafts should also be borne in mind, as tea masters incorporated into their *Gesamtkunstwerk* developments in landscape architecture, ceramics, and flower arrangement. With wamono objects celebrated for their aesthetic of austerity and imperfection, a tea gathering could take place without expensive Chinese rarities. But soon export industries on the Korean peninsula and in China developed, followed quickly by a thriving trade in domestically produced import substitutions. These enabled tea aficionados to develop personal collections of both

wamono and karamono implements that they could creatively combine at their gatherings. As such, Guth in "Import Substitution" proposes that the seemingly ascetic wabi tea indeed represented a "radical ideology of consumption," instantiating what in Bourdieuian terms can be called "ostentatious poverty" (56).

7. Both translations appear in Cooper's vivid analysis of foreign observations of tea and tea preparation in "Early Europeans and Tea," 121–22, 124–26.

8. Amino Yoshihiko has written extensively on mu'en. See, inter alia, Amino, *Sōhō Mu'en*. In her analysis of the tea diaries of the time, Berry discusses the extent of mixing, with social hierarchies often disassembled in the hierarchy of guests at a gathering. See Berry, *Culture of Civil War*, 265–67.

9. See Slusser, "Transformation of Tea Practice," for a Bourdieuian analysis of these relations. As Ikegami has shown in *Bonds of Civility*, the tea ceremony during the Momoyama and beginning of the Tokugawa eras resembled other group-based (*za*) arts of the time, such as linked poetry, which provided a venue for a caste-cutting "aesthetic sociability" within an otherwise rigid status order. While the Tokugawa shogunate repressed political association, it did not have the institutional infrastructure to thoroughly police society, and therefore tolerated the growth of horizontal networks in the performing and polite arts, themselves propelled by economic growth, urbanization, improved transport and communications systems, and print culture. In the resulting "network revolution," energies denied political expression found form in aesthetic activities. These liberating spaces of mu'en brought together prosperous commoners, bored samurai, monks, and even villagers around artistic pursuits, cultivating an aesthetic sensibility that made beauty an instinctive value in a broad swathe of the populace.

10. Bodart, "Tea and Counsel," 50. See Watsky, "Commerce, Politics, and Tea," for an analysis of the relationship between Nobunaga and Sōkyū and a discussion of how this once most powerful tea master was superseded by Rikyū when Hideyoshi succeeded to power.

11. On the ways Nobunaga interwove aesthetic pleasures and military conquest, see Lamers, *Japonius Tyrannus*; and Tanihata, *Kuge Chadō*, 48–57.

12. Quotation in Ikegami, *Bonds of Civility*, 122.

13. For insightful histories of Nobunaga's and Hideyoshi's tea practice, see Watsky, "Commerce, Politics, and Tea"; Slusser, "Transformation of Tea Practice"; and Bodart, "Tea and Counsel"; as well as Tanihata, *Kuge Chadō*, 48–77.

14. Quotation in Kumakura, "Kan'ei Culture and *Chanoyu*," 37. Plutschow, *Rediscovering Rikyu*, offers a biography of this figure.

15. The reasons for Hideyoshi's order remain the subject of much musing and mythologizing, but it seems likely that as the target of his military ambitions moved from Kansai to Kyushu and then toward Korea, so did the requisite power networks—realignments that disfavored Rikyū, who had potentially grown too powerful. On this, as well for as an overview of Rikyū's relationship with the hegemon, see Bodart, "Tea and Counsel."

16. See Tanimura, "Tea of the Warrior"; and Varley, "*Chanoyu*: From the Genroku Epoch" on daimyo tea and the transformations of this period.

17. Omotesenke was affiliated with the Kii branch of the Tokugawa house, Mushanokōjisenke with the Takamatsu domain, and Urasenke with the Maeda house of the Kanazawa domain.

18. Wilson even notes, in "Rethinking Nation," that many in the upper strata did not see themselves as part of the same ethnic grouping as those of lower status (4–5).

19. On the de-militarization and artistic training of samurai, see Ikegami, *Bonds of Civility*, 142; and Tanimura, *Ii Naosuke*, 13–49; and on *meikun* and tea ceremony, see Varley, "*Chanoyu*: From the Genroku Epoch," 169, 170; and Tanimura, "Tea of the Warrior," 140–41.

20. See Pitelka, *Handmade Culture*, 136. On Fumai and tea, see Kumakura et al., *Shiryō ni yoru*, 417–21; Kumakura, *Mukashi no Chanoyu*, 156–63; and Kramer, "Tea Cult," 175–79.

21. On Sadanobu's aestheticism, see Screech, *The Shogun's Painted Culture*; and on his relationship to tea, see Tanihata, *Kinsei Chadōshi*, 242–44; Varley, "*Chanoyu*: From the Genroku Era," 170–72; and the materials in Kumakura et al., *Shiryō ni yoru*, 430–35.

22. Indeed, twenty-one out of the twenty-three chapters constituting his *Ichie Isshū* concern the etiquette of tea preparation. Tanimura, *Ii Naosuke*, provides the most extensive account of Naosuke's tea practice. Though a prominent example of the development of strata-crossing artistic activities in the Momoyama era, it is noticeable that the tea ceremony does not figure in Ikegami's list of aesthetic practices facilitating the emergence of horizontal networks—logically, given the use of chanoyu to reinforce rather than cross social divisions by mid-Tokugawa. See Ikegami, *Bonds of Civility*, 370.

23. See Tanihata, *Kinsei Chadōshi*, 245, 271. In this period merchants too could be expected to be well versed in the other arts, including poetry composition, flower arrangement, music, and dancing; see Ikegami, *Bonds of Civility*, 143.

24. For lively examples of such criticism, see Varley, "*Chanoyu*: From the Genroku Era," 171–72, 174–75; and Kramer, "Tea Cult," 59, 74.

25. See Graham, *Tea of the Sages*, for the most thorough treatment of sencha in English; see also Kramer, "Tea Cult," 78–87. In Japanese, see Ōtsuki, *Sencha Bunkakō*.

26. Graham, *Tea of the Sages*, 4, 96, 115, 168.

27. As Kramer notes in "Tea Cult," "the lack of any outstanding political connection either with the bakufu or with the Meiji leaders in a narrative of *sencha* history in Japan indicates why there has been such enormous interest in the topic of *matcha* in the latter half of the sixteenth century" (83).

28. See Corbett, "Learning to Be Graceful," for a pioneering examination of Tokugawa-era women's tea practice. Kagotani, *Josei to Chanoyu*, provides short biographies of twelve women who practiced tea between the sixteenth and twentieth centuries.

29. See Nagatomo's modern reprint of Namura Jōhaku, *Onna Chōhōki* and *Nan Chōhōki* (21–22, 266–75).

30. Lindsey, *Fertility and Pleasure*, discusses the role of these lifestyle guides in allowing commoners access to elite worlds (10–12, 14).

31. Corbett, "Learning to Be Graceful," 83.

32. Among the male criticisms of the practice, the historical record does not indicate any complaints of the intrusion of women, as would become common in the twentieth century. Precise numbers are hard to come by, but the records of the Yabunouchi school provide an indication. Between 1801 and 1879, a total of 1,678 new students were recorded, and of these 25 were women. Though is possible that in some cases the name of a male family member was recorded when female students took up study, the figures suggest the overwhelming predominance of men. Figures cited in Hayashiya, *Zuroku Chadōshi*, 558.

33. This is the argument Ikegami presents in her sweeping account of aesthetics and civil society in Tokugawa Japan. She notes that a German visitor arriving in Japan in the late seventeenth century was so impressed by the cultivation of manners among all levels of society, "from the meanest countryman to the greatest Prince or Lord," that he even wrote that "the whole Empire might be called a School of Civility and good manners." See Ikegami, *Bonds of Civility*, 20. In Europe, the more popular notion of civility triumphed over courtesy, or comportment at court, only with the spread of bourgeois culture.

34. Ikegami, *Bonds of Civility*, 24, 140–41, 231. "Native Learning" (*kokugaku*) scholars laid some of the groundwork for such nationalizing articulations, but their writings were produced and consumed only by a minority, with not nearly the breadth of impact of the popular networks of aesthetic practice. For analyses of kokugaku, see Harootunian, *Things Seen and Unseen*; and Burns, *Before the Nation*.

35. Kido, *Diary*, 80–81, 94, 96, 120. In retirement, he constructed a tea room in the gardens of his residence.

36. For a trenchant account of this collapse, see Anderson, *Lineages of the Absolutist State*, 458–61.

37. Translation in Guth, *Art, Tea, and Industry*, 94. See Guth's book for an incisive analysis of Masuda Takashi and the world of businessman tea he anchored, which remains a touchstone in sukisha research. See also Kumakura, *Kindai Chadōshi*, 193–270.

38. In Guth, *Art, Tea, and Industry*, 130; see also 129.

39. However, it was often difficult for sukisha to lay their hands on famous utensils associated with Nobunaga and Hideyoshi, even into the early twentieth century, as many former daimyo families held on to these assets. Guth, *Art, Tea, and Industry*, 89–90; see also Kumakura, *Kindai Chadōshi*, 244–51.

40. The Daishikai, in fact, was named after the ninth-century founder of the Shingon Buddhist sect, Kōbō Daishi, and was first held to display Buddhist relics. Initially regarded with a wary eye, the exhibition of such artifacts in a tea setting would eventually be praised as a creative adaptation of fine objects in line with the freedom of tea in the Momoyama era. See Guth, *Art, Tea, and Industry*, 100–128, on the Daishikai.

41. Masuda's utensil choices, for example, more commonly derived from the in-

fluence of Enshū's ornate daimyo tea rather than the somber wabi style promoted by Rikyū.

42. Guth makes this point in *Art, Tea, and Industry*, 129.

43. The term used for "taste," *shumi*, conveyed a sense of connoisseurship and cultivation, and—in the bourgeois ideology of the time—individual expression. Contributors to the popular eponymous journal identified its cultivation as a national problem, which they attempted to rectify by developing a "Japanese taste" in contradistinction to Western sensibilities. On *shumi* in general, see Sand, *House and Home*, 95–103. On taste and sukisha, see Kumakura, *Kindai Chadōshi*, 18.

44. Quotation in Tanaka, *Chadō Kairyōron*, 15.

45. Takahashi, "Oraga Chanoyu," 441. Takahashi stressed that doing tea is an end in itself. "A person may read Moto'ori Norinaga for moral, religious, or quotidian reasons, but when he looks at a cherry tree, he's not thinking about firewood. If one enjoys tea as a connoisseur, secondary considerations are unnecessary. . . . I don't follow a particular school, so there are no boring, strict, severe rules." He ended by asserting that tea is not about morality or loyalty to the emperor, but fundamentally about taste. Quotation in Kumakura et al., *Shiryo ni yoru*, 475–76.

46. Tanaka, *Chadō Kairyōron*, 68–72. See also the discussion of the debate in Kumakura, "Chadōron no Keifu," 34–39.

47. Takahashi, "Chanoyu," 680.

48. Takahashi, *Chadō*, 100.

49. See Doak, *History of Nationalism*, on the early years of the variegated development of a modern national conceptualization (36–82).

50. On the debates waged and consensus struck during nation-formation, see Gluck, *Japan's Modern Myths*; and Doak, *History of Nationalism*. See McClintock, *Imperial Leather*, on the use of familial iconography—a trope that allows a hierarchy to be reestablished within a putative organic unity—to imagine the nation in other contexts.

51. Mackie, *Feminism in Modern Japan*, 25; and Nolte and Hastings, "Meiji State Policy," 157. Secondary school attendance reveals a high, though declining, attrition rate, with about 70,000 girls attending high school in 1910 (Inagaki, *Jogakkō to Jogakusei*, 184).

52. Translation in Jansen, *Making of Modern Japan*, 406.

53. See Gluck, *Japan's Modern Myths*, 102–56.

54. On the development of women's education, see Nolte and Hastings, "Meiji State Policy." See Koyama's *Ryōsaikenbo to Iu Kihan* and *Katei no Seisei* for analyses of the "good wives and wise mothers" standard.

55. Translation in Mackie, *Feminism in Modern Japan*, 25.

56. Translation in Czarnecki, "Bad Girls from Good Families," 51.

57. Quotation in Kobayashi, "Kyoiku toshite no Hana," 139.

58. Offering an example is the manual by Yoshimori Kingo, *Kokumin Sahō Yōgi* (123–26).

59. These arguments are based on a sample of thirty instructional books published between 1890 and 1919 (ten textbooks per decade) drawn from the Meiji- and

Taisho-era collections in the National Diet Library. While the process by which books enter the library's collection is unclear, there is no indication of a selection bias that would affect arguments concerning gender and national framings.

60. Watanabe, *Nihon no Reishiki*, introduction; Kondo, *Gengo Sahō*, 1–2.

61. Kondo, *Gengo Sahō*, 1–2.

62. Tsuboya, *Nihon Joreishiki*, 1–2.

63. On these debates, see Pyle, *New Generation*, 53–75.

64. Seikōkan, ed., *Katei Komon*, introduction.

65. Uno, *Katei no Takara*, introduction.

66. Matsui, *Fujo no Shiori*, 1.

67. Ikeda, *Joshi no Ōkoku*, 1.

68. On women's education and household management, see Tipton, "How to Manage a Household"; and Sand, *House and Home*, 55–62.

69. Tsuboya, *Nihon Joreishiki*, 347.

70. While some historians locate the feminization of the practitioner base of the tea ceremony in the Taisho era (see, for example, Kumakura, *Kindai Chadōshi no Kenkyū*, 303–4), the number of extant manuals suggests it may have came earlier. The frequency of explanations such as "while the tea ceremony is a path once followed by the samurai, now it is something that women learn" suggests that even by the first years of the twentieth century a feminized image could be taken for granted.

71. *Katei Setsuyō*, 172–73; Teikoku Fujin Gakkai, *Fujoshi no Honbun*, 216–17; Kobayashi, *Fujin Shjūyō to Jissai*, 102–3.

72. For an examination of the role of fūryū in the formation of a distinctively Japanese literary canon at the time, see Mostow, "Modern Constructions," 106–7.

73. Kumakura et al., *Shiryo ni yoru*, 457–58. This use of tea as a means of cultivating good subjects echoes earlier writings by Chikushin (1678–1745), a Confucian scholar adopted into the Yabunouchi tea family, who wrote that "for ordinary people of the towns and villages in our country, the way of tea is superior to both Confucianism and Buddhism as a path for learning the way to serve one's lord and to associate with friends" (quotation in Varley, "*Chanoyu*: From the Genroku Era," 177).

74. Kobayashi, *"Hana" no Seiritsu*, 237. Kobayashi has carried out the most thorough historical research on tea instruction at girls' schools, and her multi-sited fieldwork has unearthed much evidence countering the common assertions that tea practice spread through the school system due largely to the efforts of the iemoto, and that women began to take up the practice en masse in the 1920s.

75. Inagaki, *Jogakkō to Jogakusei*, 185–86.

76. Quotation in Kobayashi, "Shokominchi Taiwan no Kōtō Jogakkō," 2.

77. See ibid. for a path-breaking study of tea training at girls' schools in Taiwan under Japanese imperial rule.

78. Quotation in Kobayashi, "Kyoiku toshite no Hana," 32.

79. See Sato, *The New Japanese Woman*, on empowerment and subversion through women's magazines during the early twentieth century (78–113); and Sato, "Commodifying and Engendering Morality," on the role of these magazines in promoting self-cultivation among the burgeoning middle classes (99–130).

80. Examples include Ono, "Chanoyu no Kokoro"; and Kameyama, "Meiki."

81. Ōuchi, "Nihon no Cha."

82. "Ryokucha Manwa."

83. Quotation in Kumakura, *Kindai Chadōshi*, 312–13.

84. See ibid., 173–91. The effect of his structural reforms was largely cosmetic. The position of the president has since been passed down to the first son in the family in iemoto style, and its holder treated with the same regard as other iemoto.

85. Quotation in Kumakura, *Kindai Chadōshi*, 177.

86. See, for example, the collected essays published in 1987 by Tanka Senshō under the title *Chadō Kairyōron*.

87. Ibid., 9.

88. Ibid., 12.

89. These ideas were set out in a 1936 essay published in *Nihon no Chadō*. See Tanaka, *Chadō Kairyōron*, 9–13.

90. See also Tanaka Hidetaka, *Kindai Chadō*, for a penetrating analysis of Tanaka Senshō's nationalist efforts, penned by his grandson (28–34, 350–60).

91. For Okakura's career as a bicultural dilettante, competent in both Japanese and American society, but fully comfortable in neither, preferring the shock effect of inhabiting a creatively crafted Japanese persona in the United States and a Western personae in Japan, see Notehelfer, "On Idealism and Realism."

92. On this little-read text, see Notehelfer, "On Idealism and Realism," 330.

93. Okakura, *Ideals of the East*, 1, 244.

94. Ibid., 5.

95. The success of these books abroad is no less due to the globe-trotting authors' use of Western conceptual categories. On Nitobe's Western idioms, see Morris-Suzuki, *Re-Inventing Japan*, 68–69; for Okakura's, see Duara, "Discourse of Civilization," 75–76.

96. Okakura, *Book of Tea*, 31–32. The formulation inverts Nitobe's famous description of *bushidō* as the "Art of Death."

97. Ibid., 30.

98. Ibid., 29.

99. On the foreign reception of *The Book of Tea*, see Benfey, *Great Wave*, xvii–xviii, 106–7, 268. Tanaka, *Kindai Chadō*, provides an extensive analysis of nationalism in Okakura's writings, as well as in the work of other intellectuals in the early twentieth century (121–231).

100. Takahashi, *Chadō*, 306–7.

101. Ibid., 306. See Tanaka, *Kindai Chadō*, 62–64.

102. Although his given name was Muneyoshi, Yanagi was generally known by the alternative reading of the characters, Sōetsu. On Yanagi, see Kikuchi, *Japanese Modernization*; for a penetrating investigation of the tensions running through his thought, see Brandt, *Kingdom of Beauty*.

103. Yanagi, *Cha to Bi*, 130.

104. See Tanaka, *Kindai Chadō*, on the role of such national understandings in Yanagi's writings on tea (292–315).

105. Quotation in Kumakura, *Kindai Chadōshi*, 27.

106. Both quotations in Tanaka, *Kindai Chadō*, 70–71.

107. For a history of this department and the JTB, see Leheny, *Rules of Play*, 58–71.

108. Fukukita, *Tea Cult of Japan*, 12.

109. Tea utensils were on display at the Paris Exhibition of 1878, but it is unclear whether a tea performance was included as well. See Guth, *Tea, Art, and Industry*, 36.

110. "Sadō no Reijō."

111. "Chanoyu no Yōkō," *Asahi Shinbun*, February 28, 1933, 2.

112. See also Kumakura, *Kindai Chadōshi*, 305; and Pitelka, *Handmade Culture*, 155–56.

113. The centrality of intellectuals in gluing a national veneer onto cultural practices is also discussed by Ferguson in her analysis of the development of French cuisine in *Accounting for Taste*.

114. Duara, "Discourse of Civilization," and McClintock, "'No Longer in a Future Heaven,'" also describe the complementary yet fraught gendered division of labor in constructing and symbolizing the nation.

## Chapter 3

1. See Rath, *Ethos of Noh*, 116–18, on the legal transformations, and Ooms, *Tokugawa Ideology*, 60–62, on the deification of Ieyasu.

2. These family ties, however, are hardly straightforward. The early bloodlines were complicated, and the tradition was not passed down to the eldest son—the person who in most cases would continue the main family line. Sōtan, Rikyū's grandson, was the child of Shōan, the son of Rikyū's second wife and a different father. It is alleged that Sōtan's mother was Rikyū's daughter, Okamae, though historical evidence is weak. Rather than through Doan, his biological son, Rikyū's line was passed down through Shōan, his adopted son, and on to his child, Sōtan, who had four sons. The eldest chose not to continue in the tea business, which was divided among his three younger brothers, who became the heads of Mushanokōjisenke, Omotesenke, and Urasenke.

3. And when, much later, they did—as with the Dainihon Sadō Gakkai in 1898—their leaders invariably justified their new beginnings as a return to the original teachings of Rikyū. No upstart school, however, was ever to dominate the field.

4. In traditional poetry, a successor was selected from among the most accomplished students, whereas in archery and etiquette the oldest son inherited the leadership position. Though female iemoto can today be found in flower arrangement, all of the iemoto in Noh theater are men. In Japanese dance (*Nihon buyō*), accomplished practitioners may establish themselves as new iemoto, but the number of iemoto in incense enjoyment is limited to two. Under the Tokugawa, iemoto could be found in Shinto, Buddhist, and Confucian practices; in such arts as calligraphy, singing, poetry, and painting; and in games such as igo and shogi. See Bellevaire, "Japan: A Household Survey," on the historical emergence of the *ie* as a basic social unit, and Kumakura, "Iemoto Seika," for discussion of iemoto systems in general.

Nishiyama, *Iemoto no Kenkyū*, still provides the definitive account on iemoto systems in general.

5. See Smith, "Transmitting Tradition," for a descriptive overview.

6. See Nishiyama, *Iemoto no Kenkyū*, 381–89; and Pitelka, *Handmade Culture*, 89–109, on the consolidation of the iemoto system in the tea world; and Rath, *Ethos of Noh*, for the case in Noh theater.

7. On the relationship between popular texts and the codification of knowledge transfer, see Pitelka, *Handmade Culture*, 114.

8. Ibid., 94. On the spread of konomi, see Isozaki, *Japan-ness in Architecture*, 291–305.

9. See Pitelka, *Handmade Culture*, 102.

10. Pitelka's critical analysis in *Handmade Culture* deals extensively with the relationship between iemoto and utensil production, and on the Raku family in particular.

11. See Graham, *Tea of the Sages*, for a historical dissection of the sencha world.

12. Original in Tanaka, *Kindai Chadō*, 3; English translation in Kramer, "Tea Cult," 145. On how the various iemoto weathered these years, see Tsutsui, "Iemoto no Fukkō."

13. See Kumakura, *Kindai Chadōshi*, 303.

14. Ibid., 177–78. For a sense of the oeuvre, see his essays in Tanaka, *Kindai Chadō*.

15. See also Kato, *Tea Ceremony and Women's Empowerment*, on the importance of women in shoring up the power base of the iemoto, particularly following the Second World War (61–68).

16. See Guth, *Tea, Art, and Industry*, 4, 161.

17. The translation is of Section Five. The original is available online at www.j-texts.com/showa/kokutaiah.html.

18. See Tanaka, *Kindai Chadō*, 90–18, on the two tea gatherings; Guth, *Tea, Art, and Industry*, 70; and Kumakura, *Kindai Chadōshi*, 102, 110, on historical precedents in tea. For a history of the use of such spectacles in forging the Japanese nation, see Stefan Tanaka, *Japan's Orient*.

19. See Cross, *Ideologies of Japanese Tea*, 82–83.

20. Original in Tanaka, *Kindai Chadō*, 92.

21. Takeuchi, *Rikyū*, 2–3.

22. Cross, *Ideologies of Japanese Tea*, 103–4, discusses these publications.

23. On the development of the discourse of tea ceremony as a "cultural synthesis," see Kato, *Tea Ceremony and Women's Empowerment*, 71–99.

24. Sen, "Ningen Sonchō."

25. Sen, "Shinnen no Kotoba."

26. Sen, "Gochisō no Kokoro."

27. Indeed, an intensive course for foreigners—fully subsidized by the iemoto—was established in 1973 in order to train teachers to be dispatched across the world.

28. Sen, "Jo'ō Heika ni."

29. Sen, "Ichiwan no Kakehashi."

30. Sen, "'Shacha' no Deai"; Sen, "Hinshu Gokan."

31. Sen, "Hinshu Gokan."

32. Sen, "Tomo ni Heiwa o."

33. Currently, Urasenke's Tankōkai consists of 17 blocks containing 167 branches within Japan and 99 offices in thirty-five countries outside Japan. Omotesenke adopted this Rotary-based model in 1975, when the Dōmonkai became a corporation and opened its membership beyond teachers to include regular members. The Dōmonkai has since established 53 branches in Japan and 3 overseas.

34. Membership is difficult to estimate. According to the Shakai Keizai Seisansei Honbu's survey, *Reijaa Hakusho*, 2.3 million Japanese in 2006 claimed to practice the tea ceremony. Of these, about 710,000 participated in the ceremony at least two or three days a month, suggesting that they were taking lessons. Citing an anonymously written newspaper article from 1997, Pitelka, "Introduction to Japanese Tea Culture," puts Tankōkai membership at 300,000 (6), but this figure might be a bit higher. Given that Omotesenke had 114,000 Dōmonkai members in 2006 and Urasenke is between three and four times its size (see Mori, "The Tea Ceremony," 89), a rough estimate suggests that Tankōkai may count upward of 400,000 members.

35. Legally, tea schools fall under the purview of the Traditional Culture Section of the Cultural Properties Division of the Cultural Affairs Agency in the Ministry of Culture, Science, and Education. In exchange for generous tax breaks and financial assistance for the maintenance of assets considered Important Cultural Properties, the government may make demands on the schools, commonly requests from the Ministry of Foreign Affairs for tea gatherings in honor of foreign dignitaries.

36. See Bourdieu and Johnson, *Field of Cultural Production*, 75–76; and Bourdieu, *Rules of Art*, 141–76.

37. www.tankosha.co.jp/corp/index.html (accessed March 2009).

38. www.sabie-group.com/greeting/index.html (accessed March 2009).

39. www.sabie-group.com/business/kougei/index.html (accessed March 2009).

40. www.wanogakkou.com/aisatu.html (accessed March 2009).

41. www.urasenke.or.jp/textm/headq/recruit/wanogakko/wanogakko001/wanogakko001.html (accessed March 2009).

42. www.urasenke.ac.jp/school/gakuen/gakuen.html (accessed March 2009).

43. www.chado.or.jp/bunkakyokai/recruit/member.html (accessed March 2009).

## Chapter 4

1. Not only standard fare in textbooks and reference materials, family trees are even reproduced on the pocket calendars carried by many tea aficionados and on the small folding fans they always have to hand in the tea room. Teachers commonly ensure that students are versed in the lineage by selecting a different iemoto each month as the person who putatively carved the tea scoop used at lessons, thus encouraging students to memorize the dynastic succession over the course of the year. Sets of tea scoops made in each iemoto's style and bearing their source's name on the back connect lineage training to implement identification skills through a

pedagogical device that ensures the near impossibility of not committing to memory the chain linking the current iemoto to the ur-ancestor of chanoyu.

2. Such name-taking practices are common in other traditional arts as well.

3. Like Western dress, kimonos come in a variety of patterns and levels of formality, and the inappropriateness of wearing the bright, repetitive patterns of a *fudangi*—the casualwear of the kimono world—to a wedding, or a black *tomesode*, its sobriety interrupted only by a splash of color at the bottom hem, to a summer festival is clear. The most formal kimonos carry one, three, or five family crests. On kimonos, see Dalby, *Kimono*; and Goldstein-Gidoni, "Kimono."

4. While some teachers explicitly state the amount of "gift money" they expect on such occasions, most are oblique, relying on the student to query her seniors for information about the proper response to the name conferral—an opportunity to engage the hierarchy of adherents and confirm one's place within it.

5. The shift away from articulate explication may itself be verbally forewarned. One teacher cautioned two students about to receive their first instruction in upper-level procedures: "Look at the scroll and how it's written, how it is set. Look to the left very closely and notice what flowers are arranged there. Now that you are entering the upper levels, you must learn with your eyes. These deeper lessons build on what you learned before, but the instructions are not as explicit. You must watch very closely and learn with your eyes."

6. While an iemoto's signature or inscription can increase the monetary and prestige value of most utensils, extremely valuable historical antiques are an exception. In one practitioner's words, "With utensils like that, you don't need a signature. They're valuable enough on their own." A thin stratosphere of elite tea gatherings today—much like those of the sukisha of the past—bypasses this nod to recent iemoto in utensil selection, and relies on either the antique worth or the endorsements of more ancient figures to call forth their value.

7. A teacher I observed getting ready for a formal gathering cautioned a student against displaying a small piece of writing by an iemoto in the waiting area if she did not have a scroll by him in the tea space. "It would be an affront to put the iemoto here [in the waiting area] while hanging a scroll by any old monk in the main room."

8. Much of the time organizing a tea gathering—large or small—is spent acquiring such pieces through purchase or loans, with the stature of the main guest determining the appropriate rank of the utensils (and this, in turn, decided by the generation of the iemoto endorsing them, along with the prominence of the craftsman and sometimes the pedigree of prior ownership). If inviting a respected teacher to a tea gathering, the host will seek out such valued implements months in advance—an endeavor that is hardly cheap. Utensil shops keep down overall costs for their customers by buying back the utensils they sell, though at a cut in price, effectively renting out their wares. And these shops themselves are networked, circulating among themselves expensive utensils that have made an appearance at a large gathering but have returned to the store, or simply those that have sat on the shelf for more than six months. According to a utensil dealer I spoke with in Tokyo, the rule of thumb for an exceptional utensil that has debuted at a large gathering

and been bought back by the shop is that it spends ten years out in the countryside before returning to the metropolis.

9. At the headquarters this breach is contained by the assistants to the iemoto, who, with steely glances, note that "looking at the waterfall painted on the scroll should be enough to invoke the feeling of coolness." Recalling one of "Rikyū's Seven Rules" that commands adherents to bring forth a sense of the cool in summer and warm in winter, this injunction against surrender to the heat defends against the derogatory suggestion that the iemoto has not faithfully lived up to the edicts of his ancestor.

10. In taking part in the iemoto's service, practitioners may even overproject themselves as a part of the entourage. At one point during a kencha ritual in Nara, the emcee invited all participants in connection with the iemoto to stand. As his assistants rose, the tea practitioners in the audience began to hesitantly stand up as well—a false step quickly corrected by the anxious handwaving of the iemoto's aides.

11. Yet the shift in status can be difficult to maintain. At a kencha service I attended, the Mushanokōjisenke iemoto, rather than the host, controlled the conversation about the utensils. Breaking the tension that lay thick in the room (the man in charge of the service was so nervous that he sat blocking the entrance of the person preparing the tea and had to be told to move), the iemoto began with an inquiry about the flower vase—an asymmetrical, dark brown bamboo container with a large indentation on one side. Offering a comic cause of the aesthetically subtle asymmetry, he joked, "I have to ask about the flower vase. What was it, a car?" Laughter spread across the room, the shock value and clever temporal disjuncture overriding the atmosphere demanding polite restraint, as the host explained, blushing with embarrassment, that it came in a box signed by the grandson of Rikyū.

12. When an iemoto appears to transgress such boundaries, it is through a "strategy of condescension" that asserts his authority while bringing him momentarily to the same plane as practitioners, who simultaneously embrace the closeness while reaffirming his aura. See Bourdieu, *Language and Symbolic Power*, 124.

13. While the iemoto was waiting to go on stage to greet the local group, she explained: "The air conditioner was on, apparently ruffling his hair. He didn't say anything—he just looked up at it, and his assistant came over to us and told us to do something about it. What were we supposed to do? We had to go around to the building manager to try to figure out how to turn it off, which of course we couldn't."

14. For an overview of the Sekishū style of tea and its current practitioners, see Nomura, *Sekishūryū*.

15. The statistical data are drawn from the Shakai Keizai Seisansei Honbu's *Reijaa Hakusho*, carried out in 2001 and 2006. This nationwide study of 200,000 people in 80,000 households has been implemented every five years for over three decades by the statistics bureau of the Ministry of Internal Affairs and Communications. Since 1986, one question has been asked about participation in the tea ceremony. Though the raw numbers are not open to the public, tables are provided in published reports and online at www.stat.go.jp/english/data/shakai/index.htm. At the

time of writing, the figures from the 2006 survey were the most recent available. Prefectural-level breakdowns and information about incomes are accessible to the public only in the 2001 survey.

16. Unmarried women under fifty years of age are, on average, almost twice as likely to learn tea as married women. Wives who are childless are also are more likely to engage in the practice. Men, less burdened with the second shift, exhibit little such variation.

17. On the postwar changes in family patterns, see Ochiai, *Shinpan*.

18. Shakai Keizai Seisansei Honbu, *Reijaa Hakusho* (2001), www.stat.go.jp/english /data/shakai/index.htm.

19. Ibid. I was granted access to the Omotesenke membership figures in 2007.

20. On the early history of these bridal lessons, see Suzuki, "Taishō, Shōwashoki ni okeru Josei Bunka."

21. Ochiai, *Shinpan*, 47–48.

22. Their responses, as well as those of the younger women and men I spoke with, concur with those found by Kato, *Tea Ceremony and Women's Empowerment*, 150–93.

23. On the importance of self-improvement in the leisure activities of working men, see Mathews, "Can 'a Real Man' Live for His Family?"

24. In the words of one practitioner, dissatisfied with the laxness of her lessons, "My teacher has completely given up on me. The lessons are just easy fun, and she doesn't correct me any more. But to teach strictly takes a lot more energy from the teacher. Some get old and they don't have that any longer, or they give up on students like me."

25. On junior–senior relationships in other settings, see Ogasawara, *Office Ladies and Salaried Men*, for business offices; Kondo, *Crafting Selves*, for confectionary factories; and Haase, "Learning to Be an Apprentice," for pottery benches.

26. As she once reprimanded the class for moving too slowly, invoking the considerateness discussed in Chapter 1, "You have to calculate the time backward—you can't leave anything up to chance. Take, for example, the moist ashes [lining the sunken hearth]. You have to time it so that only the middle is a bit dry when the guests arrive. If you do it correctly, they'll be impressed. That sort of thing is showing consideration. There's no time to talk when preparing. With time, that becomes natural, though, and it comes into your everyday life. People who do tea have good timing in everyday life."

27. Some teachers instruct for longer stretches of five or six hours during which students will come and go as their schedules permit. A unison formal greeting is dispensed with in these cases without an official start time, but as at all tea lessons, each individual tea preparation begins with the student on deck making a formal bow and asking the teacher for instruction.

28. The suspended kettle requires extra care when ladling tea. As another teacher I observed once warned a student who set the pendulum swinging too hard, "You should invoke a breeze for your guests, not a gale-force wind!"

29. This can even become a source of momentary anxiety. At a summer lesson

when the heavens suddenly opened with rain, a student in the back room preparing the next temae let out an audible groan. "I was going to use 'water springing from stones' (*iwashimizu*)!" Her more advanced neighbor came swiftly to her aid: "Why not use 'rain from the bright sky' (*haku'u*)?"—a selection that garnered the immediate praise of the teacher.

30. Such self-conscious learning through observation is common in other traditional arts as well, and in some forms of training, the first year will be spent solely engaged in menial jobs—such as dishwashing for those aiming to become a kaiseki chef. Apprentices are expected to use the opportunity to observe and absorb as much as possible.

31. As another teacher explained to me, "With the tea ceremony, you watch and remember it. Eighty percent is watching and remembering, and then twenty percent is doing it yourself and learning. But watching is the most important, which is why when there is a new temae, you watch it first and then do it yourself."

32. The most orthodox tea instructors forbid notetaking under the stricture that everything must be learned through the body; still, many teachers encourage jottings to facilitate self-study. Though textbooks are available, the most diligent students copy down after class the various procedures learned, and check the following week with the teacher that they have in fact noted all the steps. In the words of one veteran, "If it's not my own writing, then I don't remember it. It's through writing and rewriting that you learn the procedure."

33. Though I was not directly involved in the interaction—I sat outside of the room and out of the participants' line of sight—and had been visiting the class for more than a year, my presence in the tea complex may have nonetheless encouraged the explicit references to Japaneseness that followed. This is less a complication for the present analysis, which concerns not *that* such marking is done, but rather *how* it is done. Other examples examined in this chapter and the next show that explicit references to Japaneseness are often made unprompted by even the ancillary attendance of foreigners, and are not merely an artifact of my presence.

34. Tabi covers protect the split-toed socks worn with a kimono.

35. In an interview, for example, an aging owner of a successful publishing house who studied tea with one of the high-ranking teachers assisting an iemoto described the utensils used at lessons and then added the praise, "He gives such detailed explanations; teachers out in the city don't do that sort of thing."

36. The ritual hand cleansing before entering a shrine is similar to that before entering a tea room.

37. These "Edo period manners" have received popular attention in recent years through an Edo etiquette book boom.

38. This trope extends far beyond the tea world. See Duara, "Regime of Authenticity"; Ueno, *Nashonarizumu to Jendaa*; and Yuval-Davis and Anthias, *Woman-Nation-State*, on women as bearers of national culture.

39. On this manner of national deixis, see Billig, *Banal Nationalism*, 94.

40. This government program, run from 2004 to 2007, was introduced to integrate children into their community by inviting local adults to give short lectures or

demonstrations at schools of their specialized knowledge or abilities. If a volunteer stepped forward, tea demonstrations were included as a part of the program.

41. Yamane, "Chadō to Watashi."
42. Wada, "Chadō to Deatte."
43. Ogawa, "Jibun ga Kawaru."
44. Suzuki, "Chadō wo Jugyō de."
45. Yanagita, "Chadō tōshite."
46. Ueda, "Shunpū ni Nabikareta."
47. Yanagita, "Chadō tōshite."
48. Ogawa, "Jibun ga Kawaru."
49. Noguchi, "'Dō.'"
50. Yamane, "Chadō to Watashi."

*Chapter 5*

1. Others have analyzed the importance of such institutions in disseminating national imaginings and creating a shared set of national referents. On museums, see Anderson, *Imagined Communities*, 178–85; on the radio, see Wedeen, *Peripheral Visions*, 42–49; and on newspapers, see Billig, *Banal Nationalism*, 111–19.

2. Examples include Inoue and Kasawara's 1980 *Yōsetsu Nihonshi*, 92; Hōgetsu's 1966 *Nihonshi*, 169; Inobe's 1937 *Shinshū Teikoku Shōshi*, 102; and Kunugi's 1912 *Kokutei Rekishi*, 173–74.

3. The English translation on the neighboring plaque renders this as "one of the world-renowned traditional cultures of Japan."

4. Other museums dedicated to the tea ceremony include the Uno Museum in Fukui Prefecture, the Tsugaru Museum in Aomori Prefecture, and the Kimura Museum in Niigata Prefecture.

5. Ivy, *Discourses of the Vanishing*, 29–65, provides an incisive analysis of exoticism as a spur for internal tourism in Japan.

6. Seasoned practitioners at the event sometimes comment that the corner-cutting spectacle is only a shadow of its true form. And even novices who, for the most part, may delight in the new experience, also recognize its abridgments. Such sensitivities do not undercut the ritual but produce "real tea" as a counter to what is happening in the present. See Shryock, "New Jordanian Hospitality." Indeed, the hostess at the Gion Corner even keeps on hand a photograph album of "real" gatherings to show interested visitors, as they whisk their bowls of tea, what the tea world is "really like."

7. At the two English-language performances I attended, I found as I mingled through the group that at least half of the audience were Japanese. Most explained their presence by pointing to a foreign visitor they had brought along to experience Japanese tradition or by citing a personal interest in learning how to explain Japanese culture in English.

8. The manga has received wide acclaim and was awarded the 2008 grand prize in the Tezuka Osamu Cultural Award manga competition, and the 2009 superior prize in the manga division at the Japan Media Arts Festival hosted by the Ministry of Culture.

9. Mori, *Shitte Tokusuru*, 12.

10. "'Kaiseki' to 'Kaiseki,'" 90.

11. "Onna o Kitaeru Okeiko Dō," 47.

12. Quotations in "Chanoyu Dezain," 30, 33, 35, 46, 54.

13. "Sen Rikyū no Kōzai," 32.

14. Quotations in "Chanoyu no Kokoro," 52.

15. This and the following exchanges are taken from my ethnographic observations in 2007 and 2008. Talk turned to the tea ceremony usually because I mentioned my research, and sometimes I followed up by asking the interlocutors about their impressions of it.

16. Consequently, scholarship on the practice is scanty, though see the volume edited by the Incense Culture Research Association, *Kōdō Bunka Kenkyūkai*, for an introduction, while Hata, *Kōsansai*, provides a more detailed history, albeit woven into a nationalist narrative.

17. On the twentieth-century trajectory of sumo, see Thompson, "Invention of the *Yokozuna*."

18. Hobsbawm, "Introduction: Inventing Traditions," 10.

19. Hobsbawm, for example, identifies "invented traditions" by distinguishing them from custom and routine ("Introduction: Inventing Traditions," 2–4), and Handler differentiates "objectified traditions" from unconscious lifeways, charting the shift of Quebecois folk dancing from the latter to the former (*Nationalism and the Politics of Culture*, 52–58).

20. Quotation in Frank, *Friedrich Ludwig Jahn*, 59. For a detailed review of Jahn's nationalist thought, see Kohn, "Father Jahn's Nationalism."

21. Quotation in Ueberhorst, *Friedrich Ludwig Jahn*, 39. While Jahn used the fraternity movement to promote his gymnastics, his centers were to be an alternative to schools—a "meeting-place for the whole of public life" (ibid., 66)—and therefore, unsurprisingly, the more systematic style of physical education laid out by Jahn's junior, Adolph Spieß, was incorporated into these institutions.

22. On the modes of masculinity cultivated by the gymnastics movement and other hobby associations in nineteenth- and early twentieth-century Germany, see Mosse, *Nationalization of the Masses*, 127–60, and for a detailed examination of Jahn's endeavors, see Ueberhorst, *Friedrich Ludwig Jahn* and *Züruck zu Jahn?*

23. Quotation in Goltermann, *Körper der Nation*, 66.

24. Quotations in Illig, *Zwischen Körperertüchtigung*, 475. As an article in the association's newspaper put it, "An enduring basis and ground should be found in the people, and, as such, the feeling of belonging together in a state is not to be aroused only through word and song, but the idea of the nation must also to some degree become embodied" (quotation in Goltermann, *Körper der Nation*, 274). See Goltermann, *Körper der Nation*, 66–69, for further discussion of national imaginings in *Turner* activities. Mosse, *Nationalization of the Masses*, gives participation figures. From 1893, the association met competition from the Workers Gymnastic League (Arbeiter-Turnerbund), which called for the overthrow of the authoritarian state (29).

25. Quotation in Illig, *Zwischen Körperertüchtigung*, 169.

26. Those entering the Turnhall in Nuremburg passed under a sign declaring "God protect this building with a strong hand / To the service and honor of the Fatherland." On the Bavarian gymnasia, see Illig, *Zwischen Körperertüchtigung*, 462–67.

27. Ibid., 353.

28. By the 1920s, the voice of the gymnastics movement, the *Turnerzeitung*, was even managing the official newspaper of the choir organization. On these close ties, see Mosse, *Nationalization of the Masses*, 147.

29. Figures in Van Dalen et al., *World History of Physical Education*, 213, 214.

30. See Mosse, *Nationalization of the Masses*, 132–35, on *Turner* activities during these years.

31. Linking him to Richard Wagner, Goebbels declared: "The desire of the Master of Bayreuth was to give spirit to the German nation, and the desire of Jahn was to coalesce German might" (Bernett, "Das Jahn-Bild," 134).

32. On the European spread of Jahn-inspired gymnastics, see Ueberhorst, *Friedrich Ludwig Jahn*, 85–95.

33. Nolte, *Sokol in Czech Lands*, provides a detailed and incisive analysis of the history of the Sokol and its role in Czech nationalist projects.

34. Quotation in Jandásek, "Sokol Movement," 73.

35. For a description, see Macháček, "Sokol Movement," 79.

36. There was not always a consensus on who this included, however, and as Nolte describes throughout *Sokol in the Czech Lands*, attitudes toward lower classes, later working classes, Jews, populations in borderlands, and Slavs in general varied in their inclusivity.

37. See Nolte, *Sokol in Czech Lands*, 158–62, on the international impact of the Sokols, as well as a vivid description of the 1907 Slet.

38. By 1930, there were over three thousand Sokol libraries stocking the works of the Sokol Publishing Company, as well as the collected works of Tyrš. A monthly, *Sokol*, hit the presses in 1871, and was accompanied afterward by several others, as well as a weekly that by 1930 had a circulation of forty thousand. Figures in Jandásek, "Sokol Movement," 71. The most popular topics in these publications and lectures were the history and ideology of the Sokols, but these were closely followed by items on Czech history, Hussite highpoints, and the gymnastic and aesthetic contributions of Greek civilization. See Nolte, "Our Task, Direction, and Goal," 48.

39. These greatly outnumbered the rival groups—the gymnastics associations established by the socialists and communists, in addition to the Catholic "Eagles." Figures in Jandásek, "Sokol Movement," 66, 71.

40. Quotation in Nolte, *Sokol in the Czech Lands*, 184.

41. On the decreasing salience of the nation in sports, see Poli, "Denationalization of Sport."

42. National spectacles in general—including parades and festivals—can be similarly characterized.

43. Training in this mode of combat is important, for, in the words of one doyen, the stave—also a classic of Indian police equipment—is essential for self-defense among the "world's foremost believers in non-violence." See Alter, "Somatic Nationalism," 567.

44. See Andersen and Damle, *Brotherhood in Saffron*, for an overview of the RSS, and Alter, "Somatic Nationalism," for its relationship to other forms of physical training in India. For a more critical assessment, see Basu et al., *Khaki Shorts*.

45. Golwalkar, in his collection of essays, *Bunch of Thoughts*, sets down the organization's mission: "Realizing the national character of Hindu People, the RSS has been making determined efforts to inculcate in them burning devotion for Bharat and its national ethos; kindle in them the spirit of dedication and sterling qualities and character; rouse social consciousness, mutual good-will, love and co-operation among them all; to make them realize that castes, creeds and languages are secondary and that service to the nation is the supreme end and to mold their behavior accordingly; instill in them a sense of true humility and discipline and train their bodies to be strong and robust so as to shoulder any social responsibility; and thus to create all-round *Anushasana* in all walks of life and build together all our people into a unified harmonious national whole, extending from Himalayas to Kanyakumari" (quotation in Sharma, *Encyclopedia of Eminent Thinkers*, 97–98).

46. Quotation in Sharma, *Encyclopedia of Eminent Thinkers*, 97–98.

47. Roy, *Beyond Belief*, offers a perceptive analysis of how the Indian state and other actors maintain a national self-concept of "unity in diversity" though banal channels.

48. On the political interpretations of opera in the Risorgimento, see Stamatov, "Interpretive Activism."

49. Quotation in Curtis, *Music Makes the Nation*, 156–57.

50. Wagner, "Vorwort zur Gesamtherausgabe," vii.

51. Wagner, "Über deutsches Musikwesen," 159.

52. Quotation in Curtis, *Music Makes the Nation*, 322.

53. See Pasler, *Composing the Citizen*, 515.

54. Ibid., 174–205, 308–24.

55. See Mosse, *Nationalization of the Masses*, 136–48.

56. On food, see Palmer, "From the Theory to Practice," 187–74; Cusack, "Pots, Pens and 'Eating Out the Body'"; and Appadurai, "Gastro-politics." On dance, see Daniel, *Rumba*; and Savigliano, *Tango*. On spectacles, see Spillman, *Nation and Commemoration*; and Roy, *Beyond Belief*, 66–104. On sports, see the contributions in Tomlinson and Young, *National Identity and Global Sports*; Fox, "Consuming the Nation," 225–31; and Ehn, "National Feeling in Sport." On landscapes, see Sears, *Sacred Places*; and Palmer, "From the Theory to Practice," 190–94. On built environments, see Waldron, "Representing China"; and Hagen, "Most German of Towns." On anthems and flags, see Cerulo, *Identity Designs*.

57. Postwar productions such as Harry Kupfer's "Laser Ring" of 1992—its sci-fi

costumes recalling *Bladerunner* more than ancient sagas—could be read as expressions of a postmodern Germany.

58. See, for example, Foster's analysis in *Materializing the Nation* of how a national identity has gained a foothold in even Papua New Guinea.

59. Duara provides a powerful argument on this division of labor in "Regime of Authenticity."

60. Weber, in his writings on the nation, was quick to point out the centrality of prestige in its creation. Weber, *Economy and Society*, 925–96.

61. Smith, "Limits of Everyday Nationhood," 571.

# Bibliography

Alter, Joseph S. "Somatic Nationalism: Indian Wrestling and Militant Hinduism." *Modern Asian Studies* 28 (1994): 557–88.

———. *The Wrestler's Body: Identity and Ideology in North India.* Berkeley: University of California Press, 1992.

Amino Yoshihiko. *Sōho Mu'en, Kugai, Raku: Nihon Chūsei no Jiyū to Heiwa.* Tokyo: Heibonsha, 1996.

Andersen, Walter K., and Shridhar D. Damle. *The Brotherhood in Saffron: The Rashtriya Swayamsevak Sangh and Hindu Revivalism.* London: Westview, 1987.

Anderson, Benedict. *Imagined Communities.* 2nd ed. London: Verso, 1991.

Anderson, Jennifer L. *An Introduction to Japanese Tea Ritual.* Albany: State University of New York, 1991.

Anderson, Perry. *Lineages of the Absolutist State.* London: Verso, 1974.

Appadurai, Arjun. "Gastro-politics in Hindu South Asia." *American Ethnologist* 8, no. 3 (1981): 494–511.

Balibar, Etienne. "Racism and Nationalism." In *Race, Nation, Class: Ambiguous Identities*, edited by Etienne Balibar and Immanuel Maurice Wallerstein, 37–68. London: Verso, 1992.

Barth, Fredrik. "Introduction." In *Ethnic Groups and Boundaries: The Social Organization of Cultural Difference*, edited by Fredrik Barth, 9–38. Boston: Little, Brown, 1969.

Barthes, Roland. *Mythologies.* London: Vintage, 2009.

Basu, Tapan, Pradip Datta, Sumit Sarkar, Tanika Sarkar, and Sambuddha Sen. *Khaki Shorts and Saffron Flags: A Critique of the Hindu Right.* Hyderabad: Orient Longman, 1993.

Beauvoir, Simone de. *The Second Sex.* New York: Random House, 1989.

Befu, Harumi. *Hegemony of Homogeneity.* Melbourne: Trans Pacific Press, 2001.

Bell, Catherine. *Ritual Theory, Ritual Practice.* Oxford: Oxford University Press, 1992.

Bellevaire, Patrick. "Japan: A Household Society." In *A History of the Family*, vol. 1, edited by A. Burguière, C. Klapisch-Zuber, M. Segalen, and F. Zonabend, 523–65. Cambridge, MA: Harvard University Press, 1996.

Benfey, Christopher. *The Great Wave: Gilded Age Misfits, Japanese Eccentrics, and the Opening of Old Japan.* New York: Random House, 2004.

Berezin, Mabel. "Cultural Form and Political Meaning: State-Subsidized Theater, Ideology and the Language of Style in Fascist Italy." *American Journal of Sociology* 99 (1994): 1237–86.

Bernett, Hajo. "Das Jahn-Bild in der nationalsozialistischen Weltanschauung." In *Internationales Jahn-Symposium*, 225–47. Leiden: Brill, 1979.

Berry, Mary Elizabeth. *The Culture of Civil War in Kyoto*. Berkeley: University of California Press, 1997.

———. *Hideyoshi*. Cambridge, MA: Harvard University Press, 1982.

Billig, Michael. *Banal Nationalism*. London: Sage, 1995.

Bodart, Beatrice. "Tea and Counsel: The Political Role of Sen Rikyu." *Monumenta Nipponica* 32 (1977): 49–74.

Borneman, John. *Belonging in the Two Berlins*. Cambridge: Cambridge University Press, 1992.

Bourdieu, Pierre. *Language and Symbolic Power*. Cambridge, MA: Harvard University Press, 1991.

———. *The Logic of Practice*. Stanford, CA: Stanford University Press, 1990.

———. *The Rules of Art: Genesis and Structure of the Literary Field*. Stanford, CA: Stanford University Press, 1996.

Bourdieu, Pierre, and Randal Johnson. *The Field of Cultural Production: Essays on Art and Literature*. New York: Columbia University Press, 1993.

Brandt, Kim. *Kingdom of Beauty: Mingei and the Politics of Folk Art in Imperial Japan*. Durham, NC: Duke University Press, 2007.

Breuilly, John. *Nationalism and the State*. Chicago: University of Chicago Press, 1993.

Brook, Timothy, and Andre Schmid. *Nation Work: Asian Elites and National Identities*. Ann Arbor: University of Michigan Press, 2003.

Brubaker, Rogers. "Ethnicity, Race, and Nationalism." *Annual Review of Sociology* (2009): 21–42.

Brubaker, Rogers, Margit Feischmidt, Jon Fox, and Liana Grancea. *Nationalist Politics and Everyday Ethnicity in a Transylvanian Town*. Princeton, NJ: Princeton University Press, 2006.

Brubaker, Rogers, Mara Loveman, and Peter Stamatov. "Ethnicity as Cognition." *Theory and Society* 33 (2004): 31–64.

Burns, Susan L. *Before the Nation: Kokugaku and the Imagining of Community in Early Modern Japan*. Durham, NC: Duke University Press, 2003.

Calhoun, Craig. *Nationalism*. Minneapolis: University of Minnesota Press, 1997.

Cerulo, Karen. *Identity Designs: The Sights and Sounds of a Nation*. New Brunswick, NJ: Rutgers University Press, 1995.

"Chadō to Tokonoma." *Fujin Gahō*, April 1939, 84–86.

"Chanoyu Dezain." *PEN*, January 2007, 30–93.

"Chanoyu Dezain 2." *PEN*, February 2008, 38–112.

"Chanoyu no Kokoro." *Ryōri Tsūshin*, October 2007, 16–49.

Chiba Nozomi and Gotō Masakaze. *Omotenashi no Genryū: Nihon no Dentō ni Saabisu no Honshitsu o Saguru*. Tokyo: Eiji Shuppan, 2007.

Collins, Patricia Hill. *Black Feminist Thought*. New York: HarperCollins, 1990.

————. *Fighting Words*. Minneapolis: University of Minnesota Press, 1998.

Comaroff, John L., and Jean Comaroff. *Ethnicity, Inc.* Chicago: University of Chicago Press, 2009.

————. *Ethnography and the Historical Imagination*. Boulder, CO: Westview, 1992.

Connerton, Paul. *How Societies Remember*. Cambridge: Cambridge University Press, 1989.

Cooper, Michael. "The Early Europeans and Tea." In *Tea in Japan: Essays on the History of Chanoyu*, edited by Paul Varley and Kumakura Isao, 101–34. Honolulu: University of Hawai'i Press, 1989.

Corbett, Rebecca. "Learning to Be Graceful: Tea in Early Modern Guides for Women's Edification." *Japanese Studies* 29 (2009): 81–94.

Cox, Rupert A. *Zen Arts: An Anthropological Study of the Culture of an Aesthetic Form in Japan*. London: RoutledgeCurzon, 2003.

Creighton, Millie. "Maintaining Cultural Boundaries in Retailing: How Japanese Department Stores Domesticate 'Things Foreign.'" *Modern Asian Studies* 25 (1991): 675–709.

Crenshaw, Kimberle. "Demarginalizing the Intersection of Race and Sex: A Black Feminist Critique of Antidiscrimination Doctrine, Feminist Theory and Antiracist Politics." In *The Politics of Law: A Progressive Critique*, edited by David Kairys, 195–218. New York: Pantheon, 1990.

Cross, Tim. *The Ideologies of Japanese Tea: Subjectivity, Transcendence, and National Identity*. Folkestone, Kent: Global Oriental, 2009.

Curtis, Benjamin. *Music Makes the Nation: Nationalist Composers and Nation Building in Nineteenth-Century Europe*. London: Cambria, 2008.

Cusack, Igor. "Pots, Pens and 'Eating Out the Body': Cuisine and the Gendering of African Nations." *Nation and Nationalism* 9 (2003): 277–96.

Czarnecki, Melanie. "Bad Girls from Good Families: The Degenerate Meiji Schoolgirl." In *Bad Girls of Japan*, edited by Laura Miller and Jan Bardsley, 49–64. New York: Macmillan, 2005.

Dalby, Liza. *Kimono: Fashioning Culture*. New York: Vintage Books, 1993.

Dale, Peter N. *The Myth of Japanese Uniqueness*. London: Palgrave Macmillan, 1986.

Daniel, Yvonne. *Rumba: Dance and Social Change in Contemporary Cuba*. Bloomington: Indiana University Press, 1995.

Davis, Kathy. "Intersectionality as a Buzzword: A Sociology of Science Perspective on What Makes a Feminist Theory Successful." *Feminist Theory* 9 (2008): 67–85.

de la Pradelle, Michèle. *Market Day in Provence*. Chicago: University of Chicago Press, 2006.

DeNora, Tia. *Music in Everyday Life*. Cambridge: Cambridge University Press, 2000.

Doak, Kevin M. *A History of Nationalism in Modern Japan: Placing the People*. Leiden: Brill, 2007.

Duara, Prasenjit. "The Discourse of Civilization and Pan-Asianism." In *Nations under Siege: Globalization and Nationalism in Asia*, edited by Roy Starrs, 63–102. New York: Palgrave Macmillan, 2002.

————. "The Regime of Authenticity: Timelessness, Gender, and National History in Modern China." *History and Theory* 37 (1998): 287–308.

Edensor, Tim. *National Identity, Popular Culture and Everyday Life*. New York: Berg, 2002.

Ehn, Billy. "National Feeling in Sport: The Case of Sweden." *Ethnologia Europaea* 19 (1989): 56–66.

Elias, Norbert. *The Civilizing Process*. Oxford: Blackwell, 1994.

Eriksen, Thomas Hylland. *Ethnicity and Nationalism: Anthropological Perspectives*. 2nd ed. London: Pluto, 2002.

Espiritu, Yen Le. "The Intersection of Race, Ethnicity, and Class: The Multiple Identities of Second-Generation Filipinos." *Identities* 1 (1994): 249–73.

Evans, John C. *Tea in China: The History of China's National Drink*. Westport, CT: Greenwood, 1992.

Farnell, Brenda. "Moving Bodies, Acting Selves." *Annual Review of Anthropology* 28 (1999): 341–73.

Fearon, James D. "Ethnic and Cultural Diversity by Country." *Journal of Economic Growth* 8 (2003): 195–222.

Ferguson, Priscilla Parkhurst. *Accounting for Taste: The Triumph of French Cuisine*. Chicago: University of Chicago Press, 2004.

Foster, Robert J. *Materializing the Nation: Commodities, Consumption, and Media in Papua New Guinea*. Bloomington: Indiana University Press, 2002.

Foucault, Michel. *Discipline and Punish*. New York: Vintage Books, 1995.

Fox, Jon E. "Consuming the Nation: Holidays, Sports, and the Production of Collective Belonging." *Ethnic and Racial Studies* 29 (2006): 217–36.

Fox, Jon E., and Cynthia Miller-Idriss. "Everyday Nationhood." *Ethnicities* 8 (2008): 536–76.

Frank, Ernst. *Friedrich Ludwig Jahn: Ein moderner Rebell*. Offenbach am Main: Orion Heimreiter Verlag, 1972.

Frankenburg, Ruth. *White Women, Race Matters: The Social Construction of Racism*. Minneapolis: University of Minnesota Press, 1993.

Freud, Sigmund. *The Interpretation of Dreams: The Complete and Definitive Text*. New York: Basic Books, 2010.

Fujitani, Takashi. *Splendid Monarchy: Power and Pageantry in Modern Japan*. Berkeley: University of California Press, 1998.

Fujiwara Masahiko. *Kokka no Hinkaku*. Tokyo: Shinchōsha, 2005.

Fukukita, Yasunosuke. *Tea Cult of Japan: An Aesthetic Pastime*. 2nd ed. Tokyo: Japan Board of Tourist Industry Japanese Government Railways, 1934.

Gal, Susan. "Bartok's Funeral: Representations of Europe in Hungarian Political Rhetoric." *American Ethnologist* 18 (1991): 440–58.

Garfinkel, Harold. *Studies on Ethnomethodology*. Cambridge: Polity, 1967.

Gellner, Ernest. *Nations and Nationalism*. Ithaca, NY: Cornell University Press, 1983.

Gieryn, Thomas. "Boundaries of Science." In *Handbook of Science and Technology Studies*, edited by Shiela Jansanoff, Gerald Markie, James Peterson, and Trevor Pinch, 393–443. Thousand Oaks, CA: Sage, 1995.

Gilman, Sander. *The Jew's Body*. New York: Routledge, 1991.

Glenn, Evelyn Nakano. "The Social Construction and Institutionalization of Gender and Race: An Integrative Framework." In *Revisioning Gender*, edited by Myra Marx Ferree, Judith Lorber, and Beth Hess, 3–43. Thousand Oaks, CA: Sage, 1999.

Gluck, Carol. *Japan's Modern Myths: Ideology in the Late Meiji Period*. Princeton, NJ: Princeton University Press, 1985.

Goffman, Erving. *Interaction Ritual: Essays on Face-to-Face Behavior*. New York: Pantheon Books, 1967.

———. *The Presentation of Self in Everyday Life*. New York: Doubleday, 1959.

———. *Stigma: Notes on the Management of Spoiled Identity*. New York: Simon and Schuster, 1963.

Goldstein-Gidoni, Ofra. "Kimono and the Construction of Gendered and Cultural Identities." *Ethnology* 38 (1999): 351–70.

Goltermann, Svenja. *Körper der Nation: Habitusformierung und die Politik des Turnens 1860–1890*. Göttingen: Vandenhoeck und Ruprecht, 1998.

Graham, Patricia J. *Tea of the Sages: The Art of Sencha*. Honolulu: University of Hawai'i Press, 1998.

Guth, Christine. *Art, Tea, and Industry: Masuda Takashi and the Mitsui Circle*. Princeton, NJ: Princeton University Press, 1993.

———. "Import Substitution, Innovation, and the Tea Ceremony in Fifteenth- and Sixteenth-Century Japan." In *Global Design History*, edited by Glenn Adamson, Giorgio Riello, and Sarah Teasley, 50–59. London: Routledge, 2011.

Haase, Bill. "Learning to Be an Apprentice." In *Learning in Likely Places: Varieties of Apprenticeship in Japan*, edited by John Singleton, 107–21. Cambridge: Cambridge University Press, 1998.

Haga Kōshirō. "The *Wabi* Aesthetic through the Ages." Trans. and adapted by Martin Collcutt. In *Tea in Japan: Essays on the History of Chanoyu*, edited by Paul Varley and Kumakura Isao, 195–230. Honolulu: University of Hawai'i Press, 1989.

Hagen, Joshua. "The Most German of Towns: Creating an Ideal Nazi Community in Rothenburg ob der Tauber." *Annals of the Association of American Geographers* 94 (2004): 207–27.

Hall, Stuart. "Ethnicity: Identity and Difference." In *Becoming National: A Reader*, edited by Geoff Eley and Ronald G. Suny, 339–51. Oxford: Oxford University Press, 1996.

Handler, Richard. *Nationalism and the Politics of Culture in Quebec*. Madison: University of Wisconsin Press, 1988.

Harada Yasuko. *Wafuku Saihō Tehodoki*. Tokyo: Kokkadō, 1907.

Harootunian, Harry. *Things Seen and Unseen: Discourse and Ideology in Tokugawa Nativism*. Chicago: University of Chicago Press, 1988.

Hata Masataka. *Kōsansai: Kō to Nihonjin no Monogatari*. Tokyo: Tokyo Shoseki, 2004.

Hayashiya Tatsusaburō. *Zuroku Chadōshi: Fūryū no Seiritsu*. Kyoto: Tankōsha, 1962.

Herzfeld, Michael. *Cultural Intimacy: Social Poetics in the Nation-State*. London: Routledge, 2005.

———. *The Poetics of Manhood: Contest and Identity in a Cretan Mountain Village.* Princeton, NJ: Princeton University Press, 1985.

Higuchi Katsuya. *Nihonjin no Ningen Kankei.* Kyoto: Tankōsha, 1992.

Hobsbawm, Eric. "Introduction: Inventing Traditions." In *The Invention of Tradition*, edited by Eric Hobsbawm and Terence Ranger, 1–14. Cambridge: Cambridge University Press, 1983.

———. "Mass-Producing Traditions: Europe, 1870–1914." In *The Invention of Tradition*, edited by Eric Hobsbawm and Terence Ranger, 263–307. Cambridge: Cambridge University Press, 1983.

———. *Nations and Nationalism since 1780: Programme, Myth, Reality.* Cambridge: Cambridge University Press, 1990.

Hōgetsu Keigo. *Nihonshi.* Tokyo: Yamagawa Shuppansha, 1966.

Holland, James Henry. "Tea Records: *Kaiki* and *Oboegaki* in Contemporary Japanese Tea Practice." In *Japanese Tea Culture: Art, History, and Practice*, edited by Morgan Pitelka, 184–203. New York: Routledge, 2003.

Horibe Kōin, Horibe Emiko, and Horibe Hiroko. *Kyoto Sumiya: Omotenashi wa Ocha no Kokoro de.* Tokyo: Sōshisha, 2006.

Hsu, Francis L. K. *Iemoto: The Heart of Japan.* Cambridge, MA: Schenkman, 1975.

Huggins, Mike. *Flat Racing and British Society, 1790–1914: A Social and Economic History.* London: Frank Cass, 2000.

Iguchi Kaisen, Hisada Sōya, and Nakamura Masao, eds. *Nihon no Chake.* Kyoto: Kawahara Shōten, 1983.

Ikeda Tsunetarō. *Joshi no Ōkoku.* Tokyo: Bunpūsha, 1903.

Ikegami, Eiko. *Bonds of Civility: Aesthetic Networks and the Political Origins of Japanese Culture.* Cambridge: Cambridge University Press, 2005.

Illig, Stefan. *Zwischen Körperertüchtigung und nationaler Bewegung: Turnvereine in Bayern 1848–1890.* Cologne: SH-Verlag, 1998.

Inagaki Kyoko. *Jogakko to Jogakusei.* Tokyo: Chuokoron Shinsha, 2007.

Inobe Shigeo. *Shinshū Teikoku Shōshi.* Tokyo: Mitsugane, 1937.

Inoue Mitsutaka and Kasawara Kazuo. *Yōsetsu Nihonshi.* Tokyo: Yamagawa Shuppansha, 1980.

Isozaki, Arata. *Japan-ness in Architecture.* Cambridge, MA: MIT Press, 2006.

Itō Kimio. "The Invention of *Wa* and the Transformation of the Image of the Prince Shōtoku in Modern Japan." In *Mirror of Modernity: Invented Traditions of Modern Japan*, edited by Stephen Vlastos, 37–47. Berkeley: University of California Press, 1998.

Ivy, Marilyn. *Discourse of the Vanishing: Modernity, Phantasm, Japan.* Chicago: University of Chicago Press, 1995.

Jahn, Friedrich Ludwig. *Deutsches Volksthum.* Lübeck: Niemann und Co., 1810.

Jandásek, Ladislav. "The Sokol Movement in Czechoslovakia." *Slavonic and East European Review* 11, no. 31 (1932): 65–80.

Jansen, Marius B. *The Making of Modern Japan.* Cambridge, MA: Belknap/Harvard University Press, 2002.

Jenkins, Richard. *Being Danish: Paradoxes of Identity in Everyday Life*. Copenhagen: Museum Tusculanum Press, 2011.

———. *Rethinking Ethnicity: Arguments and Explorations*. London: Sage, 1997.

Kagotani Machiko. *Josei to Chanoyu*. Kyoto: Tankōsha, 1985.

"'Kaiseki' to 'Kaiseki.'" *Fujin Gahō*, November 2006, 66–90.

Kameyama Sōgetsu. "Meiki." *Fujin Gahō*, November 1937, 122–23.

Kang Sang-jung. *Han-Nashonarizumu: Teikoku no Mōsō to Kokka no Bōryoku ni Kōshite*. Nagoya: Kyōiku Shiryō Shuppankai, 2003.

———. *Nashonarizumu: Shikō no Furontia*. Tokyo: Iwanami Shōten, 2001.

———. *Orientarizumu no Kanata e: Kindai Bunka Hihan*. Tokyo: Iwanami Shōten, 1996.

*Katei Setsuyō*. Tokyo: Joshi Saihō Kōtō Gakuin, 1910.

Kato, Etsuko. *The Tea Ceremony and Women's Empowerment in Modern Japan: Bodies Re-Presenting the Past*. London: Routledge, 2004.

Kedourie, Elie. *Nationalism*. London: Wiley-Blackwell, 1993.

Kenmochi Takehiko. *Ma no Nihon Bunka*. Tokyo: Kōdansha, 1978.

Kido Takayoshi. *The Diary of Kido Takayoshi*. Edited by Sidney Devere Brown. Tokyo: University of Tokyo Press, 1983.

Kikuchi, Yuko. *Japanese Modernization and Mingei Theory: Cultural Nationalism and Oriental Orientalism*. London: Routledge, 2004.

Killoran, Moira. "Good Muslims and 'Bad Muslims,' 'Good' Women and Feminists: Negotiating Identities in Northern Cyprus (or, The Condom Story)." *Ethnos* 26 (1998): 183–208.

Kobayashi Hikogorō. *Fujin Shūyō to Jissai*. Tokyo: Isseisha, 1911.

Kobayashi Yoshiho. "Chadō to Reihō: Jogakkō ni Miru sono Sōkan." Report for the Chanoyu Bunkagakkai. Ikenobō Tanki Daigaku, July 7, 2008.

———. *"Hana" no Seiritsu to Tenkai*. Osaka: Izumi Shōin, 2007.

———. "Kōtō Jogakkō ni okeru 'Hana' 'Cha' no Juyō." *Josei Shigaku* 12 (2001): 45–59.

———. "Kōyūkaishi 'Kishino Himematsu' ni Miru Sennan, Kishiwada Kōtō Jogakkō." *Izumi Kōkō Hyakunenshi* (July 2001): 885–914.

———. "Kyoiku toshite no Hana: 'Hana' 'Cha' wa Dono yōni Shite Josei no Nasubeki Mono to Natta no ka." *Kenkyū Kiyō* 15 (2006): 13–40.

———. "Meijisho-, chūki Joshi Chūtō Kyōiku in okeru 'Hana' 'Cha' no Juyō." *Kenkyū Kiyō* 11 (2002): 12–22.

———. "Shokuminchi Taiwan no Kōtō Jogakkō to Reigisahō Kūkan." Kyoto: Nichibunken, 2009.

Kōdō Bunka Kenkyūkai, ed. *Kō to Kōdō*. Tokyo: Yūzankaku Shuppan, 2002.

Kohn, Hans. "Father Jahn's Nationalism." *Review of Politics* 11 (1949): 646–61.

*Kokoro no Nooto*. Tokyo: Ministry of Education, Culture, Sports, Science, and Technology, 2002.

Kondo, Dorinne. *Crafting Selves: Power, Gender, and Discourses of Identity in a Japanese Workplace*. Chicago: University of Chicago Press, 1990.

———. "The Way of Tea: A Symbolic Analysis." *Man* 20 (1985): 287–306.

Kondo Yoshimi. *Gengo Sahō Kijo no Kokoroe.* Tokyo: Eisai Shinshisha, 1893.

Koyama Shizuko. *Katei no Seisei to Josei ni Kokuminka.* Tokyo: Keisō Shobō, 1999.

———. *Ryōsaikenbo to Iu Kihan.* Tokyo: Keisō Shobō, 1991.

Kramer, Robert. "The Tea Cult in History." PhD diss., University of Chicago, 1985.

Kumakura Isao. "Chadō no Keifu." In *Chadō Bunkaron,* edited by Kumakura Isao and Hidetaka Tanaka, 7–46. Kyoto: Tankōsha, 1999.

———. *Chajin to Chanoyu no Kenkyū.* Kyoto: Shibunkaku Shuppan, 2003.

———. *Chanoyu no Rekishi: Sen no Rikyū made.* Tokyo: Asahi Shinbunsha, 1990.

———. "Iemoto Seido no Bunseki." In *Metafaa toshite no Kazoku,* edited by Ryōsuke Yasue, 161–77. Vol. 7 of *Henbōsuru Kazoku.* Tokyo: Iwanami Shōten, 1992.

———. "Iemoto Seika ni okeru Geidō no Tokushitsu." *Geinōshi Kenkyū* 136 (1998): 1–14.

———. "Kan'ei Culture and *Chanoyu.*" In *Tea in Japan: Essays on the History of Chanoyu,* edited by Paul Varley and Isao Kumakura, 135–60. Honolulu: University of Hawai'i Press, 1989.

———. *Kindai Chadōshi no Kenkyū.* Tokyo: Nihonhōsō Shuppankai, 1980.

———. "Kindai no Chanoyu." In *Kindai no Chanoyu,* edited by Kumakura Isao, 73–85. Vol. 6 of *Chadō Jukin.* Tokyo: Kogakkan, 1985.

———. *Mukashi no Chanoyu, Ima no Chanoyu.* Kyoto: Tankōsha, 1985.

———. "Reexamining Tea: *Yuisho, Suki, Yatsushi,* and *Furumai.*" Translated and adapted by Peter McMillan. *Monumenta Nipponica* 57 (2002): 1–42.

Kumakura Isao, Hiroichi Tsutsui, Nakamura Toshinori, and Nakamura Shuya, eds. *Shiryō ni yoru Chanoyu no Rekishi.* 2 vols. Tokyo: Shufu no Tomosha, 1994–1995.

Kunugi Mosaku. *Kokutei Rekishi Kyōkasho Sōga Kaisetsu.* Tokyo: Kaihatsusha, 1912.

*Kyō no Maccha Mon.* Rakutabi Bunkō Series. Kyoto: Ōfusha, 2007.

Laitin, David D. *Identity in Formation: The Russian-Speaking Populations in the Near Abroad.* Ithaca, NY: Cornell University Press, 1998.

Lamers, Jeroen. *Japonius Tyrannus: The Japanese Warlord Oda Nobunaga Reconsidered.* Amsterdam: Hotei, 2001.

Lamont, Michèle, and Virag Molnár. "Study of Boundaries in the Social Sciences." *Annual Review of Sociology* 28 (2002): 167–95.

Lampland, Martha. "Family Portraits: Gendered Images of the Nation in Nineteenth-Century Hungary." *East European Politics and Societies* 8 (1994): 287–316.

Leheny, David. *The Rules of Play: National Identity and the Shaping of Japanese Leisure.* Ithaca, NY: Cornell University Press, 2003.

Linde-Laursen, Anders. "The Nationalization of Trivialities: How Cleaning Becomes an Identity Marker in the Encounter of Swedes and Danes." *Ethnos* 58 (1993): 275–93.

Lindsey, William R. *Fertility and Pleasure: Ritual and Sexual Values in Tokugawa Japan.* Honolulu: University of Hawai'i Press, 2007.

Löfgren, Orvar. "The Nationalization of Culture." *Ethnologia Europaea* 19 (1989): 5–23.

Ludwig, Theodore M. "*Chanoyu* and Momoyama: Conflict and Transformation in Rikyū's Art." In *Tea in Japan: Essays on the History of Chanoyu,* edited by Paul

Varley and Isao Kumakura, 71–100. Honolulu: University of Hawai'i Press, 1989.

Macháček, Fridolín. "The Sokol Movement: Its Contribution to Gymnastics." *Slavonic and East European Review* 17, no. 49 (1938): 73–90.

Mackie, Vera. *Feminism in Modern Japan*. Cambridge: Cambridge University Press, 2003.

Mann, Michael. "A Political Theory of Nationalism and Its Excesses." In *Notions of Nationalism*, edited by S. Periwal, 44–64. Budapest: Central European University Press, 1995.

Marx, Anthony. *Making Race and Nation: A Comparison of the United States, South Africa, and Brazil*. Cambridge: Cambridge University Press, 1996.

Mathews, Gordon. "Can 'a Real Man' Live for His Family? *Ikigai* and Masculinity in Today's Japan." In *Men and Masculinity in Contemporary Japan*, edited by James E. Roberson and Nobue Suzuki, 109–25. London: Routledge, 2003.

Matsui Senpu. *Fujo no Shiori: Kaji, Keizai*. Tokyo: Miwa Shin'ichi, 1901.

Mauss, Marcel. *The Gift: The Forms and Reason for Exchange in Archaic Societies*. London: Routledge, 2000.

———. "Techniques of the Body." In *Techniques, Technology and Civilization*, edited by N. Schlanger, 77–98. Oxford: Berghahn Books, 2006.

McCall, Leslie. "The Complexity of Intersectionality." *Signs: Journal of Women in Culture and Society* 30 (2006): 1771–1800.

McClintock, Anne. *Imperial Leather: Race, Gender, and Sexuality in the Colonial Contest*. London: Routledge, 1995.

———. "'No Longer in a Future Heaven': Nationalism, Gender, and Race." In *Becoming National: A Reader*, edited by Geoff Eley and Ronald Suny, 260–85. Oxford: Oxford University Press, 1996.

McVeigh, Brian. *Nationalisms of Japan: Managing and Mystifying Identity*. Lanham, MD: Rowman and Littlefield, 2004.

Miller, Laura. *Beauty Up: Exploring Contemporary Japanese Body Aesthetics*. Berkeley: University of California Press, 2006.

Mori, Barbara Lynne Rowland. *Americans Studying the Traditional Japanese Art of the Tea Ceremony: The Internationalizing of a Traditional Art*. San Francisco: Mellen Research University Press, 1992.

———. "The Tea Ceremony: A Transformed Japanese Ritual." *Gender and Society* 5 (1991): 86–97.

———. "The Traditional Arts as Leisure Activities for Contemporary Japanese Women." In *Re-Imaging Japanese Women*, edited by Anne Imamura, 117–34. Berkeley: University of California Press, 1996.

Mori Kayō. *Shitte Tokusuru: Wa no Keiko*. Tokyo: Chikuma Shobō, 2000.

Morris-Suzuki, Tessa. *Re-Inventing Japan: Time, Space, Nation*. Armonk, NY: M. E. Sharpe, 1998.

Mosse, George L. *Nationalism and Sexuality: Middle Class Morality and Sexual Norms in Modern Europe*. Madison: University of Wisconsin Press, 1988.

———. *The Nationalization of Masses: Political Symbolism and Mass Movements in*

*Germany from the Napoleonic Wars through the Third Reich.* New York: Howard Fertig, 1975.

Mostow, Joshua. "Modern Constructions of *Tales of Ise*: Gender and Courtliness." In *Inventing the Classics: Modernity, National Identity, and Japanese Literature*, edited by Haruo Shirane and Tomi Suzuki, 96–119. Stanford, CA: Stanford University Press, 2001.

Mouer, Ross, and Yoshio Sugimoto. *Images of Japanese Society.* London: Routledge, 1986.

Mukai, Shutaro. "Characters That Represent, Reflect and Translate Culture in the Context of the Revolution in Modern Art." In *The Empire of Signs: Semiotic Essays on Japanese Culture*, edited by Yoshihiko Ikegami, 57–83. Amsterdam: John Benjamins Publishing, 1991.

Murai Yasuhiko. "The Development of *Chanoyu*: Before Rikyū." Trans. by Paul Varley. In *Tea in Japan: Essays on the History of Chanoyu*, edited by Paul Varley and Kumakura Isao, 3–33. Honolulu: University of Hawai'i Press, 1989.

Namura Jōhaku. *Onna Chōhōki, Nan Chōhōki.* Annotated by Nagatomo Chiyoji. Tokyo: Shakai Shisōsha, 1993.

Nilan, Pam. "Membership Categorization Devices under Construction: Social Identity Boundary Maintenance in Everyday Discourse." *Australian Review of Applied Linguistics* 18 (1995): 69–94.

Nishiyama Matsunosuke. *Iemoto no Kenkyū.* Tokyo: Yoshikawa Kōbunkan, 1959.

Nitobe, Inazo. *Bushido: The Soul of Japan.* Radford, VA: Wilder Publications, 2008.

Noguchi Aya. "'Dō.'" In *Gakkō Chadō Taiken Ronbunshū*, 4–7. Kyoto: Chadō Urasenke Tankōkai Sōhonbu, 2002.

Nolte, Claire E. "'Our Task, Direction, and Goal': The Development of the Sokol National Program to World War I." In *Die slawische Sokolbewegung: Beiträge zur Geschichte von Sport und Nationalismus in Osteuropa*, edited by Diethelm Blecking, 37–52. Dortmund: Forschungsstelle Ostmitteleuropa, 1991.

———. *The Sokol in the Czech Lands to 1914: Training for the Nation.* London: Palgrave Macmillan, 2002.

Nolte, Sharon, and Sally Ann Hastings. "The Meiji State Policy toward Women, 1890–1910." In *Recreating Japan Woman, 1600–1945*, edited by Gail Bernstein, 151–74. Berkeley: University of California Press, 1991.

Nomura Zuiten. *Sekishūryū: Reikishi to Keifu.* Kyoto: Kōsonsui Koshoin, 1984.

Notehelfer, Fred G. "On Idealism and Realism in the Thought of Okakura Tenshin." *Journal of Japanese Studies* 16, no. 2 (1990): 309–55.

O Sonfa. *Nihon no Aimai Chikara.* Tokyo: PHP Shinsho, 2009.

Ochiai Emiko. *Shinpan. 21-Seiki Kazoku e.* Tokyo: Yūhikaku Sensho, 1997.

Ogasawara Keishōsai. *Utsukushii Furumai.* Text edition. Kyoto: Tankōsha, 1999.

———. *Utsukushii Furumai.* Photo edition. Kyoto: Tankōsha, 1999.

Ogasawara Tadamune. *Nihonjin no Reigi to Kokoro: Ogasawararyū Dentōsho no Oshie.* Tokyo: Karuchaa Shuppansha, 1972.

Ogasawara, Yuki. *Office Ladies and Salaried Men: Gender, Power, and Work in Japanese Companies.* Berkeley: University of California Press, 1998.

Ogawa Maiko. "Jibun ga Kawaru." In *Gakkō Chadō Taiken Ronbunshū*, 20–21. Kyoto: Chadō Urasenke Tankōkai Sōhonbu, 2002.

Oguma Eiji. *A Genealogy of "Japanese" Self-Images*. Melbourne: Trans Pacific Press, 2002.

———. *Minshū to Aikoku: Sengo Nihon no Nashonarizumu to Kōkyōsei*. Tokyo: Shinyōsha, 2002.

———. *Nihonjin no Kyokai: Okinawa, Ainu, Taiwan, Chōsen Shokuminchi Shihai kara Fukkiundō made*. Shinyōsha: Tokyo, 1998.

———. *Tan'itsu Minzoku Shinwa no Kigen*. Tokyo: Shinyōsha, 1995.

Okakura, Kakuzo. *The Awakening of Japan*. Ithaca, NY: Cornell University Library, 2009.

———. *The Book of Tea*. Tokyo: Kōdansha, 1989.

———. *Ideals of the East: The Spirit of Japanese Art*. New York: Cosimo Classics, 2007.

"Onna o Kitaeru Okeiko Dō." *CREA*, March 2008, 44–96.

Ono Keni'chirō. "Chanoyu no Kokoro." *Fujin Gahō*, November 1937, 120–21.

Ooms, Herman. *Tokugawa Ideology: Early Constructs, 1570–1680*. Ann Arbor: University of Michigan Press, 1989.

Ōtsuki Mikio. *Sencha Bunkakō: Bunjincha no Keifu*. Kyoto: Shibunkaku, 2004.

Ōuchi Shiratsuki. "Nihon no Cha, Shina no Cha." *Fujin Gahō*, June 1935, 72–73.

Outka, Elizabeth. *Consuming Traditions: Modernity, Modernism, and the Commodified Authentic*. Oxford: Oxford University Press, 2009.

Pachucki, Mark A., Sabrina Pendergrass, and Michèle Lamont. "Boundary Processes: Recent Theoretical Developments and New Contributions." *Poetics* 35 (2007): 331–51.

Palmer, Catherine A. "From Theory to Practice: Experiencing the Nation in Everyday Life." *Journal of Material Culture* 3, no. 2 (1998): 175–99.

Pasler, Jann. *Composing the Citizen: Music as Public Utility in Third Republic France*. Berkeley: University of California Press, 2009.

Pitelka, Morgan. *Handmade Culture: Raku Potters, Patrons, and Tea Practitioners in Japan*. Honolulu: University of Hawai'i Press, 2005.

———. "Introduction to Japanese Tea Culture." In *Japanese Tea Culture: Art, History, and Practice*, edited by Morgan Pitelka, 1–17. New York: Routledge, 2003.

———, ed. *Japanese Tea Culture: Art, History, and Practice*. New York: Routledge, 2003.

Plutschow, Herbert. "An Anthropological Perspective on the Japanese Tea Ceremony." *Anthropoetics* 5 (1999). www.anthropoetics.ucla.edu/apo501/tea.htm.

———. *Historical Chanoyu*. Tokyo: Japan Times, 1986.

———. *Rediscovering Rikyu and the Beginnings of the Japanese Tea Ceremony*. Folkestone, Kent: Global Oriental, 2003.

Poli, Raffaele. "The Denationalization of Sport: De-ethnicization of the Nation and Identity Deterritorialization." *Sport in Society* 10, no. 4 (2007): 646–61.

Presner, Todd Samuel. *Muscular Judaism*. London: Routledge, 2007.

Pyle, Kenneth B. *The New Generation in Meiji Japan: Problems of Cultural Identity.* Stanford, CA: Stanford University Press, 1969.

Rath, Eric C. *The Ethos of Noh: Actors and Their Art.* Cambridge, MA: Harvard University Press, 2004.

Ries, Nancy. *Russian Talk: Culture and Conversation during Perestroika.* Ithaca, NY: Cornell University Press, 1997.

Rouse, Joseph. "Practice Theory." In *The Handbook of Philosophy of Science,* edited by Stephen Turner and Mark Risjord, 499–540. Amsterdam: Elsevier BV, 2006.

Roy, Srirupa. *Beyond Belief: India and the Politics of Postcolonial Nationalism.* Durham, NC: Duke University Press, 2007.

"Ryokucha Manwa." *Fujin Gahō,* January 1932, 5.

"Sadō no Reijō." *Fujin Gahō,* April 1933, 6.

Sahlins, Marshall D. *Island of History.* Chicago: University of Chicago Press, 1985.

Sand, Jordan. *House and Home in Modern Japan: Architecture, Domestic Space, and Bourgeois Culture, 1880–1930.* Cambridge, MA: Harvard University Press, 2005.

Sato, Barbara. "Commodifying and Engendering Morality: Self-Cultivation and the Construction of the 'Ideal Woman' in 1920s Mass Women's Magazines." In *Gendering Modern Japanese History,* edited by Barbara Molony and Kathleen Uno, 99–130. Cambridge, MA: Harvard University Press, 2005.

———. *The New Japanese Woman: Modernity, Media, and Women in Interwar Japan.* Durham, NC: Duke University Press, 2003.

Saure, Felix. "Beautiful Bodies, Exercising Warriors, and Original People: Sports, Greek Antiquity, and National Identity from Winckelmann to 'Turnvater Jahn.'" *German History* 27 (2009): 358–73.

Savigliano, Marta. *Tango and the Political Economy of Passion.* San Francisco: Westview, 1995.

Schivelbusch, Wolfgang. *Tastes of Paradise: A Social History of Spices, Stimulants, and Intoxicants.* New York: Vintage Books, 1992.

Screech, Timon. *The Shogun's Painted Culture: Fear and Creativity in the Japanese States, 1760–1829.* London: Reaktion Books, 2000.

Sears, John. *Sacred Places: American Tourist Attractions in the Nineteenth Century.* Oxford: Oxford University Press, 1989.

Seikōkan, ed. *Katei Komon.* Tokyo: Seikōkan, 1903.

"Sen Rikyū no Kōzai." *PEN,* February 2009, 32–95.

Sen Sōshitsu, ed. *Chadō Gaku Taikei.* 11 vols. Kyoto: Tankōsha, 1999–2000.

———. "Gochisō no Kokoro." *Tankō,* June 1986, 22–23.

———. "Hinshu Gokan." *Tankō,* January 1988, 22–23.

———. "Ichiwan no Kakehashi." *Tankō,* June 1982, 30–31.

———. *The Japanese Way of Tea: From Its Origins in China to Sen Rikyū.* Honolulu: University of Hawai'i Press, 1998.

———. "Jo'ō Heika ni Ichiwan o." *Tankō,* June 1975, 20–21.

———. "Makoto no Kokusaijin." *Tankō,* June 1998, 22–23.

———. "Ningen Sonchō." *Tankō,* January 1965, 18–19.

———. "'Shacha' no Deai." *Tankō,* January 1981, 22–23.

———. "Shinnen no Kotoba." *Tankō*, January 1967, 22–23.

———. "Tomo ni Heiwa o." *Tankō*, January 1984, 22–23.

Seton-Watson, Hugh. *Nation and States*. Boulder, CO: Westview, 1977.

Shakai Keizai Seisansei Honbu. *Reijaa Hakusho*. Tokyo: Bun'eisha, 2006.

Sharma, Jai Narain. *Encyclopedia of Eminent Thinkers*. Vol. 20, *M. S. Golwalkar*. New Delhi: Concept Publishing, 2008.

Shimazu, Naoko, ed. *Nationalisms in Japan*. London: Routledge, 2006.

Shirane, Haruo. "Curriculum and Competing Canons." In *Inventing the Classics: Modernity, National Identity, and Japanese Literature*, edited by Haruo Shirane and Tomi Suzuki, 220–49. Stanford, CA: Stanford University Press, 2000.

Shryock, Andrew. "The New Jordanian Hospitality: House, Host, and Guest in the Culture of Public Display." *Comparative Studies in Society and History* 46, no. (2004): 35–62.

Shūbunkan, ed. *Joshi Kajikun*. Tokyo: Shōeidō, 1901.

Slusser, Dale. "The Transformation of Tea Practice in Sixteenth-Century Japan." In *Japanese Tea Culture: Art, History, and Practice*, edited by Morgan Pitelka, 39–60. New York: Routledge, 2003.

Smith, Anthony D. *The Ethnic Origins of Nations*. Oxford: Blackwell, 1986.

———. *Ethno-Symbolism and Nationalism: A Cultural Approach*. London: Routledge, 2009.

———. "The Limits of Everyday Nationhood." *Ethnicities* 8 (2008): 563–73.

———. *The Nation in History: Historiographical Debates about Ethnicity and Nationalism*. Cambridge: Polity, 2000.

———. *National Identity*. Las Vegas: University of Nevada Press, 1993.

Smith, Robert. "Transmitting Tradition by the Rule: An Anthropological Interpretation of the *Iemoto* System." In *Learning in Likely Places: Varieties of Apprenticeship in Japan*, edited by John Singleton, 23–34. Cambridge: Cambridge University Press, 1998.

Spillman, Lynette P. *Nation and Commemoration: Creating National Identities in the United States and Australia*. Cambridge: Cambridge University Press, 1997.

Stamatov, Peter. "Interpretive Activism and Political Uses of Verdi's Operas in the 1840s." *American Sociological Review* 67, no. 3 (2002): 345–66.

Starrs, Roy, ed. *Japanese Cultural Nationalism*. Leiden: Global Oriental, 2004.

Sugimoto Yoshio and Ross Mouer. *Nihonjinron no Hōteishiki*. Tokyo: Chikuma Shobō, 1995.

Surak, Kristin. "'Ethnic Practices' in Translation: Tea in Japan and the US." *Ethnic and Racial Studies* 29 (2006): 828–54.

———. "Making Tea Japanese." In *Making Japanese Heritage*, edited by Rupert Cox and Christoph Brumann, 21–30. London: Routledge, 2009.

Suzuki Mami. "Chadō Jugyō de." In *Gakkō Chadō Taiken Ronbunshū*, 59–60. Kyoto: Chadō Urasenke Tankōkai Sōhonbu, 2002.

Suzuki Mikiko. "Taishō, Shōwashoki ni okeru Josei Bunka toshite ni Keikogoto." In *Josei no Bunka*, edited by Aoki Tamotsu, Kawamoto Saburō, Tsutsui Kiyotada, Mikuriya Takashi, and Yamaori Tetsuo, 49–71. Tokyo: Iwanami Shōten, 2000.

Tagsold, Christian. *Spaces of Translation: Japanese Gardens in the West.* Unpublished manuscript, forthcoming.

Takahashi Doan [Yoshio]. "Chanoyu." In *Chadō Zenshū*, vol. 1, edited by Iguchi Kaisen et al., 680. Osaka: Sōgensha, 1936.

———. "Oraga Chanoyu." In *Nihon no Chasho*, vol. 2, edited by Hayashiya Tatsusaburō, Yokoi Kiyoshi, and Narabayashi Tadao. Tokyo: Heibonsha, 1971.

Takahashi Gishio. "Chanoyu no Kokoro." *Fujin Gahō*, March 1933, 122–23.

Takahashi Tatsuo. *Chadō.* Tokyo: Ō'okayama Shōten, 1929.

Takeuchi Yasu. *Rikyū.* Tokyo: Sōgensha, 1939.

Tanaka Hidetaka. *Kindai Chadō no Rekishi-Shakaigaku.* Kyoto: Shibunkaku, 2007.

Tanaka Senshō. *Chadō Kairyōron.* Commentary by Tanaka Hidetaka. Tokyo: Kōdansha, 1987.

Tanaka, Stefan. *Japan's Orient: Rendering Pasts into History.* Berkeley: University of California Press, 1995.

Tani Akira. *Chajintachi no Nihon Bunkashi.* Tokyo: Kōdansha, 2007.

———. *Chakaiki no Kenkyū.* Kyoto: Tankōsha, 2001.

Tanihata Akio. *Kinsei Chadōshi.* Kyoto: Tankōsha, 1988.

———. *Kuge Chadō no Kenkyū.* Kyoto: Shibunkaku Shuppan, 2005.

———. *Yokuwakaru Chadō no Reikishi.* Kyoto: Tankōsha, 2007.

Tanimura Reiko. *Ii Naosuke: Shūyō toshite no Chanoyu.* Tokyo: Sōbunsha, 2001.

———. "Tea of the Warrior in the Late Tokugawa Period." In *Japanese Tea Culture: Art, History, and Practice*, edited by Morgan Pitelka, 137–50. New York: Routledge, 2003.

Tanizaki Jun'ichirō. *In Praise of Shadows.* Translated by Thomas J. Harper and Edward G. Seidensticker. Stony Creek, CT: Leete's Island Books, 1977.

———. *In'ei Raisan.* Tokyo: Chūōkōron Shinsha, 1975.

Tei Munetetsu. *Seiza to Nihonjin.* Tokyo: Kōdansha, 2009.

Teikoku Fujin Gakkai. *Fujoshi no Honbun.* Tokyo: Kōbundō, 1905.

Thompson, Lee. "The Invention of the *Yokozuna* and the Championship System, or Futahaguro's Revenge." In *Mirror of Modernity: Invented Traditions of Modern Japan*, edited by Stephen Vlastos, 174–90. Berkeley: University of California Press, 1998.

Tilly, Charles. *Coercion, Capital, and European States, AD 990–1992.* Cambridge, MA: Blackwell, 1992.

Tipton, Elise. "How to Manage a Household: Creating Middle Class Housewives in Modern Japan." *Japanese Studies* 29 (2009): 95–110.

Tomlinson, Alan, and Christopher Young, eds. *National Identity and Global Sports Events: Culture, Politics, and Spectacle in the Olympics and the Football World Cup.* Albany: State University of New York Press, 2006.

Tsuboya Zenshirō. *Nihon Joreishiki.* Tokyo: Hakubunkan, 1891.

Tsutsui Hiroichi. *Chasho no Keifu.* Tokyo: Bun'ichi Sōgō Shuppan, 1978.

———. "Iemoto no Fukkō." In *Chadō no Rekishi*, edited by Tanihata Akio, 408–50. Kyoto: Tankōsha, 1999.

Tuchman, Gaye. *Edging Women Out.* London: Routledge, 1989.

Turner, Victor. *The Ritual Process: Structure and Anti-Structure*. New York: Aldine de Gruyter, 1969.

Uchida Shigeru. *Chashitsu to Interia: Kurashi no Kūkan Dezain*. Tokyo: Kōsakusha, 2005.

Ueberhorst, Horst. *Friedrich Ludwig Jahn 1778/1978*. Bonn: Inter Nationes, 1978.

———. *Züruck zu Jahn? Gab es kein besseres Vorwärts?* Bochum: Universitätsverlag Bochum, 1969.

Ueda Riko. "Shunpū ni Nabikareta Kokochi Yosa." In *Gakkō Chadō Taiken Ronbunshū*, 41–43. Kyoto: Chadō Urasenke Tankōkai Sōhonbu, 2002.

Ueno Chizuko. *Nashonarizumu to Jendaa*. Tokyo: Seidosha, 1998.

Uno Chōji. *Katei no Takara*. Tokyo: Nihon Gunkoku Kyōkai, 1909.

Van Dalen, Deobold B., Elmer D. Mitchell, and Bruce L. Bennett. *A World History of Physical Education: Cultural, Philosophical, Comparative*. Upper Saddle River, NJ: Prentice Hall, 1953.

Varley, Paul. "*Chanoyu*: From the Genroku Epoch to Modern Times." In *Tea in Japan: Essays on the History of Chanoyu*, edited by Paul Varley and Isao Kumakura, 161–94. Honolulu: University of Hawai'i Press, 1989.

Varley, Paul, and George Elison. "The Culture of Tea: From Its Origin to Sen no Rikyu." In *Warlords, Artists, and Commoners: Japan in the Sixteenth Century*, edited by George Elison and Bardwell L. Smith, 187–222. Honolulu: University of Hawai'i Press, 1981.

Varley, Paul, and Isao Kumakura, eds. *Tea in Japan: Essays on the History of Chanoyu*. Honolulu: University of Hawai'i Press, 1989.

Verdery, Katherine. *National Ideology under Socialism: Identity and Cultural Politics in Ceauşescu's Romania*. Berkeley: University of California Press, 1991.

Vermeulen, Hans, and Cora Govers. "Introduction." In *The Anthropology of Ethnicity: Beyond "Ethnic Groups and Boundaries,"* edited by Hans Vermeulen and Cora Govers, 1–10. Amsterdam: Het Spinhuis, 1994.

Wacquant, Loïc J. D. *Body and Soul: Notebooks of an Apprentice Boxer*. Oxford: Oxford University Press, 2006.

———. "Carnal Connections: On Embodiment, Membership, and Apprenticeship." *Qualitative Sociology* 28 (2005): 441–71.

Wada Sakiko. "Chadō to Deatte." In *Gakkō Chadō Taiken Ronbunshū*, 15–17. Kyoto: Chadō Urasenke Tankōkai Sōhonbu, 2002.

Wagner, Richard. "Über deutsches Musikwesen." In *Richard Wagner Sämtliche Schriften und Dichtungen*, vol. 1, 149–66. Leipzig: Breitkopf und Härtel, 1871.

———. "Vorwort zur Gesamtherausgabe." In *Richard Wagner Sämtliche Schriften und Dichtungen*, vol. 1, i–vii. Leipzig: Breitkopf und Härtel, 1871.

Waldron, Arthur. "Representing China: The Great Wall and Cultural Nationalism in the Twentieth Century." In *Cultural Nationalism in East Asia*, edited by Harumi Befu, 36–60. London: RoutledgeCurzon, 1993.

Watanabe Yoshio. *Nihon no Reishiki*. Tokyo: Kyōdō Shuppansha, 1892.

Watsky, Andrew. "Commerce, Politics, and Tea: The Career of Imai Sōkyū (1520–

1593)." In *Japanese Tea Culture: Art, History, and Practice*, edited by Morgan Pitelka, 18–28. London: Routledge, 2003.

Weber, Eugen. *Peasants into Frenchmen: The Modernization of Rural France, 1870–1914*. Stanford, CA: Stanford University Press, 1976.

Weber, Max. *Economy and Society*. Berkeley: University of California Press, 1978.

Wedeen, Lisa. "Ethnography as Interpretive Enterprise." In *Political Ethnography: What Immersion Contributes to the Study of Power*, edited by Edward Schatz, 75–96. Chicago: University of Chicago Press, 2009.

———. *Peripheral Visions: Publics, Power, and Performance in Yemen*. Chicago: University of Chicago Press, 2008.

Wilson, Sandra. "Rethinking Nation and Nationalism in Japan." In *Nation and Nationalism in Japan*, edited by Sandra Wilson, 1–20. New York: RoutledgeCurzon, 2002.

Wimmer, Andreas. "Herder's Heritage and the Boundary-Making Approach: Studying Ethnicity in Immigrant Societies." *Sociological Theory* 27 (2009): 244–70.

———. *Nationalist Exclusion and Ethnic Conflict: Shadows of Modernity*. Cambridge: Cambridge University Press, 2002.

Wodak, Ruth, Rudolf de Cellia, Martin Reisigl, and Karin Liebhart. *The Discursive Construction of National Identity*. 2nd ed. Edinburgh: University of Edinburgh Press, 2009.

Yamane Mayuko. "Chadō to Watashi." In *Gakkō Chadō Taiken Ronbunshū*, 2–3. Kyoto: Chadō Urasenke Tankōkai Sōhonbu, 2002.

Yanagi Sōetsu. *Cha to Bi*. Tokyo: Kōdansha, 2000.

Yanagita Eriko. "Chadō tōshite Mananda Koto." In *Gakkō Chadō Taiken Ronbunshū*, 39–41. Kyoto: Chadō Urasenke Tankōkai Sōhonbu, 2002.

Yatabe Hidemasa. *Tatazumai no Bigaku*. Tokyo: Chūōkōron Shinsha, 2004.

———. *Utsukushii Nihon no Shintai*. Tokyo: Chikuma Shobō, 2007.

Yoshimori Kingo. *Kokumin Sahō Yōgi*. Tokyo: Kinkō Kōsho, 1916.

Yoshino Kosaku. *Bunka Nashonarizumu no Shakaigaku: Gendai Nihon no Aidentiti no Yukikata*. Nagoya: Nagoya Daigaku Shuppankai, 1997.

———. *Cultural Nationalism in Contemporary Japan: A Sociological Enquiry*. London: Routledge, 1992.

Yurchak, Alexei. *Everything Was Forever, Until It Was No More*. Princeton, NJ: Princeton University Press, 2006.

Yuval-Davis, Nira. *Gender and Nation*. Thousand Oaks, CA: Sage Publications, 1997.

Yuval-Davis, Nira, and Floya Anthias, eds. *Woman-Nation-State*. London: Palgrave Macmillan, 1989.

# Index

Oribe. *See* Furuta Oribe
others, consideration of, 47, 106, 205n64, 206n66; in demonstrations, 146–47, 150; in essays, 154; in lessons, 140, 143; nonverbal, 31, 51–53; and popular impressions, 169–70

Paris Exhibition (1878), 214n109
"peace through a bowl of tea" (*ichiwan kara "piisufurunesu"*), 107
*PEN* (magazine), 166–67
Perry, Matthew, 68, 73
Pitelka, Morgan, 11–12
Plutschow, Herbert, 11
poetry, 59, 61, 105, 208n9, 214n4; aesthetics of, 77, 207n6
political power: vs. civil society, 67–68; and culture, 3–4; and gymnastics, 179; and *iemoto* system, 98, 105, 115–18; and Japaneseness, 55; in media, 164; and men, 172; and nationalism, 1–2; and nation-work, 185; and RSS, 181; in Showa period, 90; and tea ceremony, 8–9, 11, 13–14, 55, 61–66, 68, 87, 171, 185
Pound, Ezra, 83
practitioners, tea, 119–56; authority of, 125–26; Chinese, 107; class distinctions among, 135–36; foreigners as, ix–xiii; hierarchy of, x–xi, 139–40; and *iemoto* system, 94–95, 109, 119–31, 135, 156; and Japaneseness, 14–15, 18–19, 137, 156, 173–74, 220n33; language of, 46–47, 205n61; male, 137–38; male vs. female, 171–72, 210n32; and movement, 28; and nationalism, 54, 156; numbers of, 157, 216n34; popular impressions of, 168–69; by region, 135; in tea spaces, 25–26; in Tokugawa period, 95; types of, 9, 135–38; warriors as, 9, 59, 61, 64, 138; women as, 9, 11, 18, 67, 72, 74, 77–81, 86–89, 135–37, 139, 152, 171–72, 210n32, 212n70, 212n74, 219n16. See also *sukisha*
publishing, mass, 92, 95, 112, 178
purification, 154, 181–82; in tea ceremony, 24, 32, 41, 43–44, 46, 49, 131

Queen of England, 86, 106

*rakugo* comedy, 21, 170, 199n8
Raku Museum, 158
Raku pottery, 12, 36, 97, 164
Rakutabi Bunkō booklets, 160

Rashtriya Swayamsevak Sangh (RSS), 180–81, 185
Rikyū. *See* Sen Rikyū
*Rikyū* (film), 164
*Rikyū* (Nishibori Kazuzō), 103
Rodrigues, João, 60
Roppongi (Tokyo), 19–20
Rotary Club, 107, 115, 216n33
Russo-Japanese War (1904–05), 82, 89, 99
*Ryōri Tsūshin* (magazine), 168

Sakai, 59–61
*sankin kotai* system, 63
Satō Kashiwa, 166
*Sazaesan* (cartoon), 163
schools: clubs in, xiii, 108, 113, 135, 137, 148, 152–54, 158; demonstrations in, 146–52; and Japaneseness, 144; nation-work in, 4–6, 183–86; seasonality in, 38–39; tea ceremony taught in, 157–58, 171, 185, 212n74; textbooks in, 75–76, 88–89, 100, 118
scrolls, 22, 39, 123, 127, 132, 140, 151; in alcoves, 24, 26–27, 29, 37–38, 202n34; Chinese, 59; and Japaneseness, 54, 154, 173
seasonality, 38–40, 140–41, 153, 156, 168, 174, 203n38
*seiza* (correct sitting), 26–28
Sekishū style, 109, 118, 198n41; vs. *iemoto* system, 133–34
*sencha* (steeped-leaf tea), 66–67, 209n27
*Sen no Rikyū* (film), 164
Sen Rikyū: aesthetic of, 107, 211n41; and architecture, 166–67; and genealogy, 120, 214n2; and Hideyoshi, 62–63, 103, 208n15; and *iemoto* system, 92–95, 99, 102–3, 117; in media, 103, 163–64, 168; and national essence, 80; popular knowledge of, 75–76, 79, 157–59, 169–70; and tea utensils, 96–97
*Sen Rikyū* (Takeuchi Yasu), 103
*Sen Rikyū Zenshū* (Suzuki Keiichi), 103
Sen Sōtan, 63–64
Seton-Watson, Hugh, 2
Shinto, 129–31, 142, 214n4
*Shitte Tokusuru: Wa no Keiko* (Know and Benefit: Lessons on Japaneseness), 164
Showa Kitano Tea Gathering (1936), 102
Showa period: *iemoto* system in, 101–3, 105; nationalism in, 79, 89–90, 101, 172; and nation-work, 185

Made in the USA
Middletown, DE
11 September 2017